# Buying a Second-hand Car

Tony Bosworth was the editor of *Which Car?* magazine from 1983–89 and he also helped create *The Good Van Guide* and *Car Hi-fi*. He is now a freelance journalist regularly contributing to a variety of publications, including the *Independent*, the *Daily Telegraph* and the *Financial Times*. He also takes part in a regular phone-in on Talk-Back Radio. Tony Bosworth lives in Reigate, Surrey.

# Buying a
# Second-hand Car

## TONY BOSWORTH

ROBERT HALE · LONDON

ISBN 0 7090 4825 4

Robert Hale Limited
Clerkenwell House
Clerkenwell Green
London EC1R 0HT

Photoset in North Wales by
Derek Doyle & Associates, Mold, Clwyd.
Printed in Great Britain by
St Edmundsbury Press, Bury St Edmunds, Suffolk.
Bound by Hunter & Foulis Limited.

# Contents

**Mazda**
| | |
|---|---|
| 121 | 97 |
| 323 | 97 |
| MX-5 | 98 |
| 626 | 98 |
| RX-7 | 99 |

**Mercedes-Benz**
| | |
|---|---|
| 190 | 100 |
| W124 | 101 |
| 230 coupé | 102 |
| 300 coupé | 102 |
| Sports coupé | 103 |
| Sports convertible | 103 |
| S-Class | 104 |
| G-Wagen | 104 |

**Mitsubishi**
| | |
|---|---|
| Lancer | 105 |
| Colt | 106 |
| Galant | 107 |
| Spacewagon | 108 |
| Starion Turbo | 109 |
| Shogun | 110 |

**Nissan**
| | |
|---|---|
| Micra | 111 |
| Cherry | 112 |
| Cherry Europe | 113 |
| Sunny | 113 |
| Bluebird | 114 |
| Primera | 115 |
| Stanza | 115 |
| Prairie | 116 |
| 200 ZX | 117 |
| 300 ZX | 117 |
| Patrol | 119 |

**Opel**
| | |
|---|---|
| Manta | 118 |
| Senator | 120 |
| Monza | 120 |

**Peugeot**
| | |
|---|---|
| 205 | 120 |
| 305 | 122 |
| 309 | 123 |
| 405 | 124 |
| 505 | 125 |
| 605 | 126 |

**Porsche**
| | |
|---|---|
| 924 | 127 |
| 944 | 128 |
| 911 | 128 |
| 928 | 129 |

**Proton**
| | |
|---|---|
| Proton | 130 |

**Range Rover**
| | |
|---|---|
| Range Rover | 131 |

**Reliant**
| | |
|---|---|
| Scimitar SS1 | 132 |
| Scimitar SST | 132 |

**Renault**
| | |
|---|---|
| 5 | 133 |
| Clio | 135 |
| 9 | 135 |
| 11 | 136 |
| 19 | 137 |
| Chamade | 137 |
| 21 | 138 |
| 25 | 139 |
| Espace | 140 |
| GTA V6 | 141 |

**Rover**
| | |
|---|---|
| 200 | 142 |
| 400 | 143 |
| SDI | 143 |
| 800 | 145 |

# Introduction

Basic Checks • Mechanical Checks • Bodywork Checks •
Other Checks • The AA and RAC • How to Use this Book •
Cars which are Excluded • Registration Dates

Choosing a good second-hand car is one of the hardest tasks there
is. Even though much of today's legislation helps the used car
buyer a lot more than it did even five years ago, there is still
always the uncertainty. Has it really only covered that mileage?
Will it last for two or three years, or will it break down on the way
home? Has it ever been involved in a serious accident?

All of these questions can be answered by carefully carrying out
a number of standard checks but the real problem all potential
car buyers come across is how to find out exactly what goes wrong
with each car. In other words, does the 1988 Rover Metro have
the same potential costly suspension fault as did the 1984
version, and just which year was it that a faulty batch of
camshafts were fitted to Vauxhall Astras?

Most car buyers will have seen the car price guides which are
readily available in high street newsagents, but the drawback is,
they can only give an idea of likely second-hand car prices, they
don't tell you the faults to look out for. And there are magazines
which cover the subject of buying second-hand cars but most will
only cover a maximum of five or six cars a month. In this book we
cover hundreds.

Armed with this information you can go along to a dealer or a
private buyer safe in the knowledge that you know exactly what
you're looking for. It becomes easier to avoid the cars which you
know are potential disasters.

Alongside our comprehensive lists of specific faults there are
other basic checks which should always be carried out before
buying any second-hand car, even when buying from a reputable
dealer. You don't have to be any kind of expert, you just need to
carefully go through the list of checks, and then you'll be well on
the way to getting the right car for you.

## Basic Checks

First thing to make sure of is that you have a firm idea about the type of car you want. All too often buyers go along to a dealership and are seduced by what they see, rather than sticking to what they actually want. Before you set out it's best to make a list of the cars you're really interested in, but keep it to around three or four different cars.

When you find the one that looks right for you, you should carry out mechanical checks, bodywork checks, and check also to see that the car legally belongs to the seller. This is especially important if buying from a private seller, simply because some unscrupulous dealers try and masquerade as private sellers – an offence under the law. If buying privately there is always a chance that the car is stolen or wanted by a finance company because the payments are not up-to-date. So, check ownership by looking at the registration document. If buying from a private seller, the name should tally with the name of the person who is selling the car. If you're told the documents are not available, or it's being re-registered, then you should leave that car well alone, something is amiss.

Other documents which should be examined are the service record which should be completely up-to-date (this should also help you check the truth of the car's mileage), and the MOT certificate which ideally should have some time to run. Don't buy a car without a current MOT. Even if you do get a good discount because of that, there will almost certainly be a good and potentially expensive reason why there is no current MOT.

If there are receipts for any repairs that have been carried out, all well and good. This will also give you some idea of the overall running costs of the car.

On the mechanical side, carry out the following checks.

## Mechanical Checks

The top of the engine should be free of weeping oil, as should the bottom of the engine (the sump) and the base of the spark plugs. While checking for signs of oil also check the dipstick. Ideally the oil on it should be clean, but if there are any white deposits, or if the oil is dirty and sludgy, or the oil level is low, beware, there will be engine problems.

Look inside the radiator and make sure that the water is clean. Rusty coloured water can reveal a dodgy, inefficient cooling system.

With the engine running, push the clutch down and listen for any mechanical thrashing. If it's loud there could be problems with the gearbox bearings. Keep the handbrake on and gently let the clutch come up, as if you're hill-starting the car, and check for any slipping or shuddering through the pedal.

The gearbox can be checked by going through each of the gears and listening for any untoward noises. If it's an automatic car, place the gear selector in 'drive' and then take it through to reverse. There should be no more than a couple of second's delay as the gearbox moves in from one gear to the other, and there shouldn't be any major clunking or shunting.

When the engine is running, check the smoke coming out of the exhaust. Ideally it should be invisible, if there is either excessive white or blue smoke there is a problem. Lastly, rev the engine hard and look out for any black smoke. You will find this with diesel cars, and it doesn't mean there's a problem, but if it's a petrol-engined car, leave it well alone.

**Bodywork Checks**
The bodywork should also be examined, especially for resprays – check around the edges of badges and bumpers, some paint overspray will always have got on to them if the car has been resprayed. A respray in itself is not a problem, an enthusiastic previous owner might have had it done to keep the car in tip-top condition, but there is always the fear that it's hiding some more serious bodywork problems.

Perhaps the car has been involved in a serious accident? To check this, look at the body panels and doors for a proper fit. Look along the sides of the car to see if the metal is even. If it isn't, it's a sign of accident damage and that could mean there is also serious damage to the chassis of the car.

Body panels which have been badly repaired are often best spotted with the aid of a strong magnet. Run it around the body and where it isn't attracted to the body it's likely that filler has been used to hide damage, or rust. (Obvious exceptions to this are the few aluminium, plastic and fibreglass cars which of course will not attract a magnet.)

Rust is rarely a problem on most of today's cars but if you're looking at a car over five years old it still pays to be careful. Check for corrosion around door sills, in the boot, along the sides of the engine and in joins between panels. If the car is five years old or more and it's recently been undersealed be very wary, the underseal could be there to hide problems, such as rusting chassis supports, or holes in the floorpan.

Once you've carried out these checks, there are others which are not as major but which are nevertheless just as important.

**Other Checks**
Electrics should all be checked over, and this is especially important if the car has central door locking, electric windows, electric sun-roof, or electric door mirrors. If any of these are not working they can be expensive to put right and it can also mean there's a question mark over the electrics system as a whole.

Suspension can easily be checked. Just push down hard on each corner of the car and when the springs are compressed, release the corner. It should bounce once, and then come to a stop. If it bounces more than once then the shock absorbers are worn and will need replacing.

The steering should be checked for play. There shouldn't be any, but off-road four-wheel-drive vehicles often have play engineered into their steering so that it doesn't snap back suddenly when travelling over rough ground.

The exhaust should be examined for any corrosion because once it takes a hold the high temperatures and noxious gases being pumped through the exhaust pipes soon hasten its end.

It is obviously important to check the brakes, and the main faults to look out for are spongy brakes with little bite, or a brake pedal which has a long travel before it bites. Either of these problems can mean there's a leak in the braking system, potentially an expensive repair, or problems with the brake pads and discs, again, a potentially expensive fault.

Check the tyres for wear, including the spare. A tyre or tyres which are worn on the edge is usually evidence of either bad tracking or damage to the suspension system. In extreme cases this might have been caused by damage resulting from a serious accident, so it can often be a tell-tale sign of more serious problems. Where there is uneven tyre wear on a four-wheel-drive vehicle it can mean the 4x4 system is out of alignment, and this could prove horrendously expensive to cure.

**The AA and RAC**
It may be that you don't want to carry out all of these checks yourself, or perhaps you just feel intimidated by the salesman — lots of buyers are. For you the sensible alternative could be an AA or RAC inspection. There are two advantages to this. Firstly, it's an impartial inspection and, secondly, any dealer who refuses to let you call in the AA or RAC to inspect the vehicle has probably

got something to hide. But just what does one of these inspections entail? Is it worth having? In many ways the answer is yes. The inspections stop short of damning a car but they do reveal the sort of condition which major mechanical and body parts are in.

Both the RAC and AA inspections cover bodywork, the underbody, engine, cooling system, steering, gearbox, brakes, clutch, drive shafts, suspension, electrics, wheels/tyres, interior trim and security. Where possible they also include a short road test.

There follows a full written report, which you will usually get within twenty-four hours, and it gives a series of marks. A tick means that the component is satisfactory for the age of the vehicle. Clearly, this is open to interpretation but in essence it means that a particular component is not in bad condition.

The reports also distinguish between items which are unserviceable, and which therefore need immediate attention, and areas where repairs are desirable in the near future. In addition, there's a summary which outlines the overall vehicle condition, which for most potential buyers will prove the most important part of the inspection.

Costs vary, depending on the engine size, but as an example, the RAC's Category A covers all cars up to 2500cc, although excluding four-wheel-drive and turbo cars, which are covered in a separate category. A test of a vehicle which falls into this group will cost £75 if you are an RAC member, and £88 if you're not. If you're thinking of buying a car which costs several thousand pounds then this sort of outlay is often well worth considering.

### How to Use this Book

All makes and models of cars produced in the last eleven years are covered here, and they've been arranged alphabetically, so it's simply a matter of finding the relevant make and then reading the specific report. Following each report, there's an overall verdict which tells you whether the car is good, bad or average when bought second-hand.

### Cars which are Excluded

There are a number of cars which we haven't included in this guide, for a variety of good reasons. Firstly there are those which were, or are still, built in such few numbers that they are rarely available on the second-hand market. In addition, it's often hard to come to any firm conclusions about the overall reliability of such cars simply because so few of them are available. I felt it would have been unfair both to potential owners and the car manufacturers to include these cars, amongst whom are Maserati, Bristol and Ferrari.

The second group of excluded cars are those which are not now readily available on the second-hand market, for a number of different reasons. For example, cars such as the Vauxhall Chevette are excluded, simply because there are so few left on the second-hand circuit, and those which are still motoring around are fetching second-hand prices in the bottom hundreds. For potential buyers of these types of cars the fact that they are still running at all is the major requirement.

There is a third group of excluded cars which were produced, or imported into the UK, in such small numbers and they sold so few, that again, there is little point in covering them in any detail. Such cars include the Lancia Gamma and Talbot Tagora.

And finally, there are a few cars which were last produced in 1981–82 and of which there will now be only a handful available on the second-hand market. Amongst these must be numbered the Fiat Mirafiori and Lancia Monte Carlo.

**Registration Dates**
Finally, here's a list of registration dates so that you can quickly find which year any car you're looking at was registered in. For the first three, the registration year letter came at the end of the number plate, while from August 1983 it was at the beginning.

W   August 1980–July 1981
X   August 1981–July 1982
Y   August 1982–July 1983
A   August 1983–July 1984
B   August 1984–July 1985
C   August 1985–July 1986
D   August 1986–July 1987
E   August 1987–July 1988
F   August 1988–July 1989
G   August 1989–July 1990
H   August 1990–July 1991
J   August 1991–July 1992

# The Cars
# from A to Z

## ALFA ROMEO ALFASUD and SPRINT

A range of front-wheel-drive hatchbacks (Alfasud) and front-wheel-drive coupés (Sprint).

### History

*June 1982* Limited edition Sprint Trofeo.
*July 1982* Alfasud 1.3SC, 1.5 Cloverleaf and 1.5TiX.
*October 1982* Limited edition Sprint Speciale.
*January 1983* Alfasud 1.3Ti.
*February 1983* Alfasud 1.5Ti renamed 1.5Ti Green Cloverleaf, 1.5 Cloverleaf changes to Gold Cloverleaf. 1.5 Sprint Veloce now becomes simply, Sprint.
*May 1983* Sprint 1.3 and Green Cloverleaf 1.5 launched in UK with new trim; bonnet air intakes, body side mouldings, alloy wheels.
*March 1984* Alfasud discontinued.
*December 1987* Sprint 1.7 and 1.7 Veloce launched, using a 1721cc engine, five-speed gearbox, tinted glass and alloy wheels. Veloce has an extra body kit and colour-keyed spoilers.

### Fault Finder

On any Alfasud or Sprint the first check must be for rust. Check around the window rubbers for rust bubbling up from underneath, the bottom edge of all doors, and the tail-gate lip. Slam the tail-gate down quite hard and watch to see if grains of rust drop out, likewise with the doors. Under the bonnet, check the engine bay for structural rust along each of the insides of the wings, and check the suspension mounts for rust. Electrics are always suspect, so check that all of the gauges are reading properly and that any electrically operated items – windows, sun-roofs – are working properly. It is not always an easy job to repair electrical faults in an Alfa Romeo. On Alfa Sprints in particular, check the interior trim carefully, paying particular attention to front seats. They had a tendency to sag and even split if subjected to hard use, or high mileage. Gearboxes can be stripped of their synchromesh, especially on second gear. Aside from that the gearboxes are normally quite strong, although the quality of the gearchange varies widely from car to car. They should be strongly sprung, but slot into each gear smoothly. If any gear will not engage smoothly, leave that car alone, these are the beginnings of gearbox problems, and they will worsen. Brakes often squeal, but premature disc wear is not a major problem – the squeal is usually because of a build-up of brake dust. The brakes on all of these cars are exceptionally good, with plenty of progression and weight, and with a legendary ability to stop the car very quickly. If there is any sponginess through the pedal, or a lack of progression there may well be a leak in the system, or the brake pads have been worn right down. Shock absorbers take a pounding and need to be changed frequently. Both the Alfasud and the Sprint corner flatly, with no noticeable body roll, and they ride with a taut suppleness. If there is serious body roll, or too much bouncing through the springs, the shock absorbers will need replacing – not a major job. Engines are generally very reliable but watch for engine misfires due to incorrect tuning. Early versions of the Alfasud – up to the end of 1983 – frequently stall when hot, so make sure that you drive the car you are looking at for around 10 miles, some of it in heavy town traffic. Regular kerbing of the front wheels can cause premature wear to the steering rack, a fault which can be recognized by hard-to-turn steering and a loud creaking when the wheel is turned. This problem is most common on cars built between 1982 and 1985, and is more of a problem on the Alfasud than on the Sprint.

**Verdict**
Great to drive – when they are in a good state of tune. Prices are attractively low but this is due to the niggling electrical problems and the lurking spectre of rust. Best choice is a late-registration Sprint, a car which is attractively styled and which has higher resistance to corrosion than an Alfasud.

**ALFA ROMEO ARNA**
Front-wheel-drive hatchback.

**History**
*November 1984* 1.2SL five-door launched, 1186cc engine, five-speed gearbox.
*March 1985* 1.3SL with 1351cc engine.
*May 1985* 1.5Ti with 1490cc engine.
*September 1986* Range discontinued.

**Fault Finder**
In spite of the body coming from Nissan, rust is a problem, due mainly to the thin metal and poor paintwork finish. Check the body very carefully because even small dents and scratches caused by careless parking can soon deteriorate into quite serious rust. Engines do not suffer from major ills, being sturdy and durable, but the 1.3-litre can go off-tune if not properly looked after. Look for a full service record. The gearchange is often sloppy, the worst ones demanding quite a lot of stirring round to find the correct gear. The warning bells should ring if it's hard to slot the gear-lever into any gear, it should slot in lightly. Interiors do not stand the test of time, with splitting seats and sagging rear seats. Electrics are much better on this car than on other Alfa Romeos, but still carry out checks to see if all electrics are working properly, paying particular attention to warning lights. The Arna has much more body roll than other Alfas, and the ride is not so supple, a touch harsher, but shock absorbers last longer than on the Alfasud. Brakes should be precise and work swiftly. Any sponginess indicates a leak which is allowing air to get into the system. Check the brake fluid reservoir to see if there are any air bubbles in there – if there are there is a problem.

**Verdict**
An unfortunate marriage between Alfa Romeo engines and Nissan Cherry bodywork. Mechanically quite a reliable car, but the chief problem with the Arna is that the body is too wide and therefore

suffers from too much body roll when cornering. Straight-line performance is good and the Arna keeps predictable second-hand value. But for real Alfa enthusiasts this will always be a Nissan.

## ALFA ROMEO 33
Front-wheel-drive and four-wheel-drive hatchbacks and four-wheel-drive estate.

### History
*June 1983* Front-wheel-drive, five-door hatchbacks, all with five-speed gearboxes. 1.3-litre, 1.5 and 1.5 Gold Cloverleaf.

*June 1984* 1.5-litre Green Cloverleaf launched, more powerful than previous 1.5.

*May 1985* Four-wheel-drive estate with 1.5 litre engine.

*January 1986* Both engines get more power, and there are trim changes.

*May 1987* Revised range. 1.5Ti and Veloce get the more powerful (105bhp) engine. Also, launch of 1.7-litre Cloverleaf and Veloce. All models have new close-ratio five-speed gearbox, and a host of equipment improvements. Veloce models have extra body skirts.

*July 1987* Sportwagon estate launched to replace previous 4x4 estate. New model available in Veloce and Cloverleaf trim. Both versions feature high equipment and Veloce has additional body skirts.

*June 1988* Veloce trim changes slightly to give sportier look.

*June 1990* 1.7IE and 1.7 Boxer 16 valve Cloverleaf with more powerful engines, and both models get new styling.

*September 1990* 1.5IE with enhanced equipment.

*March 1991* 1.7-litre 16-valve Cloverleaf Permanent 4 hatchback and 1.7-litre 16-valve Sportwagon. Permanent 4 has an advanced four-wheel-drive system and copious equipment. Sportwagon gets close-ratio five-speed gearbox.

*July 1991* hatchback 16-valve 1.7-litre launched, similar equipment to 1.7IE.

### Fault Finder
Rust is not the problem it is on the Alfasud, but look just in case.

Mechanically, fairly sound, but all gearboxes built before 1989 tend to dissolve with monotonous regularity. Check for a restrictive gearchange, it spells expensive trouble. There are problems with engine tuning on carburettor cars built before 1987, making them hard to restart once the engine is warm. This can be solved by tinkering with the carburettor setting, but always expect rather jerky town performance from the frenetic 1.5-litre carburettor engine – it's simply due to the design of the carburettor. As with all Alfas, check for worn shock absorbers, and on all versions made before 1986 check for front shock absorber leaks. Electrics must be checked, dials have a habit of misinforming the driver, and electric windows sometimes work and sometimes don't. Even the latest 33s need a careful electrical check. There is a large amount of torque steer (in this case, pulling the car to the left) when accelerating hard in the 1.5-litre injection and 1.7-litre models. This is not a fault, merely a result of the design of the front drive shafts. However, if the car pulls from side to side when accelerating quickly, or there is a loud creaking from the front, check the rubber boots around the front drive shafts to see if they are split and leaking fluid. This is more a problem with cars built before 1986.

## Verdict

Successor to the much-loved Alfasud, the 33 never came close in terms of image and desirability because it was thought by many to be a watered-down Alfa. Nevertheless, the 33 is fast becoming a classic car, and if you can find one in good condition it's a great car to drive. Best engine is the 1.5-litre injection, as long as it is regularly serviced.

## ALFA ROMEO ALFETTA AND GTV ▼

Rear-wheel-drive saloon (Alfetta) and coupé (GTV) sharing common mechanical components.

## History

*February 1982* GTV has choice of 2.0-litre or 2.5-litre V6 engines. GTV gets revised gear ratios and standard sun-roof.
*October 1982* 2000 and 2000SL mark 2 Alfetta saloons appear.
*May 1983* Improved equipment for both GTV models.
*January 1984* Gold Cloverleaf Alfetta with high equipment level.
*August 1985* Alfetta discontinued.
*October 1987* GTV discontinued.

## Fault Finder

Two of the worst Alfa Romeos for rust. It gathers spectacularly quickly around the front lights, along the door sills and around the bottom of the tailgate. If that weren't enough, it also collects around the side window rubbers and the sun-roof, especially if the roof's drain channels haven't been cleaned out regularly. These are two of the few cars of their era to also suffer from severe corrosion underneath and it was common for early models, pre-1985, to have welding work carried out to enable them to pass the MOT test. Mechanically, the best engine is the 2.0-litre, the V6 is not the most reliable, suffering from blown engine head gaskets with monotonous regularity. To check for this, make sure you keep a close eye on the temperature gauge when driving, looking for any signs of overheating, and look for creamy gunge on the inside of the oil cap, a sure sign that water is getting into the oil via a broken head gasket. If a V6 is your choice, take the car on as long a run as possible and look for a very smoky exhaust – this can signal the end of the engine's valve guides. The brakes also need close scrutiny because pads wear down quickly, especially on the V6. Check the front pair very carefully because the GTV is a very nose-heavy car, and that means the front brakes have to work hard. Gearchanges have never been very smooth, mostly because the gearbox is slung over the rear wheels, so there's a long and torturous gear linkage. A good GTV gear change should be heavily sprung and quite weighty, but it should slot into gear easily. Quite often, first gear is a touch tricky to get into. Forcing the gear-lever does

4444444

no good, you have to get the engine ticking over at just the right revs, and then gently push the lever in. Second gear synchromesh can often be beaten by an enthusiastic gear change, but this is not necessarily a sign that the synchro is wearing. Check for clutch slippage because GTVs go through them very quickly, especially the V6 engined cars. The 2.0-litre engine is a safer bet but listen for any undue rattles, this could signal the end of the timing chain, and if you can hear it rattling there might already be damage to the engine.

**Verdict**
The GTV is already a classic car, and when they are good they are very good. But when they are bad ... Best choice is the 2.0-litre but the V6 offers smooth, fluid performance. There will be few good Alfettas around now, and it's not as alluring a car as the GTV.

**ALFA ROMEO GIULIETTA**
Rear-wheel-drive saloon.

**History**
Choice of 1.6, 1.8, 2.0-litre petrol engines.
*February 1982* Revised range with improvements to equipment.
*October 1983* Further revisions, centred around equipment. Engines remain virtually as when originally launched.
*1986* Giulietta discontinued.

**Fault Finder**
Not so disastrous a rust bucket as many of its brothers, but still needs a careful look for corrosion. All three engines are prone to head gasket problems and timing chains need replacing at regular intervals, so look for a full service history and check for a heavily smoking exhaust. Listen for rattles from the engine on tick-over, a sign that the timing chain or the camshaft belt needs replacing. If there are rattles, damage may already have been caused. Check that proper Alfa Romeo spark plugs have been fitted because many other makes melt their tips at the high operating temperatures produced by these Alfa engines, and this can cause damage to the pistons. Oil leaks from main feeder pipes are quite common on 1.6-litre cars and there's very little warning that most of the oil has gone, before the engine seizes. Gearchanges vary tremendously, some are precise and light, others are heavy and slow. But the major point is to watch for worn synchromesh because this often means that the gearbox is on its last legs. You have to drive the car until the engine is well warmed before you will notice synchromesh failure, and on some Giuliettas, especially the 1.8-litre cars, it can happen after just 10,000 miles. On all Giuliettas the synchro is likely to have failed on second gear, at least, by the time the car has covered 40,000–50,000 miles. The disc brakes can have brake fluid leak on to them, causing loss of pressure, and eventual failure of the braking system, but also causing loss of braking due to the fluid making the discs slick. A similar problem occurred with many 2.0-litre cars, although this was due to main engine oil leaking onto one front disc, causing braking to be uneven and dangerous. Corrosion can also attack the brake calipers

on all versions, causing the calipers to seize. They are expensive to replace. Electrics are always suspect in the Giulietta, so check everything over carefully. It is quite common to find warning lights coming on when there is nothing wrong. Trim is not well put together and on surviving Giuliettas it could be rather poor by now. Check for good fit and finish of all trim, and carefully check the seat fabric – it was never strong, and can rip along the side of the seat cushion. Worn shock absorbers and collapsed suspension mounts, the former due to hard driving, the latter due to corrosion in the tops of the mounts, are common problems. Check these areas carefully. Look at the tyres closely for any signs of uneven wear, because the front wheels often got knocked out of line by regular kerbing. Look inside the boot for water leaks and corrosion, especially at the back of the boot.

## Verdict
As with most Alfas, if you get a good one you will enjoy it, but if not, it can be a real headache. It helps to have a full service record which details all repairs, because then you can see if timing chains, camshaft belts, and brake discs have been replaced. Best model is a 2.0-litre because the engine performs well and is relatively reliable, and it's fast becoming a collectable classic car, unlike most of its rather humdrum rivals.

## ALFA ROMEO ALFA 75
Rear-wheel-drive saloon.

## History
*June 1986* 1.8 and 2.5-litre launched.
*May 1987* Veloce versions arrive, with body styling kit.
*September 1987* 2.0i Twin Spark and 3.0i unveiled in standard and Veloce trim. High equipment levels for both versions, Veloce models have a sporty body kit.
*November 1987* 2.5i Auto with similar equipment to Twin Spark manual.
*June 1989* Equipment and trim up-date for all models, 3.0i gets new alloy wheels.
*October 1989* 3.0-litre Special Edition Lusso launched with full equipment.
*September 1990* 3.0-litre Cloverleaf. More powerful engine (192bhp), more efficient brakes, and improved suspension.

## Fault Finder
Faulty electrics are the most common Alfa 75 fault, and they usually show themselves with false warnings, or the failure of items such as electric windows. Check all of the electrics very carefully because if there is a problem it demands specialist help, and that can be expensive. Rust is generally not a problem on the 75, Alfa Romeo learnt their lesson with the Alfasud. However, check for stone chips on the front valance, under the bumper, and the bonnet because if left untreated stone chips can quickly lead to corrosion. Check also along the window rubbers for any creeping rust getting in underneath and

then spreading to the doors. Check carefully for accident damage – these Alfa Romeos were often driven with verve but not always with a lot of skill. An Alfa which has suffered a serious accident is a car well worth avoiding. On the V6 engined cars, check for engine head gasket failure. This can most easily be checked by lifting the oil cap off and checking to see if there is any creamy, sludgy gunk on the cap. If there is, the car has almost certainly suffered, or is suffering, a head gasket problem. Because the Alfa's engine block is alloy this may well have meant that the engine has overheated and the block needs replacing. On the V6 engine this can happen as early as 25,000 miles. Gearbox synchromesh often wears quite quickly, especially on second gear, due in the main to the rather long throw of the gear-lever, and the fact that the gearbox is placed at the back of the car, so giving a long and rather torturously complicated linkage. The gearchange on all 75s varies tremendously, but the best should be weighty but smooth and quite heavily sprung, while the ones which are likely to lead to trouble will be very heavy to use, and hard to slot into at least one of the gears. Brakes are all round discs and while the pads do seem to last for a good time, the discs can suffer from warping. This will manifest itself in a major judder every time the brakes are applied, so it's easy to spot.

## Verdict
The Alfa is a fine car – as long as you can find a good one, and that is not easy. The best choice is the 2.0-litre Twin Spark which pro-

vides almost V6 power, yet without the bigger engined car's often troublesome engine. Buying privately is the best bet in many ways, because dealers are pricing at the top end to try and stabilize rather dire second-hand values.

## ALFA ROMEO ALFA 90
Rear-wheel-drive saloon, slightly bigger than the Alfa 75.

## History
*February 1985* 90 Gold Cloverleaf launched.
*September 1986* Discontinued.

## Fault Finder
Suffers from all the usual Alfa faults. Check the body extensively and carefully for rust, including underneath the car. A full service history is a must, and should include bills for any work which has been carried out. The V6 engine is not the best, suffering regularly from blown gasket and cylinder heads. Check the inside of the oil cap for the creamy gunge which reveals a blown gasket, listen for any rattling on tick-over which could mean the camshaft belt is on its way out. If the rattle is severe it will mean serious damage has already been caused to the camshaft. Bounce each corner of the car to check for worn shock absorbers. Make sure that brakes are efficient and progressive and not spongy. Any brake squeal could herald the near demise of the brake pads. Feel the brake discs carefully to see if they are scored – if they are, they will need replacing. The gearchange is not usually precise, but it should be relatively smooth. If there is a

reluctance to slot into any gear there could be problems on their way. Gearboxes can last as little as 40,000 miles. Electrics are always suspect in the 90. Check all electrics work properly. If they don't it can be expensive and time consuming to get them sorted out. Check the top of the exhaust manifold, they crack away from the engine regularly, even after fairly short mileage.

**Verdict**
Not a good Alfa, in fact, one of the least desirable. While the V6 engine has plenty of power, and sounds terrific, it is not reliable, and not as tough as you might expect. Better to go for one of the rivals, most of their engines might not sound as good, but you will end up walking home less often.

**ALFA ROMEO ALFA 6**
Rear-wheel-drive executive saloon.

**History**
*February 1982* launched with carburettor fed engine.
*July 1983* fuel injection replaces carburettors.
*April 1984* Discontinued.

**Fault Finder**
At all costs avoid the carburettor-engined Alfa 6. This uses six separate carburettors and they never seem to be in tune together, no matter how regular the servicing. Rust is not a major problem on the Alfa 6, but as with all Alfas of this era, check in any case. This car doesn't have the tautness of other Alfas, it wallows a lot around corners, placing lots of weight on its shock absorbers, so they tend to

wear quite quickly. Check the suspension mounts in the engine bay for leaks, and for any rust because this will weaken the mounts. Check the discs for scoring. The auto gearbox can slip its gears, a common fault on original carburettor models, and it's a very expensive unit to replace, if you can find anywhere that stocks them. V6 engines blow cylinder head gaskets regularly, so check for any water in the oil, usually revealed by creamy white sludge on the inside of the oil filler cap. Rear drive shafts have been known to snap. When moving away from rest check for a clunk sound from the back of the car. If it's there, leave the car well alone, it's an expensive repair. It's imperative that the engine timing chain has been replaced regularly. Make sure this replacement is mentioned in service records. Electrics should all be examined closely, in particular the gauges inside, because rogue readings are commonplace. Check also that electric windows and the sun-roof are working properly, and that all exterior lights work.

**Verdict**
One of the least popular Alfa Romeos, the 6 has not proved itself to be reliable. The carburettor arrangement is awful, and while the injected version is better, this car is not desirable. Second-hand prices are rock bottom, reflecting its unpopularity. All rivals are better.

**ALFA ROMEO ALFA 164**
Front-wheel-drive executive saloon.

## History

*October 1988* 3.0-litre V6 and Lusso launched.

*June 1989* Both models available with extra cost automatic transmission.

*June 1990* 2.0-litre Twin Spark and Lusso 2.0-litre. Lusso has ABS brakes, alloy wheels and electric sun-roof.

*December 1990* 3.0-litre V6 with more powerful engine, catalytic convertor, uprated suspension with switchable dampers, air conditioning and leather trim.

## Fault Finder

Rust is not a problem on this Alfa. Electrics are good, engines are tough and durable. Check manual gearboxes for worn synchromesh on second and third gear, but this will signal a hard-worked gearbox, rather than one which is heading for more elaborate problems. Check front drive shafts for leaks, examine the rubber boots on the drive shafts to make sure that they are intact. Check for accident damage by looking along the sides of the car for any rippling of the metal. Brakes must be checked because the brake discs can be scored easily if the brake pads have been allowed to wear down low. Only buy a 164 which comes with a full service history.

## Verdict

Alfa prove they can get their act together. The 164 is a well engineered car which also looks good, attributes which ensure it is keeping a healthy second-hand value. Best choice is the Twin Spark which has virtually the performance of the V6 but without the fuel thirst.

## AUDI 80

The original range is rear-wheel drive, and is later replaced by front-wheel drive and four-wheel drive saloons.

## History

*October 1982* Turbo Diesel with 1.6-litre engine.

*March 1983* 80GL gains carburettor 1.8-litre petrol engine.

*April 1983* 80 Sport launched with 1.8-litre fuel injected engine, uprated suspension, alloy wheels.

*August 1983* 80 Quattro 4x4 unveiled with 2.2-litre injection engine, uprated suspension and high level of equipment.

*October 1983* CL gets an uprated carburettor 1.6-litre engine. CD gains uprated 2.0-litre injection engine.

*April 1984* SC launched with 1.8-litre engine and choice of five-speed manual or three-speed auto.

*October 1984* heavily revised across the range.

*November 1986* Range discontinued and replaced by new Audi 80.

New range is front-wheel drive and four-wheel drive. Range is, 1.6-litre, 1.6 Turbo diesel, carburettor 1.8S, injection 1.8E, 1.8E Quattro.

*August 1989* Base version gets 90bhp fuel injected engine, 2.0E and Quattro get 2.0-litre injection engine. ABS brakes standard on Quattro.

*October 1989* 2.0-litre Sport.

*September 1990* 2.0-litre Sport 16-valve, Quattro Sport, both with 137bhp engine. Quattro Sport has ABS brakes.

*January 1991* Range discontinued,

AUDI

AUDI

replaced by new range.

**Fault Finder**
Later Audi 80s have galvanized
bodies, so rust is not a problem on
the major areas of sheet metal.
However, on rear-wheel-drive
models, check under the wheel
arches and at the bottoms of the
doors inside, water has been
known to get trapped and cause
the beginning of corrosion. Mechanically this is a fairly sound car,
but check the rubber mountings on
the radiator. If they have worn it
can cause the radiator to shift, and
this can cause water leaks from
the rubber hoses. Let the car stand
running for some time to check
that the electric engine fan is
cutting in. Audi 80s run very hot so
it is imperative that this fan is
working. While waiting for the fan
to cut in, keep a careful eye on the
temperature gauge, this will tell
you if the car has overheated
before. If it has the needle will
quickly climb into the red. Engine
fan electric switches often failed on
cars built in 1982–4. Engine valve
clearance is something that needs
to be checked, as are the valve
stem oil seals which often perish,
and the inlet valves can fail. These
problems are most acute on cars
made up to 1985, but even on more
recent Audis you should check for
these problems. The tell-tale sign
here is lots of blue smoke when
accelerating hard, and it's most
common on Audis which have
covered around 50,000 miles or
more. Brake discs need to be
checked for scoring because while
it is not a common problem with
the 80, a scored disc does have to
be replaced, and this is expensive.
Scored discs also point to a
previous owner who has been less
than diligent about servicing.
When braking, check to see if the
car pulls, especially to the left. If it
does it will be a sticking piston on
the brake caliper, quite a common
fault on cars made up to 1987. This
is not serious and it's not expensive
to put right. However, pulling to
the right may well signal accident
damage that's been poorly
repaired. On front-wheel-drive
models, even the latest versions,
check the condition of the rubber
boots around the front drive shafts.
If these are split and fluid has
leaked out and dirt has got in, this
could mean new CV joints, and
these are not cheap. The good news
is that Audi 80 boots are stronger
than most, and less susceptible to
splits. Rear suspension dampers
can leak. You can spot this by
looking under the wheel arches and
examining the suspension struts. If
there is a leak, the struts will have
to be replaced.

**Verdict**
A quality car, the 80 is well worth
looking at. Disadvantages include
a very small boot and high labour
charges from Audi dealers. Parts
prices are now a little more in line
with rivals, but some are still too
expensive. Best models are those
with the 2.0-litre injection engine.

**AUDI 90**
Rear-wheel-drive and front-wheel-
drive saloons, with the same body
as the Audi 80, but using a range
of five cylinder engines.

**History**
*February 1985* Rear-wheel-drive
CD and Quattro 4x4 unveiled.

CD uses the 2.0-litre engine, Quattro gets the bigger engine.
*December 1986* Range discontinued, replaced by new front-wheel-drive 90.
*June 1987* 90 has 2.0-litre engine, 2.2E and Quattro share the 2.2-litre engine. 2.2E has alloy wheels, sports seats, Quattro has ABS brakes.
*August 1989* 2.3-litre injection engine replaces 2.2-litre. 20-valve engines launched, giving 170bhp and mated to sports suspension and ABS anti-lock brakes. Sport and Special Equipment packs at extra cost. All models have catalytic converters.
*June 1990* Quattro Sport 2.3 20-valve, with alloy wheels, ABS brakes, de-chromed bodywork.
*December 1991* Electronic four-speed auto gearbox offered on 2.3E and 20-valve. Driver can pick Sport or Economy settings.

**Fault Finder**
Mechanically identical to the Audi 80, and with the same pluses and minuses. An additional point on the 90, though, is to watch for occasional engine misfires caused by cracked spark plug leads. ABS brakes must be working. If they have failed it will not affect the braking ability as such but the fault will cause the car to fail an MOT test. ABS brakes are very expensive to repair or replace, and there have been failures of the system on 90s produced in late 1989, early 1990.

**Verdict**
The 90 is a rather expensive car when compared to the 80, and aside from the five-cylinder engine

it's hard to see why buyers would want to pay more for a 90. Save your money and look at an 80.

**AUDI 100 AND AVANT**
Four-door saloons and five-door estates with four and five-cylinder engines, front-wheel and four-wheel drive.

**History**
*January 1983* CC, CS and CD models launched. CC uses five-cylinder 2.0-litre carburettor engine, CS and CD have fuel injected 2.1-litre engine.
*August 1983* Avant CD estate, mechanically identical to CD saloon with exception of Avant's uprated suspension.
*October 1983* Diesel and Turbo Diesel versions launched. Diesel has 1.8-litre, TD has 2.0-litre. TD equipment similar to CD petrol model.
*October 1983* Avant CC and TD estates.
*October 1984* CD and CD Avant get 2.2-litre engine. All models have engine modifications, improved heating and ventilation, and uprated sound insulation.
*February 1985* Quattro 4x4 and Avant Quattro with high equipment, and new 2.2-litre engine.
*April 1988* Range revised, with redesigned interiors and wider rear track. Quattro models get the more modern Torsen differential for their four-wheel-drive system.
*August 1988* Further revisions. Range consists of base model and 2.0E, both using the 2.0-litre engine, Turbo diesel, 2.2E, and Quattro.

*November 1988* 2.3E saloon appears. Standard catalytic converter. Specification similar to 2.2E saloon.

*August 1989* More revisions. All of the petrol models come with a standard catalytic converter. Petrol turbo models (front-wheel-drive and Quattro versions) get new 165bhp 2.2-litre engine, ABS brakes and alloy wheels.

*March 1991* Range discontinued, replaced with new Audi 100.

**Fault Finder**

Check mileages carefully, by checking the service documents, because the 100 is a favourite company car so is often subjected to high mileage. On the plus side, these cars have usually been run by senior managers and have been looked after well. Engines with high mileage – above 60,000 – often suffer worn valve seals, a pointer to this being clouds of black smoke when accelerating. This problem is more common to the four-cylinder engines than the more robust five-cylinder units, and is more common to Avant models fitted with tow bars, due to the additional engine strain caused by hauling trailers. The four-cylinder engines can also suffer from blocked oil breather pipes. A good way to pinpoint this is to check for sprayed oil in the engine compartment. At its most extreme, a blocked breather pipe can cause the engine to clog up, and eventually to seize. It's a potential problem in any Audi over 80,000 miles but is most commonly seen around 100,000 miles. Every 40,000 miles the camshaft belt has to be replaced on all Audi 100 engines, so check this has been done if the car you're looking at has covered near this mileage. Excessive whine from the gearbox at high speeds (around 70 m.p.h.) could mean the shaft bearings have worn. This is an expensive repair. Listen to the front wheels for rumbling, which may indicate worn bearings. The problem here is that the Audi 100 suffers from excessive tyre rumble, so it's not easy to decide whether it's the road surface or wheel bearings making the noise. Vibration from the engine on tick-over is not normally a problem because all Audi 100 engines do this, especially the five-cylinder units. However, if it's excessive it could mean that the engine mounts are worn. Check this by checking for any lurching as you pull away from rest. Have a look at the exhaust to check it's in good condition. Why? They cost around £600 to replace. Finally, it's better to buy a 100 without ABS brakes as they can fail at around 60,000 miles and they cost a small fortune to replace. A car fitted with ABS which isn't working will fail an MOT test.

**Verdict**

There are more Audi 100s on the second-hand market than any other Audi, so the choice is vast. If you don't find a good one straightaway, keep looking, there are always others. Best saloon choice is a straight 2.0-litre injection model, while Avant buyers should go for a front-wheel-drive version. The Quattro Avant is a complicated piece of machinery which costs a fortune to repair when it goes wrong.

## AUDI COUPÉS
Front-wheel and four-wheel-drive coupés

### History
*March 1981* Left-hand-drive Quattro coupé with turbocharged five-cylinder engine (2144cc) and permanently engaged four-wheel drive.

*April 1981* GT5-S front-wheel-drive coupé launched.

*October 1982* Fuel-injected front-wheel-drive coupé with 2144cc engine launched with close-ratio five-speed gearbox, uprated suspension, power steering and ventilated disc brakes. Quattro Turbo comes to UK in right-hand-drive form.

*October 1983* GT coupé gets fuel injected 1994cc engine.

*October 1984* 1.8-litre coupé unveiled, offered with either a five speed manual or a three-speed automatic gearbox.

*June 1986* 2.2-litre GT launched.

*September 1986* GT 1.8i coupé.

*October 1987* Quattro improved, with new 2.3-litre engine, and modern Torsen differential for the four-wheel-drive system.

*June 1988* Front-wheel-drive coupé and four-wheel-drive Quattro (not turbo) replaced by new coupé range.

*November 1988* 2.2E and Quattro get 2226cc engine. Disc brakes all round, with ABS anti-lock brakes on Quattro.

*August 1989* Revised range, consisting of 2.0E with four-cylinder engine. 2.3E and Quattro 20-valve get new 2309cc engine producing 136bhp in normal form (10-valve engine) and 170bhp in 20-valve form.

*January 1991* Series 2 four-wheel-drive Turbo Quattro arrives with 220bhp engine.

### Fault Finder
On turbo models check that the turbo fires in smoothly, without rattling. If the car has covered a high mileage, 100,000 or so, the turbo will almost certainly be on its last legs. Engines are very reliable but a full service history is paramount, and regular servicing must have been carried out by Audi franchised dealers – these cars are not easy to work on. Cracked exhaust manifolds are quite common, and an Audi replacement exhaust for a Quattro turbo will cost around £1000, so this is worth remembering. Engine mounts should be checked carefully. The easiest way to do this is to see if there is any lurching from the engine when slowly driving forwards from rest. If there is any sign of a misfire, or explosions of black smoke, be wary. This could mean that the cylinder is cracked. Split oil cooler pipes, there are two of them, occur in older coupés – those made between April 1981 and the end of 1983 – and lead to rapid loss of oil. If not spotted early enough it can lead to complete engine seizure. On four-wheel-drive versions check the drive system. The only major problem which rears its head here is a loud clicking when the steering is on full lock. If you hear that, leave the car well alone, it signals imminent major problems with the front driveshaft joints. If buying an early Quattro, listen carefully for rattly wheel bearings because they tend to go around 80,000 miles. Whine from the five-speed manual gearbox on Quattro versions could

be a relatively minor replacement – a new constant velocity joint at the back of the gearbox – but it could also mean the gearbox is on its last legs. There's no easy way to spot this, so if you hear this whine, it's usually best to look for another coupé. On all cars fitted with ABS anti-lock brakes you have to be aware that the system can fail around 90,000 miles, reverting the braking back to a normal system. Replacing the ABS is a major expense, so if it is not working on the car you see, think again. Electrics are generally very reliable but there were a few problems with the voice synthesizer and digital arrangement on early Quattro Turbos – those made up to October 1984, often leading to misleading vocal warnings. As there is no easy way to switch the voice synthesizer off, it's better to try and get a car without one, they really are more trouble than they're worth. Suspension needs checking over very carefully, especially on high-mileage front-wheel-drive and on all four-wheel-drive coupés. On the Quattro models suspension bushes and ball joints wear out relatively quickly, they can need replacing as early as 25,000 miles. On the road this potential fault is easily recognizable. If the coupé wallows around bends, especially at the back end, then there is almost certainly a problem with the rear suspension. If it's a Quattro the repair costs – mainly labour costs – can be quite high. Brakes should be efficient and progressive. All coupés, and particularly the powerful Quattro, eat brake pads, and if they have not been replaced quickly enough the discs will easily be damaged.

Discs for any of the coupés are quite expensive.

**Verdict**
Good, solid coupés, capable of seating four as easily as most saloons. The basic coupés are rather uninspiring but keep their value well and seldom cost a lot to run. The Quattro Turbo is an exhilarating piece of machinery. Repair and maintenance costs for the four-wheel-drive models are less exhilarating. So, think carefully before buying four-wheel-drive models.

## AUDI 200
Front-wheel-drive and four-wheel-drive saloons and estates.

**History**
*March 1984* 200E and Turbo models launched, both using a fuel injected 2144cc engine.
*July 1985* Avant estate versions with turbo engine and Quattro four-wheel-drive.
*August 1988* Revamped models launched. New five cylinder 2226cc engine, restyled interior. Quattro models gain the Torsen differential.

**Fault Finder**
The Audi 200 is virtually identical to the Audi 100, the difference being that the 200 features only five cylinder engines. Check the Audi 100 Fault Finder for areas to be checked before buying.

**Verdict**
There seems little point spending the extra money on a 200 when the 100 is as good, a fact reflected in lower second-hand values for the

200. The advantage for the second-hand buyer is that there are good value 200s to be had. If you do want one, try and find a 200E or a Turbo, they are the best versions.

## AUDI V8
Four-door luxury saloon.

### History
*June 1990* Single model, the V8, launched. The engine is a 3562cc unit linked to a four-speed automatic gearbox which offers switchable Sport and Economy modes.
*April 1992* 3.5-litre engine replaced by 4.2-litre V8.

### Fault Finder
Full service history is a must, these are cars which demand regular and fully qualified servicing. Make sure that mileage is verified, because by the very nature of these cars they are often bought to cover high mileages very quickly. Listen to rumbling from the front wheels which may point to worn wheel bearings. Check the ABS anti-lock brakes. If they are not working they are very expensive to replace, repairs are rarely carried out. Such a fault here will cause the car to fail an MOT test. Check for accident damage. Look at the tyres, checking for uneven wear. This can signal incorrect wheel alignment. This is not a common problem, but when it does exist, undue strain is placed on the drive axles and the transmission, and that can lead to expensive repairs.

### Verdict
Still very new, and few have been sold, so little is known about these cars on the second-hand circuit, aside from the fact that their values plummet in the first year. This is a spectacular car to drive and thanks to its understated looks it does not attract attention. Best choice is the newest version, the 4.2-litre engined car, but whichever one you choose, remember that the boot is relatively small.

## AUSTIN MINI (from 1982)
Two-door saloon, originally launched in 1959.

### History
*April 1982* City E and HLE, using 998cc A-Plus economy engine.
*September 1982* Mayfair arrives with high level of equipment.
*October 1983* Limited edition, Sprite.
*July 1984* Special edition, Mini 25.
*June 1985* Limited edition, Ritz.
*June 1986* Limited edition, Piccadilly.
*January 1987* Limited edition, Park Lane.
*June 1987* Limited edition, Advantage.
*February 1988* Limited editions, Red Hot and Jet Black.
*June 1988* Limited edition, Designer.
*January 1989* Special editions, Rose, Sky, Flame, Racing.
*June 1989* Limited edition, Mini 30.
*February 1990* Limited editions, Flame, Racing, Checkmate.
*June 1990* Limited edition, Studio 2.
*July 1990* Limited edition, Mini Cooper.
*September 1990* Mini Cooper

launched. This is a standard model, without the extra trim of the earlier limited edition model.

*February 1991* Special edition, Neon.

*June 1991* Convertible Mini, only 75 made.

## Fault Finder

Most of the early reliability problems which occured with the Mini have been sorted out over the last thirty-three years, but it is still wise to make the following checks. Look under the car at the rear subframe, a large H-shaped girder construction which supports the back end of the Mini. These have always suffered from rust and once they disintegrate the car is past saving. Most modern Minis have their subframes protected, but check for rust, and see if any repair work has been carried out. While looking underneath the car, check the bottom of the sills for rust. It is common for the sills to rust straight through, and although this can be remedied at relatively low cost it often signals further more far-reaching rust in the bodywork of the car. Look for fluid leaks from the drum brakes at the back of the car. Seals wear and cause fluid to leak on to the drums. This causes spongy brakes – and eventually causes brake failure – but in its early stages it can cause the Mini to pull to one side quite violently when braking. Underneath at the front, check the state of the front sub-frame, although this rarely has corrosion problems as bad as the rear frame. While there, check the bottom of the sump for oil leaks and also for damage caused by grounding.

Check the front drive shafts because the rubber boots covering the CV joints often split, letting grit in which then damages the joints. A creaking sound when turning the steering wheel also points to worn CV joints. In the engine bay, examine the sides of the bay for rust, especially rust starting in the wings, because that could work its way right through. It's important to check under the carpets, particularly in the driver's and passengers' footwell because corrosion can eat through here surprisingly quickly, usually at the seam where the wing and sill meet. If you can see any daylight, look for another Mini. This is not serious structural rust, but once it has taken hold it's very hard to eradicate. Look also for rust along the edge of the windows and actually inside the window runners. If it gets bad here it can make the windows rattle as you drive along, and in bad cases they will drop down into the doors. Check for oil leaks from the top of the engine, around the rocker cover. This will mean that a head gasket needs replacing, but this is seldom serious, as long as it's caught early. Mini engines can suffer overheating – not that this happens very often – without serious engine block warping, but when test driving the car keep a close eye on the temperature gauge. If it does creep up to the red line there is a problem which needs looking at. Piston rings can wear but usually only after high mileage, around 60,000 miles plus, but if they have gone there will be plenty of blue smoke and the smell of burning oil when accelerating hard. Gearboxes are virtually unbreakable but because they share the engine's sump oil it's imperative that the oil level is correct. Too low, and it can damage the gearbox even before it damages the engine. Check the fuse box on the side of the engine bay. On Minis made up to around 1984 the fuse box could often take water in and then cause short circuits or failures of circuits. Most commonly affected were the fuses for windscreen wipers, heated rear windscreen and indicators. Check the box for cracks, and check that the windscreen wipers work because if they don't a cracked fuse box could be the culprit. Minis up to the early 1980s did not have a metal guard in front of the engine distributor. This is important because when it rains water comes through the radiator grille and directly onto the distributor, causing the car to stop, or making it near impossible to start in the first place. Later versions had a metal plate placed in front of the distributor and this solved the problem. If there is not a plate fitted, it is easy to fit one yourself. When pulling away from rest, if there is a clunk from the engine, and it lurches, it means the engine mounts have worn. They are easy and inexpensive to replace but if they are not replaced the engine's movement will soon crack the exhaust manifold and a new one will be needed. Check the state of the battery. In the Mini it's placed in the boot where it can often be forgotten about, collecting dust and grime and sometimes not working properly as a result. It should also be properly covered so that no acid can spill on luggage or the car's bodywork.

**Verdict**
Lots of second-hand Minis about, so you should be able to find a good one. Those around five years old are the best because the more recent Minis are very expensive, often costing more than a much bigger and more modern hatchback. The Mini is good fun to drive but those who hanker after more room and a more modern ride and handling package would do well to look at the Metro.

**AUSTIN METRO**
Front-wheel-drive three- and five-door hatchback.

**History**
*October 1980* Three-door versions launched. 1.0, 1.0L and 1.0HLE have 998cc engine. 1.3S and HLS use 1275cc unit. Base 1.0 model also available to special order with low compression engine. HLE is the economy special, with low compression engine as standard and higher gearing. All models have four-speed gearboxes, no five-speed option.
*January 1981* 1.3L, aimed at fleet sales.
*July 1981* 1.3 Auto.
*February 1982* 1.0 City.
*April 1982* 1.3 Vanden Plas.
*May 1982* MG Metro with 1275cc engine.
*September 1982* 1.3L and HL launched, plus trim improvements to other models.
*October 1982* MG Metro Turbo
*January 1983* 1.3HLE launched, base and L models get economy HLE engine.
*January 1984* City X launched as base model.

*October 1984* Five-door versions; City X, 1.0-litre L, 1.3L, 1.3HLE, 1.3 Vanden Plas.

*February 1986* Launch of five-door 1.0 City, 1.3 City, 1.3 Mayfair, and three-door 1.3LE and Mayfair. Trim improvements across the range and extra equipment.

*August 1987* 1.3 City three-door Auto.

*October 1988* 1.3GS, Sport and GTa.

*January 1990* 1.0-litre and 1.3-litre Clubman and Clubman L replace City, City X and L models.

*April 1990* New Metro launched. 1.1C, 1.1L, 1.1S, 1.4SL, 1.4GTa, 1.4GS. All except 1.1C and L have five-speed gearbox (optional on others).

*June 1991* 1.4GTa 16-valve.

**Fault Finder**

The worst years for Metro reliability were 1980 to 1984 but all Metros should be checked for all of the following. Poor engine running on the earliest Metros led to the engines running-on badly after they had been switched off. It could also produce bad engine back-firing and poor running at idling speed. The design of the carburettor was the culprit and no amount of adjustment could solve the problem. The car's tick-over was either too fast or it barely ticked-over at all, often stalling particularly when the engine had had time to warm up. This was most common on the 1.0-litre cars, less of a problem on the 1.3-litre. Suspension on all Metros is a Hydragas type which often suffers from leaks. This causes a corner of the car to list badly, while suspensions which have not regularly

been pumped back up – this is part of the regular servicing – causes the whole car to sit down on its springs. In severe cases the Hydragas units have to be completely changed, but in most cases it's a matter of replacing the seals and then pumping the system back up. Check for this problem by slowly walking around the car and checking that all corners are level. If the car is sitting down on its springs the sensible course is to go and look at a better Metro. Rust rears its head in a number of places on the Metro, even on fairly new ones. One of the worst areas is on the front wings, just forward of where the wing meets the front door. Rust works its way from under the wing, so when you eventually see it bubbling through the paintwork it has already taken a deep hold on the metal. Unless spotted early it's usually only cured by replacing the wing with a new one. Check the sills, especially at the front where they meet the wheel arches. Water often gets in here and is then trapped under the sill where it eventually produces rust, again eating its way from inside the sill to the outside. This can be quite serious and in the worst cases can cause an MOT failure. Look inside the engine bay for corrosion, particularly along the sides of the bay where any corrosion may lead through into the front wings. Also, check for rust on the front spoiler because this is easily damaged by stones, and soon corrodes. Rust can sometimes also be found in the roof rain channels and in severe cases this can lead to rust spots on the edges of the roof, especially at the back of the car. The tail-gate does not normally rust but check along its bottom edge and then slam it closed, looking for any rust dust flying out. Rust also gathers around the headlamps, in particular on the thin outside edge nearest the wing. Oil leaks from the top of the engine are commonplace, but not necessarily serious. Changing the head gasket usually solves the problem and as long as the Metro has not been driven like this for too long it should not have damaged the engine, as this is one of the most robust units on the market. Not so the gearchange on the earlier four-speed cars. All Metros have always suffered from gear whine, and in some cars it can be painfully noisy. Gear whine in itself is not a problem but on many early Metros (1980–5) the whine was combined with metal stripping from the gear cogs and eventually causing the gearbox to seize. So, if gear whine is excessive there could be a problem brewing. On Metros built after 1985 a new design was used so the problem did not reoccur. Five-speed Metro gearboxes are very good, and suffer no common faults. The rubber gaiters on the front drive shafts need a careful examination. They often split and once they do, grit gets in and damages the CV joints. If this problem exists, you will hear a creaking noise when turning at low speeds, and in extreme cases – when the drive shafts have been seriously damaged – there will be a loud clunk from the front of the car when moving away from rest. Water leaks through the window rubbers are common on all Metros, mostly the water will dribble through the front side window rubbers where they meet the windscreen pillar. This is not easy to spot because it only manifests itself when the car has been sitting in a rain storm. Ironically, when driving along, water rarely comes through because the air pressure forces it away from the side window. You can check for this type of leak by looking carefully at the carpets, especially in the corner where the bulkhead meets the door sill. If there is rust here, or the carpet is discoloured, or, of course, if it's damp, then this problem could exist. It is not an easy problem to cure. Replacing the entire window rubber can be the only answer and even this will not guarantee a cure. The front disc brakes on all Metros are prone to attracting grit which sticks in the calipers and quickly scores the discs, which in turn makes the brake pads wear quickly, a problem which can only be solved by fitting new discs. Metros built from 1986 had a different design of caliper, with a special guard built on, so the problem is less likely to occur. Even so, run your finger over the discs to see if they are smooth. A word of warning – do this before you drive the car, because the discs will be red hot afterwards. Engine mounts can wear out after as little as 30,000 miles, but they are not expensive to replace. As with any car with this problem, do make sure that mounts are changed as quickly as possible, if not, the movement of the engine will soon crack the exhaust manifold. If the mounts have worn, then the engine will lurch as you accelerate from rest.

**Verdict**
There are a vast number of Metros on the second-hand market, and

chosen with care you will find it a reliable and pleasant car. Best versions are those with the 1.5-litre engine and five-speed gearbox, but if they are beyond your budget try and get a 1.3-litre car, the newer the better. There are better rivals, chiefly the Peugeot 205, Ford Fiesta and Volkswagen Polo.

## AUSTIN MAESTRO
Front-wheel-drive family hatchback.

### History
*March 1983* 1.3 Base, 1.3L, 1.3HLE, 1.6L, 1.6HLS, 1.6 Vanden Plas, 1.6MG.
*October 1983* 1.6 Auto.
*October 1984* 1.3HL, 1.6HL, 2.0MG.
*August 1985* 1.3 City and City X. latter replaces Base model.
*February 1986* 1.6 Mayfair launched, plus trim and equipment improvements across the range.
*April 1987* Revised range. 1.3 Mayfair replaces HL, automatic transmission available on 1.6L.
*October 1988* 1.3 Special replaces City and City X. SL replaces Mayfair and Vanden Plas.
*January 1989* MG Turbo.
*March 1990* Revised range, 1.3 Clubman, 2.0 Clubman diesel, 1.3LX, 1.6LX Auto, 2.0DLX diesel, MG and MG Turbo.

### Fault Finder
The earliest Maestros – those built from 1983 to 1985 – suffered from appalling build quality, resulting in trim falling off and the onset of numerous rattles and squeaks

which it was virtually impossible to eradicate. In many cases, dashboards came away from the car completely. However, two years after the launch of the Maestro most of these problems had been sorted out. Maestro 1.6-litre engines often spring oil leaks from the top of the engine. Check carefully for this because it will usually mean the head gasket needs changing. If the gasket has failed, damage may already have been caused to the engine due to overheating, so look carefully at the temperature gauge when driving – if it's right up against the red line, leave that car well alone. Other oil leaks which are potentially more serious can come from the timing chain cover. Check for any evidence of major oil leaks from here, they can spell serious engine trouble. Clutches on 1.6-litre cars in particular are prone to slipping, and early failure. Make sure that the clutch on the car you're trying to buy is well weighted and doesn't slip on hillstarts. A loud rumbling sound from under the bonnet when the car is ticking over will almost certainly be a faulty distributor. This is a common fault on 1.3-litre engined cars, especially those built in 1985. Early 1.3-litre engines used an electronic carburettor which did not work well, often sending too rich a mixture to the engine, causing early engine coking and higher than average fuel consumption. Cars from around 1985 reverted back to a more orthodox carburettor set-up, linked to a manual choke, rather than the unreliable automatic choke. On all Maestros it's a good idea to take the vacuum pipe off the engine when it's

running. If the engine continues to
run it usually means that there is
a crankshaft problem which is
quite serious. Do not buy a Maestro with this fault. The easiest
engine for mechanics to work on is
the 1.3-litre unit, but try and avoid
the low compression 1.3-litre
engines, they never ran very
smoothly and while essentially
reliable they could burn out pistons at a relatively early age, often
as low as 50,000 miles. The
1.6-litre carburettor engine found
in the first MG versions was not a
good arrangement, the carburettors were forever running badly,
causing heavy fuel consumption,
indifferent performance and often
making the car stall in heavy
traffic. The 1600 MG also suffers
from a weak gearbox, with synchromesh being stripped away
very quickly and, in serious cases,
metal stripping off the gearbox's
cogs, badly damaging the gearbox.
On 1.6-litre engines the engine's
crankcase does not breathe well
and if regular oil changes have not
been carried out it means that the
valve clearance closes up, eventually causing engine failure. This
is not easy to spot, so the only way
to be reasonably sure that the car
you're looking at is not suffering
with this problem is to look for a
full service history and hope that
all of the oil changes have been
carried out. Major structural corrosion is not a Maestro problem
but corrosion does attack the
bottoms of the front doors and in
serious cases can eat its way
through. Cars produced in 1990–2
are much better. Finally, the
bumpers are rather flimsy plastic
affairs and they often crack and
splinter. They cannot cope with

any heavy knocks. Thankfully,
they are relatively cheap to
replace.

**Verdict**
Choose a good Maestro and it will
be reliable, very inexpensive to run
and very practical. The secret is to
choose as new a Maestro as
possible, preferably one which is
two or three years old, with a full
service record.

## AUSTIN MONTEGO
Front-wheel-drive        four-door
saloons and five-door estates.

**History**
*April 1984* Range consists of
1.3-litre Base, 1.6 Base, 1.6L,
1.6HL, 2.0HL, 2.0HLS, 2.0
Vanden Plas, 2.0i MG.
*October 1984* Estate car versions
launched. 1.6 Base, 1.6L,
1.6HL, 2.0HL, 2.0HLS. Same
equipment levels as equivalent
saloons.
*February 1985* Injection engine for
Vanden Plas saloon and new
VDP estate.
*April 1985* MG Turbo saloon.
*February 1986* 1.6 and 2.0-litre
Mayfair saloons and 2.0 Mayfair estate.
*January 1987* Revised 1.6L and
new 2.0Si saloons.
*April 1987* Revised range. 2.0L
saloon and estate launched. 2.0
Mayfair saloon and estate get
more powerful engine.
*October 1988* 2.0-litre diesel DL
and DSL saloons and estates
with new turbo diesel engine.
*April 1990* Clubman, LX and SLX
replace Base, L and SL.
*February 1991* Diesels get new
two-stage injection engine and
new gearbox with lower ratios.

## Fault Finder

The Montego suffers from similar faults to the Maestro, and like its hatchback brother, early Montegos – those made between 1984 and the end of 1985 – were not well put together, suffering from numerous rattles and squeaks, as well as having badly fitting dashboards and trim. Many Montegos are used as company cars so it's imperative to check the service history. The mileometer may not always be a completely reliable source of information because during the first two years of Montego production there were a whole batch of faulty speedos which were later replaced. It's also possible that a hard-worked Montego may have gone right around the clock and be on its second 100,000 miles. The 1.3-litre cars should be left alone. They leak oil from various parts of the engine and also consume large quantities of oil. This is partly because the engine is really too small to haul this large car around. On both 1.3 and 1.6-litre cars the cylinder head gasket can leak oil and eventually cause expensive problems. In 2.0-litre cars with the electronic engine management system there can often be faults, the most common being the engine running too quickly. The only sure way to solve this problem is to fit a new system, and that's quite expensive. It is imperative that regular oil changes have been carried out, otherwise the valve gear can be affected, eventually causing serious engine problems. The engine which suffers most from this is the 2.0-litre overhead cam unit. Camshaft belts on all models must be replaced at the 36,000 miles service. Check this has been carried out. If the belt is not replaced on time the engine can completely seize. Regular and comprehensive servicing is also vital to the smooth working of the gearbox, especially on 1.3 and 1.6-litre cars. If not properly serviced it can be hard to slot the gear-lever into fourth and fifth gear, a signal that the gearbox is beginning to deteriorate and will not last much longer. As with all front-wheel-drive Rover cars, check for worn front wheel bearings. A deep rumbling noise when driving at slow speed means the bearings need replacing. It's not an expensive repair. And lastly, the brittle plastic bumpers almost always shatter when hit. They are not very expensive to replace but you may have to do it quite often.

## Verdict

After the first year of pretty awful reliability and poor build quality, the Montego improved tremendously. If the car you pick has been properly serviced and has average mileage for its year it should be reliable for years to come. Best choices are the 1.6-litre and 2.0-litre, though the turbo diesel is also impressive, if a touch unrefined.

## BMW 3-SERIES

Rear-wheel-drive saloons and estates.

## History

*January 1983* Revised 316, 320i and 323i, two-door saloons.
*January 1984* Four-door 316, 318i, 320i and 323i. Four-speed auto transmission available on 320i and 323i.

*October 1985* 325i with either five-speed manual or four-speed auto. Optional anti-lock brakes.

*September 1986* 320iSE and 323iSE, high equipment models. Anti-lock brakes standard on 325iSE and Sport.

*April 1987* M3 high performance two-door, and 325iX 4WD (two- and four-door) to special order.

*October 1987* 320i Convertible launched, and 318i gets new 1795cc engine.

*April 1988* 325i Touring estate 5-door.

*September 1988* 316i saloon, 320i Touring estate, 325i Sport reintroduced in two-door form.

*June 1989* 318i Touring.

*February 1990* 316i Lux, 318i Lux launched, plus trim update for 320i and 325i SE.

*February 1991* 318i Convertible.

*April 1991* Range discontinued, new 3-Series launched.

**Fault Finder**
Generally reliable, but it's imperative that full and proper servicing has been carried out – this is the first item to check. The six-cylinder cars are not easy to work on and because of their performance they tend to be driven hard. So, check for cracked cylinder heads on the light alloy engines. This can happen because of a failed water pump, a problem with cars made in the early to mid 1980s. Check for oil leaks from the top of the engine, although this is not commonplace. Fuel injectors last for around 65,000 miles, so if the car you are looking at is nearing this sort of mileage this may well be an expense you'll soon have to face. If performance is ragged, this could be the problem.

The master brake cylinder can leak fluid. Check for any staining around the cylinder. Clutches can wear on the high performance models at around 40,000 miles, so check for a slipping clutch when accelerating. Rust is generally not a problem, but check around the tops of the front wings because it can appear there on a car which has not been well looked after.

**Verdict**
Essentially, a reliable car but do look for a full service record, and be prepared for quite hefty bills when something does need replacing. The 316 and 318 are, in many ways, the best choices, because their engines are much simpler to work on than the bigger six-cylinder units. Also, they are less likely to have been driven excessively hard.

**BMW 5-SERIES**
Rear-wheel-drive                four-door
saloons.

**History**
*October 1981* Revised range launched. 518 uses carburettor engine, 520i, 525i, 528i have injected engines. Five-speed gearbox is an option on the 518, standard on the others.

*May 1983* 525e automatic with new 2693cc economy engine.

*January 1985* M535i high performance model. 518i gets injection engine, and replaces the 518.

*September 1986* 525i SE, with high specification.

*November 1986* High specification versions of all models launched, called Lux variants.

*June 1988* Range discontinued and new range launched. Still rear-wheel drive, but with new, smoother body. Range is 520i, 525i, 530i, 535i. SE (Special Equipment) version of 535i also available.
*September 1988* 520iSE.
*February 1989* 525i Sport.
*May 1990* 518i.
*September 1990* 520i and 525i get new 24-valve engines.
*February 1991* 525i Sport.

**Fault Finder**
The 5-series is one of the most reliable cars in its class, provided it's been well looked after and fully and regularly serviced. Scrutinizing the service records is the most important check. Engines are all pretty much trouble-free but do look for oil leaks around the top of the engine, and watch for smoky exhausts, a sign that the valve seals are wearing right down. Brakes should be checked for scored discs, especially on the top performing versions, and on automatic models make sure there isn't any slipping in the gearbox as it changes up. The upward gearchanges on an auto should be barely perceptible. Look for accident damage, again, especially on the high performance models. Rust is not a problem and is only likely to occur if the paintwork has been previously damaged.

**Verdict**
Best version is the latest shape 525i which combines good performance with a fair equipment level. The secret of successful 5-series ownership is to buy as well equipped a car as possible, preferably from a dealer, and to make

sure that the service record is absolutely tip-top. Do that and the 5 will give well over 100,000 miles of motoring without any major hiccups.

**BMW 6-SERIES**
Rear-wheel-drive sports coupé.

**History**
*June 1982* Range is 628CSi, 633CSi and 635CSi.
*January 1983* Automatic models get four-speed overdrive transmission.
*January 1984* 635CSi available with optional switchable automatic transmission, giving choice of Economy and Sport modes.
*February 1985* M635CSi high performance version.
*October 1987* Trim and equipment revisions and M635CSi gets uprated 200bhp engine.
*September 1988* All models get self-levelling suspension.
*August 1990* Range discontinued.

**Fault Finder**
As with all BMWs, the secret is to get a car which has a full service history. If it hasn't, walk away quickly. Rust is a problem on some of the earliest 6-series, mostly on the front wings, so check carefully for this because once it takes hold it spreads quickly. Mechanically, it's best to try and find an automatic gearbox model, and preferably one with the Sport/Economy switchable gearbox. These are sturdy affairs which last for many thousands of miles. The five-speed manual Getrag gearbox is less successful, often stripping its gears at 80,000 miles or so.

Check for noisy rear axles, especially on the most powerful 6-series models, because owners tend to drive them briskly, with consequent wear to the drive train. Any clunking or groaning from the axle at low speeds should be viewed with suspicion. Engine valve wear is a potential problem on a 6 which has covered more than 60,000 miles – look for a smoky exhaust. Brakes can judder, a sure sign that the discs have either been scored or have warped. Repairs to brakes are quite expensive. Make sure all shock absorbers are in good condition, keeping the car level, and that they are not leaking.

## Verdict
Find one of these cars in good condition and it will just keep on going. High mileage – 100,000 plus – is not a problem, as long as the 6 has been regularly serviced. Beware, though, of high running costs, both in terms of fuel thirst and spare parts and replacement costs. Best choice is the 628CSi.

## BMW 7-SERIES
Rear-wheel-drive saloons.

## History
*February 1981* Range is 728i, 732i, 735i, 735iSE.
*January 1984* 728iSE and 732iSE.
*September 1986* Range discontinued.
*January 1987* New range of sleeker bodied cars. Range is 730i, 730iSE, 735i, 735iSE.
*October 1987* 750iL with V12 engine and long wheelbase.
*January 1988* 736iL long wheelbase.
*February 1989* 750i, with V12 engine but standard wheelbase.

## Fault Finder
Once again, a full service history is a must. Check the engine carefully for oil leaks, and leaks of fluid from the brake master cylinder. It's not easy to sort through all of the wiring under the bonnet of a 7, but take your time, checking for any chafed or partially melted wires. Smoking exhausts are a sign both of hard driving and worn valve seals, and signal major expense. Brakes can judder badly when the discs are badly worn down, and check that the ABS anti-lock braking system is working as it's very expensive to replace. Rust can appear along the wings, but is not commonplace.

## Verdict
First-class value second-hand, due to massive drops in price on the used car market. Why? The 7 lacks the svelte style of the 3 and 5-series cars, but it's still a fine machine. Best choice is the 730iSE with extra equipment and impressive performance. Make sure it's an automatic – manual gearbox models are worth much less.

## CITROËN 2CV
Front-wheel-drive four-door saloon with a two-cylinder air-cooled engine.

## History
First produced in 1949, this car has changed little since then.
*October 1981* Club version launched with folding sun-roof, Charleston with two-tone paintwork also available.
*April 1984* Limited edition. Beachcomber (only 350 pro-

duced) with special blue and white paintwork and striped 'deckchair' style seats.

*June 1985* Special edition Dolly (initially, 810 produced) with choice of three paintwork schemes.

*April 1986* New Dolly with different colour paintwork schemes.

*September 1986* Another Dolly with more differing paintwork schemes.

*July 1988* Special edition, Bamboo with special paintwork colours.

*September 1990* Range discontinued.

**Fault Finder**
Pre-1981 cars did not have disc brakes at the front, so braking was not very effective. If the brakes feel rather wooden and ineffective on a pre-1981 car it is usually this design which is at fault, rather than any inherent problem with the braking system. The engine is air-cooled so there are no problems with water leaks in the engine. But on all 2CVs check all of the air breather hoses for chafing and splits. Such problems can cause engine overheating in stop-start town traffic. The engine is a single overhead camshaft design which has proved mostly reliable. It's also a noisy unit, so it's often hard to detect any untoward noises. Do check for oil leaks from the bottom of the engine. Even if the engine has been steam-cleaned such an oil leak can usually be detected because oil will have flowed along the underside of the car. This is an important check to make, because if there has been engine overheating the engine block is often seriously damaged. Suspension is

the softest there is, so expect excessive body roll. The ride should be very comfortable, even when going over potholes. Feel for crashing from the suspension, especially at the front, because this can signal front wheel kingpin problems. This is a potential problem on all 2CVs, especially on those which have not been regularly serviced by an authorized Citroën dealer. In extreme cases it can lead to one or other of the front wheels coming loose from the drive axle. Check the rear wheels for excessive sideways movement, a sign that the rear axle or suspension bolts are loose. When empty, the 2CV should sit the road levelly. If there is any lean at all its signals problems with the suspension system, usually a worn set of springs. This is most normal on the back offside. Once mastered, the push-pull dashboard mounted gearchange is simplicity to use. It should be smooth and light to operate. There have been few problems with this mechanically simple arrangement, but if there is any resistance slotting into gears, or groaning noises when changing gears, it usually means there's a problem with the gear linkage, often caused by inattentive servicing. This is a problem which is easily cured by a specialist dealer. Check the exhaust carefully, as these very often corrode relatively quickly – sometimes in as little as 20,000 miles. This is more often a problem on the versions built during 1978–86. Because the air cooled engine is quite noisy it is hard to listen out for a defective exhaust, so make sure you get under the car, checking the system for corrosion, or holes. This is an especial problem at the exhaust manifold, where it meets the engine, and where the extreme exhaust temperatures can eat through the thin metal of the pipe quite quickly. Check also for corrosion or holes near the centre of the piping system. A new exhaust is not too expensive but it's far better to find one which is in good condition. Body rust has been a problem, even on the later versions, simply because this car's anti-corrosion treatment has never been up to the standards of more modern cars, allied to the less than clean shape of the front of the car. Check around the headlamps in particular, because it's here that rust can quickly take hold and then eat swiftly through the bonnet. Check also for stone chipping on the bonnet, because this can quickly form major rust spots. The front wings can easily be replaced, but a careful check for corrosion here is paramount, because severe rust here is often a sign that it has taken hold elsewhere in the car's body and is eating its way through and out. This car is hardly bristling with equipment, and you will find the fuel gauge will swing up and down like a pendulum as you corner. This is normal.

## Verdict
This car is mechanically very simple, so there's little that can go wrong. Add to that the 2CV's half century on the roads, which means there's been ample time to sort out any mechnical problems, and it's clear that it's one of the safest second-hand buys. But if you want performance and modern handling, look elsewhere, because while

the softly-sprung and lethargic 2CV is good fun to own, it is light years away from the modern car. For many people thereby lies its charm.

## CITROËN VISA
Front-wheel-drive hatchback.

### History
*January 1982* Visa L, mechanically similar to Super E, but with less trim and lower price.
*February 1983* Visa GT.
*October 1983* 11E and 11RE replace L and Super E, plus launch of 11E Convertible.
*October 1984* 14TRS, plus new dashboards for all models.
*May 1985* 17D and 17RD diesels, plus 1.6-litre GTi.
*October 1985* 10E.
*March 1988* Range discontinued.

### Fault Finder
Engines are sturdy but noisy. Look for oil leaks at the bottom of the engine because the sump plugs often perished slowly, letting oil seep out. Engine mountings wear quite quickly (around 30,000 miles) and is revealed by the engine lurching as you pull away from rest. Brakes have never been very effective, but if they are very spongy check the brake fluid reservoir to see if there are any bubbles in the top of the liquid. This could mean there is a leak in the system, a problem in Visas launched before December 1983. The Visa is an incredibly softly sprung car – with the exception of the GTI – so it's often hard to tell if shock absorbers are in good condition. However, while the car always wallows around corners

there should be no undue bouncing on straight roads. Bonnets are often hit by flying stones and so should be checked for rust. Paintwork is thin so corrosion can easily take hold once the paint has been damaged.

**Verdict**
Few still left on the second-hand market, flimsy bodies saw to that. However, the Visa is a cheap mode of transport with low running costs. Try and go for a 14TRS which has more power than the smaller engined models and yet retains the fine ride which the harder-sprung GTi lacks.

## CITROËN AX
Three- and five-door, front-wheel-drive hatchback.

**History**
*June 1987* Range is 10E, 10RE, 11RE, 11TRE, 14TRS.
*December 1987* GT.
*April 1988* Five-door models launched (10RE, 11RE, 11TRE, 14TZS, the latter similar to the three-door 14TRS).
*November 1988* Uprated engines for GT, TZS and TRS.
*March 1989* Three- and five-door 14RD and 14DTR diesels.
*July 1989* Five-door GT.
*October 1989* 11TGE and 11TRS.
*June 1990* 11TZX three- and five-door, replacing 11TRS.
*May 1991* Revised AX range.

**Fault Finder**
Regular servicing is a must, and make sure that the camshaft belt has been replaced at the correct mileage, all too many Citroën dealers do not replace the belt

when they should. Check the dashboard for fit and finish. Check all switches work properly, and that none are loose. Gear-leavers are flimsy, so check there isn't too much play, if there is, it should be re-tightened by a Citroën mechanic. Rust is not a problem, but check for accident damage. Engines are reliable but exhaust manifolds on 1.1-litre models can crack if engine mountings wear and allow movement of the engine. Any engine lurching when pulling away will point to worn mounts. Brakes often squeal, but this is usually caused by a build-up of brake dust, it's rarely a problem with the braking system itself. Bodywork is thin, so check for damage caused by careless parking, because such damage dramatically knocks value off this car. Check for cracks anywhere in the tail-gate glass because any stress, such as slamming the tail-gate closed, can then cause the glass to shatter.

**Verdict**
Low weight means that all versions of this car perform exceptionally well. Less welcome may be the plasticky interior, but in terms of reliability this car has so far proved pretty impressive. Best version is the 14TRS which combines sparkling performance with low fuel thirst and a first-class ride and handling package.

## CITROËN ZX
Front-wheel-drive five-door hatchback.

**History**
*June 1991* Range is 1.4-litre

Reflex, 1.4 Avantage, 1.6i Aura, 1.9i Volcane.
*September 1991* 1.4 Aura, 1.6i Avantage.
*January 1992* 1.9-litre diesel versions of Avantage, Aura.

**Fault Finder**
Brake pad warning light on. This seldom means the brake pads need replacing, it's a wiring fault. When water gets on to one of the brake wires it causes a false circuit which illuminates the light. Citroën dealers often replace the brake pads when in reality all that is needed is to move the offending cable and resecure it. A similar problem can occur with the handbrake-on warning light. Drive over muddy ground, leave the car for a while and then when you start the car again the light can flicker on and off until the wiring dries out. Both of these warning light problems apply to cars made in 1991 to mid 1992. Check all electrics. The electric windows can fail intermittently, and is usually due to a faulty control panel behind the electric window buttons on the door. When it first begins to show itself, a solid thump on the buttons' surround is usually enough to make them work again. Replacement is not expensive. Sometimes the electric windows will not work unless the sunroof is opened half an inch first, or one of the front doors is opened. This is another minor wiring fault affecting the earliest ZXs and it's a fault which a Citroën dealer can easily cure. An early batch of faulty rear wash/wipe motors should all have been replaced by now. When water got into the mechanism it meant the wiper could not be turned off. If you experience this problem it is cured in about five seconds by having a new motor slotted in. Cost is minimal. On carburettor-engined versions there is often a tendency for the car to be hard to restart after it has warmed up and been left for a while. This is due to fuel evaporation in the carburettor and while not serious, it does become annoying. The problem can be partially solved by advancing the timing on the carburettor. Check that engine tick-over is correct. Some dealers set the tick-over too high, partly to try and get around the carburettor fuel evaporation problem, but this only causes higher fuel consumption and ragged around-town driving. Look for soundproofing under the dashboard hanging down. This happens because there is very little height between the dashboard and the floor, so the material is often caught by driver's and passenger's feet. Hardly a serious problem.

**Verdict**
Still too new to be fully assessed for reliability, but so far the omens mostly look good. The ZX is the most comfortable car in its class, thanks to a superb ride, and it's also very well equipped and terrific value for money. Best choice is the Avantage which is economical, a really good performer, and very practical.

**CITROËN BX**
Front-wheel-drive and four-wheel-drive, five-door hatchbacks and estates.

## History

*August 1983* Range is 14, 14E, 14RE, 16RS, 16TRS.

*April 1984* 19RD diesel.

*October 1984* 19GT.

*August 1985* 16RS, 19TRS, 19RD estates. RD uses diesel engine.

*October 1985* 14 Leader hatchback. RD gets 1769cc diesel engine and is rebadged 17RD. 19DTR hatchback gets the 1905cc diesel engine.

*June 1986* GTi hatchback, 19TRS hatchback.

*February 1987* 16RE hatchback with 1580cc petrol engine.

*July 1987* GTi 16-valve.

*April 1988* 19TRi estate.

*May 1988* DTR Turbo hatchback and estate.

*December 1988* 17RD Turbo hatchback.

*June 1989* 14TGE and 16TGS hatchbacks.

*August 1989* Revised GTi 16-valve hatchback, changes to trim and equipment.

*December 1989* Revised range. TG models replace R models, TZ replace TR, plus trim and equipment changes.

*February 1990* GTi 4x4 hatchback and 4x4 estate.

*June 1990* Four-speed automatic available on 19TGD and TZD diesels.

## Fault Finder

Try and look for low to average mileage models because high mileage BXs can be unreliable. So, try and avoid any petrol models over 70,000 miles, the diesels do last longer. On petrol-engined BXs listen for a rattly engine on tick-over, this could mean the camshaft belt has not been replaced. This is a must because if they are not replaced before 50,000 miles they can snap and then you may well need a new engine, or at the least an expensive engine rebuild. Look for this on the service record because until around 1986 Citroën only 'recommended' replacement at 50,000 miles, but many owners were unaware of this, simply because the maintenance guide did not mention this until 1986. The same applies to diesel-engined models, but because the unit has a diesel rattle it is not so easy to spot cambelt problems by ear. The best policy is to make sure that the belt has been changed if mileage is anywhere near 50,000. When driving, make sure that the clutch has enough weight, because clutch cables are prone to failure. There may be nothing to warn you, but a floppy clutch will certainly signal imminent failure. Rust is generally not a problem, particularly so on the bonnet, because it's made of plastic. However, the sides of the BX are very thin metal and therefore susceptible to knocks in car parks. Check the bodywork carefully, especially where small dings and dents might be leading to corrosion. Check the front brake pipes underneath the car. Until 1986 they were metal and tended to rust through. Later models have plastic pipes, which are much more robust. All BXs built between 1983 and November 1990 have been recalled for a free check on the braking system, and replacement where needed. If you are looking at one of these cars – there are some 170,000 of them on UK roads – make sure the check has been carried out. Check the electrics, especially central locking

and electric windows. Central
locking sometimes fails, only working on the driver's door, and
windows often fall off their runners and drop down inside the
door. Trim is not the most robust,
even on newer models, so look for
good fit and finish. On estate
models check for wear and tear in
the cargo area. On all models make
sure that the self-levelling hydropneumatic suspension is working
properly. The BX should sit the
road squarely and evenly, no
matter what the load. If it is
dipping down on one side there is a
serious suspension problem which
will be expensive to correct.

**Verdict**
There are lots of BXs on the
second-hand market, so it isn't too
hard a job to find a good one.
Diesels are well worth looking at
because they perform as well as
most petrol cars, are capable of
very high mileages and prove very
economical.

## CITROËN CX (from 1981)
Front-wheel-drive saloons and
estates.

**History**
*August 1981* 2000 Reflex Safari
and Familiale estates with
1995cc engine. Automatic
models retain the 2347cc
engine.
*September 1982* Trim and equipment revision, plus badging
changes. New range is CX 20,
Safari estate, Familiale, CX
Pallas, CX 25D, 25D Safari,
25D Familiale.
*October 1983* All petrol injection
and diesel models get new

2.5-litre engine block. Launch of
DTR saloon and DTR Safari
turbo diesel models. TRi Safari
gets injected engine and standard auto gearbox (five-speed an
option).
*October 1984* GTi Turbo.
*October 1985* RE saloon and Safari
launched. 22TRS saloon with
2.2-litre engine. 25RI Familiale
to special order. GTi only available with three-speed automatic.
*March 1987* 25 DTR Turbo 2 Safari.
*December 1988* TGD turbo diesel
Safari.
*March 1991* Range discontinued.

**Fault Finder**
Very complex to work on and
therefore very expensive to run.
Check condition of the brakes
because renewing brake pads and
discs takes hours of labour. If the
brakes have a fault, there will be a
delayed action between touching
the pedal and the brakes biting.
Check the rear brake calipers,
because rust can get in and make
them seize. Engines are generally
reliable but carry out the usual
checks for oil leaks, especially from
the top of the engine because that
could mean there's a leak from the
head gasket which may already
have caused engine damage.
Check on the temperature gauge
for overheating, another sign that
the engine might have overheated
previously and caused serious
damage. Suspension needs careful
checking. The hydropneumatic
arrangement is generally trouble-
free but if the balls which support
the suspension and thus support
the car are leaking then repairs
are exceptionally costly and time-
consuming. If the car has been

sitting for some time it will be sitting right down on its wheels. But when the engine is fired it should rise levelly and sit level, with no sagging or dipping on any of the corners. Push the ride height lever to its maximum ride height. The CX should rise levelly, and sit well clear of the wheels. If it stays in this position then the suspension is sound, but if it slowly sinks back down there are faults which will be expensive to repair. You also need to check the colour of the hydraulic suspension fluid – known as LHM. It should be bright green, if it is any other colour there is a serious problem. And the fluid should be changed completely every 30,000 miles, so check the service history to make sure this has been done. When driving, check for any dipping when braking. The CX should stop without dipping forwards because the suspension keeps it level at all times. If this does not happen on the car you are looking at, leave it well alone. Steering self-centres very strongly – as soon as you let go of the steering wheel it sweeps back to the centre position – and there is a very serious fault if the CX you are looking at does not do this, or if it pulls to one side. Rust is a problem, but usually it's cosmetic, rather than a serious structural problem. Nevertheless, check the insides of the engine bay for any serious corrosion along the sides and into the car's wings. At the back, check that there is no corrosion under the rear wings. Also look around the light packs at the back because corrosion can often eat around them so that they eventually fall right out. And where chrome meets the bodywork

look closely for any rust creeping out from underneath, where moisture gets trapped. A minor fault is a ticking speedometer, but this can usually be cured by pumping grease into the cable. Inside, check the quality of the trim, and for any sagging or splitting in the seat material.

**Verdict**
Not for the faint-hearted, the CX is only for those who really know about CX mechanicals, or know someone who does. If you do, then prices are low and value is high, these are big cars offering the utmost in comfort and, in GTi form, the best of performance, albeit only in a straight line.

**CITROËN XM**
Front-wheel-drive hatchbacks and estates.

**History**
*October 1989* Range launched, consisting of, 2.0, 2.0i, 2.0Si, 2.0SEi, 3.0V6 Si, 3.0V6 SEi.
*March 1990* Turbo diesel models; D, SD, SED.
*May 1990* A ZF four-speed automatic transmission is fitted as standard to the V6 models, while manual five-speed becomes a no cost option. Automatic gearbox optional on 2.0-litre at extra cost.
*July 1990* High power XM 24-valve V6 launched.
*March 1991* ZF automatic gearbox available on turbo diesel models.
*November 1991* Estate versions launched. Range is 2.0i, 2.0Si, V6, 3.0i, V6 3.0SEi, SD turbo diesel.

## Fault Finder

The XM's unique suspension system should be checked for leaks, although it is very unlikely that such a problem will have occurred on this car so far. But, to be on the safe side, check that the car sits the road squarely and levelly. There have not been any problems with engines so far, so just make the usual checks for oil leaks. On models with ABS anti-lock brakes make sure that these work properly. There have been cases of ABS systems failing on one or other wheel, with potentially disastrous results. This does not appear to have happened on the XM, but it should be checked. The XM has an absurd handbrake design. It is more a footbrake than handbrake, and it is all too easy to push the brake down too far so that it is then impossible to re-release it. If this happens out on the road the only alternative is to disconnect the cable before you can drive off again. So, make sure that the hand/foot brake is working properly and that it holds the car on a hill without you having to push it down too far. Gearboxes appear to have been reliable so far. The powerful brakes do have a big appetite for brake pads, so make sure you check the brakes are working properly – there should be very little movement on the brake pedal before the brakes bite – and check also for any scoring of the discs. Citroën's on-board electrics rarely cause problems, but most XM's are stuffed with electrical gadgetry so check it is all working properly because repairs are not always easy. One problem which some owners have reported is electric windows working only intermittently. Such a fault cannot be tracked down easily, simply because it is not always there.

## Verdict

No long-term problems have arisen with the XM yet, partly because it's a relatively new car. As with any Citroën, a comprehensive service record is a must and if you are buying, it's very important to make sure that all of the electrics are working properly. One of the best all round models is the SD turbo diesel. It's refined, a good performer and the most reliable of the lot. Inside, check the quality of the trim, and for any sagging or splitting in the seat material.

## DACIA DUSTER

Four-wheel-drive utility vehicle.

### History

*May 1984* GLX with 1397cc engine and four-speed gearbox.
*January 1986* Trim improvements.
*October 1988* Roadster 4WD Soft-top.
*October 1989* GLD diesel with 1596cc engine.
*March 1991* Range discontinued.

### Fault Finder

Check the engine for oil leaks. These are Renault-derived units built in Romania and they are not renowned for their toughness. It has even been known for the engine blocks to split. If there are serious looking oil leaks, look for a Duster elsewhere. If the engine is rattly it may well be piston slap. If this is the case, walk away very quickly. Check for a leaking master brake cylinder. Brake pipes should be checked for leaks, especially at the front. The four-wheel-drive system is essentially quite rugged, but check carefully for proper uptake of four-wheel drive when it is switched in, and look for any transmission oil leaks. Check also for leaks from each of the driving axles. Gearboxes have been known to strip their gears. Make sure that the gear selector goes in smoothly and that there are no crunching noises. Brakes should stop the vehicle in a straight line. If not, a brake caliper may be seized. This often happens with Dusters which have been used off-road. Check carefully for rust, particularly underneath the Duster, and around the suspension turrets. Surface body rust is not so common, but check just in case. Look for leaks from the shock absorbers, again, especially if the Duster has been used off-road for any period. Inside the cab, check the seats for rips and tears.

**Verdict**
Bargain basement vehicle, with all that that means. Quality control has never been up to mainstream European standards and while the Duster is inexpensive that's because reliability is not good.

**DAIHATSU DOMINO (From 1986)**
Front-wheel-drive, five-door hatchback.

**History**
*April 1986* New Domino launched.
*March 1988* Restyled exterior.
*April 1990* Discontinued.

**Fault Finder**
The small engines do not last well, particularly if subjected to high speeds or extremes of engine heat. If there looks to be water mixed in with the oil – check for blobs of water on the oil dipstick – a head gasket has failed. This is not a common fault on this car, but it's wise to look for it because if the gasket does go and is not swiftly replaced the engine can overheat and quickly crack the engine block. Brakes seldom wear quickly but they can bind on the front wheels. Let the car roll down a very gentle slope to check for this. Check the bottoms of the doors for rust. It's not common but some Dominos have door drain holes which silt up and then store water in the doors, causing serious corrosion from the inside out. Check tyres for wear. Because the wheels are small the tread tends to wear down quickly. The Domino is quite near to the ground, so check the front brake pipes for damage, and the bottom of the engine for any knocks. Exhausts wear at the manifold very quickly. Check for undue noise from a blowing exhaust, although it must be said that the Domino's engine is none too quiet, so hearing a defective exhaust will not be easy. Check the top of the exhaust for any gaps between it and the engine, and when it's cold try moving the manifold side-to-side to see if it's in good condition, and firmly connected.

**Verdict**
A fairly rare sight, the Domino's territory is in town – it's not a car for the open road. Running costs can be very low because fuel economy is amazingly good, but

against that are quite high repair costs should anything go wrong, and the limited availability of spares.

## DAIHATSU CHARADE
Front-wheel-drive hatchback.

### History
*April 1983* Revised range, Base model, CS, CX, CX with high roof.
*October 1983* Diesel and Diesel High Roof five-door models.
*April 1984* Turbo three-door and five-door models.
*June 1985* Revised range; CS, CX, Turbo, with petrol and diesel engines. Petrol-engined Turbo gets uprated suspension.
*April 1987* Range discontinued and replaced by new model.
*May 1987* New range is, CS, CX, CX Auto, CS Diesel Turbo, GTi.
*April 1989* 1.3CX.
*May 1991* 1.3CXi and 1.3GXi.

### Fault Finder
The petrol turbo engine runs at high temperatures and has a thirst for oil. Check for smooth running of the turbo, if it's rattling when the engine is started then it may not last that much longer. The turbo engines do not sound too smooth when ticking over, and they can sometimes be jerky around town – this does not necessarily mean there's a problem with the car, it's merely a facet of the engine design. Transmissions are strong, but check for worn synchromesh, especially on second and third gears on petrol turbo versions, and a slipping clutch – a sure sign the car has been given a hard life around town. The turbo should

also be checked on diesel models and it's vitally important that diesels have been serviced according to the service instructions, and not run beyond their service schedules. On Charades built during 1983 there were manufacturing faults on a large number of cylinder heads which led to the cylinder heads cracking, quickly leading to overheating and damage to the engine. When driving the car, keep a watchful eye on the temperature gauge – if it is up near the red line then the cylinder head problem almost certainly exists, and that car should be avoided. Camshaft belts snap very early, often after only 20,000 miles, and when they do go they cause almost immediate damage to the engine, damage which will be very expensive to repair. Check in the service records for cambelt replacement, and if it has not been done, but the car otherwise seems in fine condition, get the cambelt replaced straight away. On diesels in particular, valve seals often wear, again, quite early in the vehicle's life, sometimes as soon as 30,000–40,000 miles. If there are clouds of black smoke from the exhaust, and performance is not good, then worn seals are almost certainly the problem, and it's a car which should be left well alone. Minor corrosion can be a problem, due to thin paintwork and thin metal bodywork. Check the bottoms of doors and under the sills. Charades produced since late 1989 have extensive wax injections into major body cavity areas, so it's very unlikely that these versions will see any major rust.

## Verdict

Well equipped and good value for money on the second-hand market, it must also be said that the petrol turbo model has a highly stressed engine which can wear out, in as little as 40,000 miles. Best choice is one of the later 1.3-litre engined cars, or a low mileage turbo diesel.

## DAIHATSU APPLAUSE

Front-wheel-drive five-door hatchback.

## History

*January 1990* Range launched, 1.6L, 1.6Xi.
*February 1991* 1.6GXi.

## Fault Finder

Look for a full and complete service history. Check second gear synchromesh, on injection cars this can wear after excessive town mileage. Listen for rattling engines on 1.6L models, it's often a sign that the camshaft belt needs replacing. Check bodywork for dings and dents caused by careless parkers, as many Applauses are used in town.

## Verdict

So far, no horror stories about reliability, so this car seems a good buy. Few of them on UK roads, and a small dealer network, combined with quite high replacement parts means the Applause may be more costly to run than some of its closest rivals.

## DAIHATSU SPORTRAK

Four-wheel-drive multi-purpose vehicle.

## History

*March 1989* Launch of DX Soft Top, EL Hard Top.
*July 1990* EFi.
*March 1991* Revised range, 1.6 STi Soft Top, 1.6 ELi, 1.6 ELXi.

## Fault Finder

Try and find out if the Sportrak you are looking at has been used off-road. In any case, check underneath for damage to the underside, leaking shock absorbers, and grit in the front brake discs. Engines are robust and reliable and as long as the Sportrak has been serviced according to Daihatsu's schedule it should give many years of service. Tyres are expensive, so check for good condition, knocking money off if any have gashes or lumps on their sidewalls. Check the freewheeling front hubs click in smoothly when four wheel drive is selected. Make sure the four-wheel drive engages easily. On the Sportrak the lever should slot in smoothly. Likewise, the gearchange. While it's notchy, and synchromesh can sometimes be caught out, the change should be quite light and slot easily into each gear. Carefully examine the interior because seats are not thickly covered and many Sportrak owners are also dog owners, so the backs of the back seats can easily be damaged – the plastic covering punctured – by dogs' claws.

## Verdict

Good fun, and comes in some wacky colour schemes, but the Sportrak also has a rather bouncy ride and the engine is not the smoothest. However, charm is high, there are not many Sportraks imported each year, and so second-hand prices are quite healthy. Remember that there's no such thing as a cheap Sportrak, and you should end up with a first-class vehicle.

## DAIHATSU CHARMANT
Four-door, rear-wheel-drive saloon.

### History
*February 1982* Launch of range, 1300LC, 1300LE, 1600LE.
*May 1984* 1600GLX.
*September 1987* Range discontinued.

### Fault Finder
Check for oil leaks from the rear axle differential, and any oil leaks at the top of the engine. Service history is vital, especially if the Charmant has been run as a high mileage company car. Gearboxes work smoothly but are not the most robust. Check for crunching or resistance when the lever is slotted into a gear. Check for rust on the bonnet, its large, flat surface easily catches stones which damage the paintwork. Check wheel rims for evidence of kerbing because in extreme cases this can damage the steering box.

### Verdict
Few problems with the Charmant, but it's quite an uninteresting car and mechanically is fast becoming dated. Best model is the very well equipped 1600GLX. Rarity will ensure that prices remain quite stable.

## DAIHATSU FOURTRAK
Four-wheel-drive multi-purpose vehicle.

### History
*June 1987* El Turbo Diesel Estate.
*February 1988* 2.8 EX Turbo Diesel.
*February 1990* EL TD gets improved equipment.
*April 1991* Revised range, 2.0GX petrol, 2.8DL diesel, and 2.8TDL and TDX, both turbo diesels.

### Fault Finder
Check gearchanges for smoothness and precision on early or high mileage Fourtraks. The original five-speed gearbox was not one of the most successful, due to lots of notchiness and a tendency for second gear to fail. Check also for oil leaks from the transmission, and both the front and rear drive shafts. Check freewheeling front hubs for corrosion and make sure that they operate smoothly, without sticking. Check bodywork for corrosion caused by bangs and dents, because Fourtrak paintwork is thin. Engines are strong, but carry out the usual checks for oil leaks. If a tow bar is fitted, or has recently been removed, check the exhaust for blue smoke. Although Fourtrak engines are strong and able, excessive towing can damage the engine's valves, causing heavy smoke and dwindling performance. Look under the vehicle to see if off-road use has damaged the underside. This is rare, though, because the Fourtrak has high ground clearance. Check interior trim for damage, as many Fourtraks are used by farmers.

## Verdict

Proven reliability, but even the latest versions are still quite agricultural, and they lack the sheer style of the Sportrak. But prices are competitive and as long as the bodywork is in good order the Fourtrak will last for many years.

## FSO

Rear-wheel-drive,        four-door saloon.

## History

*June 1981* 1300 launched.
*October 1984* 1500 saloon launched.
*November 1991* Range discontinued.

## Fault Finder

Oil leaks are commonplace, so check the entire engine carefully. Piston slap is also a common fault, even on cars with relatively low mileage (20,000 miles) so listen for any knocking from the engine, or undue rattling. Fuel pumps and water pumps have both been known to fail, so look for leaks, and listen for a banging sound when the engine is idling – this could be a faulty water pump. Brake master cylinders can leak. Check also for leaking fluid on the brake discs at the front. When driving, it's vitally important that the brakes pull the FSO up in a straight line. If they do not then it could be something as simple as a sticking caliper, but while this problem is relatively easy to cure, it does reoccur quite regularly. The brakes are very heavily servoed, so they bite almost immediately and on models made before mid 1984 this can cause alarming wheel lock-up, usually on the back wheels. The best option here is to go for one of the later models because they don't have this problem quite so badly. Look under the wheelarches to check for any leaking from the suspension struts. At the same time, make sure that the car is sitting on the road evenly, there have been a number of cases where rear suspension has collapsed on one or even both sides. Listen carefully for rumbling from the front wheels, because worn wheel bearings are common. Prise the hub caps off and look for any oil weeps from around the centre of the wheel. If serious, this could herald the end of front wheel bearings – not an expensive replacement – or, more seriously, if there are leaks on the back wheels this could signal problems with the main axle driving hubs. Check under the rear of the car for any serious oil leaks from the drive shaft in the centre of the drive axle. Also, when driving, listen carefully for any drumming, rumbling sounds from the rear axle, because this usually means that the drive shaft is nearing the end of its life. Steering is heavy on all FSOs but check for any undue stiffness when turning the wheel at moderate speed, and listen for creaking from the steering column. If present, this usually means that there is wear on the steering rack, or inside the steering column, and these problems can be expensive to cure. Electrics should all be checked, mostly the lights and indicators, and check the trim for any loose bits. Rust can be a major problem on the earliest FSO saloons, ranging right from small areas where stone chips have damaged the paint, to major corrosion inside the engine bay and right on through the front wings. At the back, the rear wings also need to be checked thoroughly for rot, and it is not uncommon to see FSOs with badly rusting bumpers, although at least these can be replaced fairly inexpensively. Look under the covering in the boot for any standing water, or corrosion which is eating its way through the boot floor.

## Verdict

If you can only afford the very cheapest second-hand car, then take a look at an FSO, at least you get a lot of metal for your money. But it is not a desirable car, and many things go wrong. It's better to try and opt for a more modern hatchback from a mainstream European maker. You might have to buy something a little older, but at least it will last longer.

## FSO POLONEZ
Rear-wheel-drive hatchback.

## History
*June 1983* Revised 1.5LE.
*July 1985* Prima 1.5-litre.
*December 1987* 1.6SLE and 1.5SCE.

## Fault Finder
Engines are generally strong, but check for oil leaks from the top of the engine, and listen for any rattling on tick-over, a sign of a worn timing chain. If there is a knocking sound, this could be a faulty water pump. Check for excessive smoke from the exhaust, as these cars often have worn engine valve seals, sometimes as early as 15,000 miles. Brakes should be checked for worn and scored discs. Check also for pulling to one side (a sign of seized calipers) because while this is not too serious, it is a fault which keeps coming back. Gearboxes are quite strong but the quality of the gearchange varies from car to car, sometimes being sloppy, while on other cars it's hard to slot the lever into a gear. There's little that can be done about these traits, but it's very important that there's no crunching as the gear-lever goes in, because this points to stripping of the gearbox cogs, a warning sign of the gearbox's imminent demise. Check the clutch for slipping, because the clutch can fail early on in the car's life – around 20,000 miles is not uncommon. Interior trim, and especially the dashboard, should be checked over, mainly because wires tend to hang down under the dashboard and are sometimes accidentally snagged by passengers, causing electrical failures. When replaced they are not always reconnected properly, as they are awkward to get at. Check all electrics carefully, in particularly the dashboard dials and switches. There have been cases where the switches have worked backwards! Rust is not as big a problem as on the FSO saloon, yet it still needs to be looked for, especially if you're looking at one of the older Polonez models. Look around the tops of the front wings, the bottoms of the front doors, and the sills right along the car. Also look in the cargo area, especially towards the back of the boot in the corners, this is where rust can take a hold and eventually eat right

through the floor. Finally, check that all of the door handles and catches work properly, because they often stick.

## Verdict

The Polonez is a whole lot better car than the FSO saloon, but it still cannot match the best from the major European and Japanese producers, not by a long way. While you do get a lot of car for the money it has to be said that a smaller, even older, major European car would be a better buy, and will also retain a healthier second-hand value.

## FIAT 126

Rear-wheel-drive, rear-engined. Originally a saloon, then a hatchback.

### History

*February 1982* Two-door De Ville.
*May 1985* Revisions to engine and trim.
*September 1987* 126 Bis, three-door launched with bigger engine (704cc).

### Fault Finder

Engines are noisy at the best of times, but they should not rattle on tick-over, as this is a sign of valve wear. It has to be said that these engines do not last long. The problem is not so much the design of the engine as its small size. This means it's revved hard by drivers and more often than not it's pushed to its limits in each gear. So, check for any oil leaks from the engine, and keep a very careful eye on the temperature gauge, these cars are renowned for overheating, mostly because of blocked oil breather pipes. The rear drive shafts which slot into each rear wheel can leak oil, look for evidence of this. Hard cornering can cause quick tyre wear, especially at the back. But if tyre wear is uneven, particularly at the back, it can be a symptom of worn suspension bushes, and these are rather tricky to replace. Check the smoothness of the gearbox. The gear-lever should slot in precisely and easily. Synchromesh wears on second gear. The exhaust is noisy at the best of times, but try and see if it's blowing, or if there are corrosion holes at the rear end, because the system is not easy to replace. Interior trim is rather flimsy, so make sure it fits well, and that everything works properly. Check electrics over very carefully, paying particular attention to the gauges. Rust is not the problem it is on some other Italian cars, but still, check the 126 over carefully, just in case. Look inside the cramped engine bay for any evidence of corrosion there.

### Verdict

Noisy and miniscule, but a mostly inexpensive little car to run. Prices second-hand are attractive on the face of it, but squeezing yourself inside the Fiat is less of an attraction.

## FIAT 127

Front-wheel-drive hatchbacks.

### History

*May 1982* Revised range, two-door 900 Comfort, three-door 1050 Comfort, 1050 Super, 1300 GT.
*September 1983* Range discontinued.

## Fault Finder

Both the 950 and the overhead camshaft 1050 are quite noisy engines, and even on tick-over the timing chains can sound quite rattly. While this is normal, any excessive growling from the engine should be treated with suspicion because it could mean that the timing belt is on its way out. On the 1050 and 1.3-litre engines it's crucial that the camshaft belts are changed every 35,000 miles, so check the service history to see if this has been done. If they are not changed in time, and they snap, serious damage can be caused to the engine. On all engines, listen for potential piston and valve problems. Piston slap can be heard quite easily, and if there is excessive smoke from the exhaust then the valve seals could be worn. Both of these problems are expensive to correct. Check for any water and oil leaks from the engine block. These can usually be cured by replacing gaskets – not a terribly big job – but any seriously leaking gaskets might also have allowed the engine to overheat, and that could have damaged the block. When driving, keep a careful eye on the temperature gauge to check it doesn't climb too near the red line. The gearchange is a touch notchy, but light enough. Nylon bushes on the gear-lever itself often wear, making for awkward selection into some gears. These are fairly easily replaced. Another, potentially more serious, fault is for the gear-lever to come completely loose, detaching itself from the gearbox. There is only one bolt holding the lever in place and it can work loose, falling into the top of the gearbox. An excessively loose gear-lever could well point to this imminent problem. Clutch cables do not last long. If there is excessive clatter from the clutch when it's pushed down, or the pedal is rather floppy, this could mean the cable has stretched and will soon need replacing. The rubber boots on the drive shafts at the front of the car should be intact. If they are split and oil has leaked out it could be that damage has already been caused to the constant velocity joints inside. If there is a knocking sound when the steering wheel is turned then this could be the problem. Front wheel bearings wear quickly. If they are wearing out they can usually be heard rumbling at low speeds. Look under the hub-caps as well, because if the bearings are about to go they will be leaking oil onto the centre of the front wheels. Look for leaks from the suspension struts. If leaking they will need to be replaced. The suspension's lower ball joints also wear on the 127. If they are worn they will groan when cornering and may make a clacking sound when going over bumps. Inside the car, check for fluid leaking down on to the brake pedal. This signals a leak from the brake master cylinder. It's also worth examining the brake drums both for wear, and for leaks from brake pipes. Rust is a problem on the 127, particularly on the very early ones. Check the paintwork carefully because bad paint application often caused paint blisters, which then led to rust. Check for rust on the sills, the bottoms of the doors, the jacking points along the sides of the car, the tail-gate, and even the tail-gate hinges.

## Verdict

To drive, the 127 is really good fun, but its rust problems and the fact that mechanically it is not easy to work on puts off a good number of potential buyers. Find a good 127 and you will enjoy it, a bad one will be a nightmare.

## FIAT PANDA

Front-wheel-drive hatchback.

## History

*July 1981* Panda three-door launched.
*September 1982* Panda Comfort.
*March 1983* Panda Super.
*September 1984* Panda 4x4
*April 1986* Revised range, 750L, 1000CL, 1000 Super, 1000 4x4.

## Fault Finder

The overhead camshaft engine is a reliable unit but on the 1000 versions do check for rattling timing chains – easily heard when the engine is ticking over – and oil leaks from the engine, especially from the engine sump gasket. To check this, look under the car for evidence of a major oil leak, both along the bottom of the car, and also on the ground. Look at the drive shafts on each front wheel because the drive shaft seals can wear and leak fluid. If left for a while this can cause serious damage to the drive shafts. Front brakes can sometimes seize on one side, and it's not always apparent, even when braking. The best way to check is to lightly touch the wheel itself and if it is very hot this could be the problem. Not an expensive repair. Rust is not a major problem, but due to the boxy shape of this car, when it does rust

in the body seams it can spread quite quickly. Look also for any accident damage to the front of the Panda. Because of the Panda's boxy shape, a frontal accident can distort the whole car, and it is none too easy to repair. When driving, make sure that the Panda doesn't pull to one side. Also check for this when braking.

## Verdict

A very inexpensive and rather basic car, but good fun to drive and, mechanically, fairly sound. Best choice is one of the 1000 models but due to the unpopularity of the slower 750, prices for this car are a snip.

## FIAT UNO

Front-wheel-drive hatchback.

## History

*June 1983* Range is launched, 45 Comfort, 45ES, 55 Comfort, 55 Super, 70 Super.
*July 1985* Turbo IE.
*August 1985* Revised range, 45 FIRE, 45S FIRE, 60, 60S, 70SL.
*July 1987* Selecta (model with auto transmission) launched.
*August 1987* 60DS diesel launched.
*January 1990* New range launched, 60S FIRE, 70SXie, 70 Selecta, Turbo ie, 60D, 60DS.
*May 1991* 1.4 ieS.

## Fault Finder

This is a very reliable car, and although timing chains sometimes rattle, and there can be engine tappet noise, there are rarely any serious mechanical problems. Check all engines for oil leaks, in particular around the sump area at the bottom of the engine. When this occurs it's usually a worn gasket which can easily be replaced. Gearboxes are mostly robust but the gearchange is quite notchy. There have been cases of the nylon bushes wearing in the gearchange remote control, so if it's very hard to get into any gear this could be the problem. Repair is not expensive. Oil leaks from the in-board driveshaft gaiters are quite common and as long as they are spotted early enough, they are inexpensive to replace. Check for this by looking under the car and following the drive shafts back from the wheels, towards the engine. Brakes have always been a touch spongy, but check that the Uno pulls up straight when braking. If not it could be seized brake calipers, quite a common problem, but again, inexpensive to repair. Electrics can suffer from damp getting in, sometimes causing false readings, and occasionally causing complete short circuits, and therefore electrical failure. Make sure that all electrics are working properly, because fault-finding can be a long process. It's important to make sure that the headlamp switch is working. This is the most common switch to fail, usually because of water getting into the system. Rust is rarely a problem, but check just in case. The area around the tail-gate window can catch water which then begins to corrode the surround. Look at the sills, because while rust is rare, stone chips can take the paint off, especially near the front wheels.

### Verdict

For many years this has been Europe's top selling car, and with good reason, for the Uno is a very reliable car which doesn't suffer the rust ravages of most of its earlier brothers. Best choices are the 60 and 70 versions, but for round-town use the smaller FIRE engine is ideal.

## FIAT TIPO
Front-wheel-drive hatchback.

### History
*July 1988* Range launched, 1.4, 1.4DGT (DGT are petrol models with digital dashboards), 1.6DGT, 1.6DGTSX, 1.9-litre turbo diesel.
*October 1988* 1.7 diesel.
*April 1990* 1.4 Formula, 1.4S.
*October 1990* 1.8ie DGTSX.
*November 1990* 1.6DGT Selecta (automatic).

### Fault Finder
All models – Check electrics carefully, both the car's overall electrical system and also any electric extra – electric windows, etc. There have been numerous problems with electrics, ranging from short-circuits to real rogue defects, for example, the rear lights failing to work, indicators coming on for no reason, the horn sounding when cornering. Oil leaks are not that common but they should be looked for, especially around the top of the engine. The camshaft belts have to be replaced every 35,000 miles. Check the service history to make sure this has been done. If not, and the engine is rattling, leave the car well alone, especially if it is well over 35,000 miles. Make sure that the radiator is filled to the proper level. Early Tipos (1988–9) did have problems with leaky radiat-

ors, and if this has happened it could have damaged the engine. Models with power steering are desirable but the power steering pumps have not been the most reliable. They should be silent when cornering. If there is any noise, there could be problems. Rust will not be a problem because the car features galvanized body panels, but on 1988 models some paintwork problems occured, leading to bubbling and blistering of paint. Check this carefully. On high performance models check for kerbing of the front wheels, this can affect the tracking, and even the suspension, leading to sloppy handling and eventual problems with the steering box. Check the dashboard for rattling, and make sure all switches work properly and fit properly. Some 1988–9 Tipos suffered from poor dashboard fitment.

**Verdict**
Not a strong seller in the UK, the Tipo is nevertheless a mostly reliable and very spacious car. Best model is the 1.9 diesel, least successful the digital dashboarded DGT. Prices are relatively low but long-life is certainly possible if professional, regular servicing is carried out.

**FIAT STRADA**
Front-wheel-drive hatchback.

**History**
*February 1982* 105TC added to the range.
*May 1983* Strada 2 range launched, 60 Comfort, 60 Comfort ES, 75 Comfort, 85 Super.
*June 1983* Strada 2 105TC.

*July 1983* Bertone Cabriolet version.
*June 1984* Abarth 130TC.
*August 1985* Trim and bodywork revisions.
*August 1988* Range discontinued.

**Fault Finder**
Engines are fairly sound, but it's imperative that they are serviced regularly, and on older Stradas this might not have happened. First check, then, is for a full service history. In particular, it's important to check that the camshaft belt has been replaced at least once, because by now, all Stradas will be high mileage cars. Look for oil leaks, especially from the top of the engine because this could signal serious engine problems. Head gaskets on these engines are renowned for failing quite quickly, and unless replaced swiftly this can lead to serious engine damage. Check inside the oil filler cap to see if there is any creamy, sludgy gunge on it. If so, the cylinder head gasket has failed, and may already have caused more serious damage to the engine. Timing belts rattle badly when they are worn, listen for this because it means a new belt will soon have to be fitted. Any knocking from the engine could well be a faulty water pump. Check the pump for leaks. Look in the brake fluid reservoir. If there are bubbles in it then there is almost certainly a leak somewhere in the piping which is letting in air. Check the master brake cylinder for fluid leaks. Gearboxes tend to lose second gear synchromesh quite early in their lives and the nylon bushes in the gearbox can wear, leading to difficult gear selection.

But, if there is a lot of crunching when trying to select third and fourth gears this almost certainly means that the gearbox needs replacing. Check front disc brakes for scoring, and check for any brake fluid on the back brake shoes, or trickling down the brake pedal. A stained carpet may point to this. Check shock absorbers for leaks, and make sure that the car is sitting the road squarely. When driving, make sure that the Strada doesn't pull to one side. If it does this could point to accident damage, because these cars are very hard to reassemble properly, once they've been damaged. When braking, check for any pulling, usually to the left, this is a sign of a seized caliper, a common problem with the Strada, but one which can easily be cured. Electrics are notoriously bad on the Strada, so make sure everything works properly, especially the switches. Interior trim often falls off, and so should be checked for fit and finish. Rust is quite a problem, especially on the earliest Stradas which suffered from severe rusting along all seams, around the headlamps, and along the sills. Look at the bottoms of the doors and the tailgate. Early Stradas, though built by robot, often had badly fitting door panels, and the tailgate in particular often did not fit correctly. Look inside the boot for rust coming through the floor panels, and water sitting in the boot.

## Verdict

All Stradas are quite old now and do not make a good second-hand buy. There are too many problem areas and though this was the car that should have taken Fiat into the modern motoring world it ultimately won few friends.

## FIAT X1/9

Rear-wheel-drive, mid-engined two seater sports car.

### History

*July 1983* VS 1500.
*March 1989* Gran Finale.
*September 1989* Range discontinued.

### Fault Finder

Check engines for oil leaks, although these are not that common. Timing chains rattle and can make the engine noisy, but they rarely need replacing. Oil pressure gauges are often faulty, suggesting, falsely, that oil pressure is low. Clearly, this needs checking properly. Carburettors can go off tune easily and it's not easy to recalibrate them properly, it calls for a professional. Look at the exhaust manifold carefully. They are subjected to high heat levels and can burn through quite quickly. Brake pads wear quickly and discs can easily become scored. Check the discs by running a finger over them, once they've cooled off! Any pulling to one side when braking points to a seized caliper. Second gear synchromesh fails very quickly but otherwise the gearboxes are strong, and gear selection is precise and easy. If the gear change is restrictive and makes crunching noises, then the gearbox may well need replacing. Steering should be taut and very precise, with no play in the system. A groaning from the steering when turning means that the joints in the steering column need lubricating. This is quite a laborious job because the whole column has to be taken to pieces. Clutch plate wear can be rapid, sometimes as early as 20,000 miles, so check for any clutch slippage, especially when accelerating in second and third gears. The pop-up headlamp motors often fail, though it's usually one of the headlamps that either stays up or down, rarely both. Corrosion is a problem, but rarely a serious one. The long bonnet occasionally suffers stone chips but its low angle means it's not as susceptible as many more modern, bulbous cars. The area around the pop-up headlamps can rust as water gets under the headlamp covers and affects the surround of the pop-up section. Rust along the sills is a problem, aggravated by this car's closeness to the ground. Check these carefully. Rust along the back panel, below the boot lid, is another favourite place and just below the back window where the window seal meets the boot lid. Rear side panels can also be affected by corrosion, although this is fairly rare. Look carefully around the targa top for any flaking paint or rust on the support rails. When it does exist it's usually only cosmetic, but it's wise to check carefully. Electrics always need checking, both gauges and switches. And if electric windows are fitted, make sure these work. The X1/9 suffers poor starting in wet weather, and sometimes it will not start at all. There is no cure for this, other than to carry around a can of damp-start to be sprayed over the engine when this problem occurs. Check interior trim for cuts and

poor fit, although it must be said that the X19 is better built than many other Fiats of the same age. Finally, look for any evidence of accident damage, for these cars are often driven hard.

**Verdict**
Still a fine car, if you can find a good one, the X1/9 doesn't keep its value very well but it's great to drive and could well become a classic and collectable car in a few years time.

**FIAT REGATA**
Front-wheel-drive saloons (Regata) and estates (Weekend).

**History**
*March 1984* Range launched, 70 Comfort, 70ES Comfort, 85 Automatic, 85 Comfort, 100 Super.
*May 1985* Weekend 85 Comfort, Weekend 100 Super.
*August 1985* DS diesel Super saloon.
*October 1986* Revised range, Saloons; 70 Comfort, 85 Comfort, 85 Super, 85 Super Automatic, 100 Super IE, Turbo diesel Super. Weekend; 85 Comfort, 100 Super IE.
*August 1990* Range discontinued.

**Fault Finder**
Engines are essentially reliable, but timing chains can be rattly, something you'll notice as soon as the engine is ticking over. This is rarely serious, but a very rattly chain should be replaced. Camshaft belts must be replaced at around 35,000 miles, so check the service record to see if this has been done. Oil leaks from the top of

the engine are rarely serious, and usually just demand the replacement of a head gasket. Check the brake fluid reservoir for bubbles, a sign that there is a leak in the system, and test the brake pedal to see if pressure is good. Bear in mind, though, that Regata brakes are quite spongy. Brake calipers can seize, you will notice this because the car will pull to one side when braking. Curing this is not expensive. Check the drive shaft gaiters at the front, because they can split and cause grit to get into the CV joint, quickly causing problems. Check for this by listening for any clonking sound as you turn the steering wheel hard over. Gearbox linkages can become worn after 40,000–50,000 miles, leading to a difficult, sloppy gearchange. This can be quite expensive to repair, because of labour time, so try and avoid such a car. If you hear lots of clanking noises when changing gear, this could be the problem. Check suspension struts for leaks. On Weekend versions look for a tow bar, or evidence of one being fitted, because these engines are not up to pulling heavy loads. On such a car, check also for excessive exhaust smoke, a sign that valve seals are worn, usually as a result of too much heavy haulage work. Rust is not a problem on the Regata, but it's always wise to look for any paint blemishes which might lead to corrosion. On Weekend versions, check that the two-piece tail-gate unlatches properly, there have been problems with sticking catches on the bottom halves. Electrics are not as bad as on earlier Fiats, but central locking often stops working properly,

sometimes locking only one door, and occasionally only unlocking the driver's door.

### Verdict
Engines are not the best, a fact underlined by the much better engines in this car's replacement, the Tempra. But Regatas and Weekends are inexpensive and the Weekend in particular is a practical car. Best choice is the Weekend Super 100 IE.

## FIAT TEMPRA
Front-wheel-drive saloons and estates.

### History
*September 1990* Range is 1.4, 1.6, 1.6S, 1.6SX, 1.8ieSX, 1.9D, 1.9Tds.
*June 1991* Estates, 1.6, 1.6S. 1.8ieSX.
*September 1991* 1.9Tds estate.

### Fault Finder
It's really too early for any major faults to have reared their heads. Make the usual checks for a full service history and try and avoid high mileage ex-company cars. Electrics should be checked, particularly on electric windows and central locking. Corrosion will not be a problem, thanks to extensive galvanized body panels. On turbo diesel versions check for a quiet and effective turbo. On estate versions, check for a sticking door catch on the bottom half of the tail-gate. Owners have already complained about the handle sticking, which means they have to force the handle, and the mechanisms can then snap.

## FIAT CROMA
Front-wheel-drive hatchback.

### History
*June 1986* Range is 2000, 2000IE, 2000IE Turbo.
*July 1987* IE SX launched, plus minor revisions to other models.
*July 1989* Revised 2000, renamed, 2.0 CHT.
*July 1991* Revised range, same model line-up but higher equipment levels.

### Fault Finder
Many are used as company cars, so check mileage is correct by cross-referencing with the service booklet. Listen for excessive rattles from the engine, which could point to a worn timing chain. Any knocks from the engine on tick-over usually signals the near demise of the water pump. Oil leaks from the top of the engine are quite common and if they have not been left for too long are easy to cure, simply by fitting new gaskets. If this is done soon enough, hopefully the engine will not have been damaged. But keep an eye on the temperature gauge when driving. If it moves into the red, the engine is damaged and will be very expensive to repair. Check the oil for leaks. Make sure that the camshaft belt has been replaced at the stipulated service interval – ideally around 36,000 miles. If this has not been done, then view the car with more scepticism. Listen for clonks from the front suspension, a sign that the bottom joints are wearing. Check the drive shaft rubber gaiters for splits, and if there are any, listen for a groaning noise when the steering is turned full over to the right or left. If there is such a noise, it could mean that grit has already got in and damaged the joints. Check the brake discs for scoring, and when driving, make sure that the Croma pulls up straight, otherwise it could be a seized caliper, a common Fiat problem, but not a major one. Look for leaks from the master brake cylinder, and check the brake fluid reservoir to see if there are any bubbles in it, evidence of air getting into the system. Check the quality of the flexible brake pipes leading to the front wheels, and check on the brake discs for any leaking fluid, especially on the back pair. On turbo models, check for clattering when the engine is turned off, a sign that the turbine's blades are out of sync and that the unit will need replacing. Also, on turbo Cromas, check the quality of the oil. If it's dirty brown there could be a corrosion problem inside the engine, a sign that proper regular servicing has not been carried out. Gearboxes are mostly robust units with a notchy but fairly precise gearchange. If there is any difficulty getting into any gear, accompanied by crunching noises, then the nylon bushes may well have perished and will need replacing – not a terribly expensive job. Suspension struts should all be checked for leaks and sagging, because the Croma is a big car which is often driven quickly, and this can affect the shock absorbers rather more than in an average mid-sized car. As with all Fiats, check the electrics over, although in the Croma there have been few horror stories. There have been some faulty electric door mirrors, and if water gets into

their innards it can cause short circuits which sometimes make them whirr back and forth by themselves. Also, check the central locking, because, as with most other Fiats, this will sometimes only work on the door which is being locked or unlocked. Corrosion is generally not a problem, but the Croma can look rather tatty, because it appears to attract more stone chips than many other cars. Interior trim is not the strongest, so look carefully for rips and tears in the fabric, and examine the dashboard closely for any loose bits.

## Verdict

Prices for Cromas are really low, and really there's little good reason for this – it's simply that the Croma doesn't have the appeal and image of many of its price rivals. A good buy for someone who chooses carefully. Turbos are quick, but the best choice is a 2.0IE with a full service record.

## FORD FIESTA

Front-wheel-drive hatchback.

## History

*December 1980* 950 Popular, 950 and 1100 Popular Plus.
*January 1981* 1300 Supersport.
*September 1981* Styling modifications.
*December 1981* XR2.
*September 1983* Heavily revised range; 950 Popular, 950 Popular Plus, 950L, 1100 Popular Plus, 1100L, 1100 Ghia.
*April 1984* 1600 Diesel Popular Plus, L. New XR2.
*January 1986* 1400L, 1400 Ghia.
*April 1986* 1.4S.

*May 1987* 1100L CTX Auto, 1100 Ghia CTX Auto.
*March 1989* Range discontinued, replaced by new range.
*April 1989* Three- and five-door range, 1.0-litre, 1.1, 1.4, 1.6, 1.8 diesel. Trim levels are Popular, Popular Plus, L, GL, Ghia, S.
*October 1989* XR2i.
*June 1990* RS Turbo.

## Fault Finder

On very old Fiestas with high mileage there may be some oil leaks from the top of the engine, but these are rarely serious, and if the offending gasket is replaced swiftly it should not lead to serious damage. Most Fiestas have virtually unbreakable engines, but on XR2 models check the head gasket. If the car is hard to start, or splutters badly out on the road, it could be water getting into the engine. This is rarely fatal on the Fiesta, but it is something which demands instant attention. Carburettors can go off tune quite easily, but if the car is serviced according to the schedule there should be little problem here. Check the front suspension for bottom ball joint wear, especially on the hard-driven XR2. Examine the shock absorbers for leaks. Brakes last well, but check the front discs for scoring, just in case. Gearboxes are tough, although synchromesh can dissolve on second gear, but usually only after very high mileage – 70,000–80,000 miles. Inside, the Fiesta is very well built and the quality of trim is good, so a tatty example will not have been well looked after, and should be avoided. Rust is not a problem on any models, but look out for cars with numerous stone chips, these can soon lead to surface corrosion, seriously affecting resale values. On some solid red cars produced in 1984–6 the paintwork on the bonnet is prone to fading. Check for this because a respray could be the only answer.

**Verdict**
Safe and reliable second-hand, as long as you opt for one of the mid to high trim levels. Avoid the early Popular and L models because they suffer from poor soundproofing and do not have five-speed gearboxes. The XR2 is much sought after, and expensive to insure, but terrific fun to drive, very sturdy, and economical to service. It's best to buy post 1983 models.

**FORD ESCORT**
Front-wheel-drive hatchbacks, estates, cabriolets.

**History**
Range is 1100, 1300, 1600. Trim levels are, base, L, GL, Ghia.
*November 1980* Three-door estates, 1100, 1100L, 1300, 1300L, 1300GL, 1600L, 1600GL.
*April 1982* Trim and equipment additions and revisions.
*October 1982* XR3i.
*March 1983* Five-door estates.
*September 1983* Major trim revisions, engine modifications.
*December 1983* Cabriolet 1300, 1600, 1600i.
*April 1984* 1100 Popular three-door hatchback and estate.
*September 1984* RS Turbo.
*March 1986* Major revisions, including new bonnet, bumpers, front grille, interior and new

suspension and more efficient engines. New 1.4-litre engine is a lean-burn unit.
*June 1986* New RS Turbo.
*September 1987* 1.4LX, 1.6LXm, plus uprating of other models' equipment.
*September 1988* 1.3-litre HCS petrol engine launched.
*September 1989* Popular Plus three- and five-door hatchbacks and estates, plus uprated engines for XR3i and XR3i Cabriolet.
*July 1990* Range discontinued, replaced by new range.
*September 1990* Hatchback and estates launched, 1.3-litre, 1.4 carburettor and injection, 1.6 carb or injection, 1.8 diesel. Trim levels, Popular, L, LX, GLX, Ghia.
*January 1991* 1.3L, 1.4L, 1.8LD.
*February 1991* 1.6S.

**Fault Finder**
The Escorts to avoid are those built between 1980–4. The first of the new front-wheel-drive Escorts had what was called the Bugs Bunny Syndrome which referred to the terribly bouncy suspension. This was changed to give a too hard suspension, then changed again after 1984 to give a whole lot better ride, with better control of damper settings. Carburettors on cars built in 1980–4 often went off tune, and cars afflicted with this proved hard to drive smoothly in stop-start traffic. Check for a quick start-up and smooth running, even when the engine is cold. If the car is fitted with an automatic choke, check firstly that it comes on properly, and check also that it cuts out at the right time; even on the newest Escorts, all too many

either cut-out within seconds of starting the car, or they do not switch off for many miles. Another engine problem, quite common in early 1.3-litre cars – those made between 1980–6 – was damp getting in to the distributor and the electrics, making the car near impossible to start, especially on damp mornings. Electrics need to be checked on all early Escorts because there were quite a number of problems; faulty readouts, failure of electric windows and rear wash/wipe, and faulty heater fan controls. Paint finish on Escorts built up to 1985 was often diabolically bad, with peeling paint, pock-marked surfaces, and rust coming through within a very short time. Better models are those made from 1985 when many of the early problems were solved. However, on all Escorts, check the engine carefully for oil leaks, and lift the oil filler cap to see if it has any creamy gunge on it, a sure sign that there are major engine problems, due to head gasket failure. Check for a smoky exhaust, a sign that the valve seals are worn, or that the engine needs a de-coke – both major jobs. Gearboxes rarely suffer from major faults, but synchromesh goes on second and third gears, and in high mileage Escorts you can lose first gear altogether. Clutches do not last long, they often have to be replaced after 20,000 miles, so check for any slipping. It usually shows in third gear when accelerating hard. Check the front MacPherson suspension struts for leaks, although this is not common. More importantly, check for rusting around the suspension turrets under the bonnet. Also check for rusting along the sides, where the wings come in to meet the engine bay. Exterior rust may well be along the tops of the wings, around the headlamps and along the sills. If caught early this is rarely a problem. Escorts built after 1986 have a much better paintwork finish, and they rarely suffer serious corrosion. On all models look for excessive tyre wear, especially on the front wheels. This is very common on pre-1986 models because of the suspension geometry. More modern versions do not wear tyres any quicker than most other front-wheel-drive cars. On all versions, look for evidence of turned-back odometers, simply because Escorts are favourites of the fleet market, and therefore clock-up miles very swiftly.

### Verdict

Avoid the earliest examples, try and find an Escort which had been privately owned, and you should have a very solid and reliable car. The ones to avoid are the XR3 (1.6-litre carburettor engine) because it's slow and the engines quickly burn-out, and the XR3i unless you are willing to pay a fortune in insurance. The Turbo is superb fun, but the car thieves think so too. Estates are good hold-alls and 1.6-litre diesels are noisy but economical. Look for good, clean 1.8D versions. They are smooth, refined and economical.

### FORD ORION
Front-wheel-drive saloon.

## History

*September 1983* Range is 1.3GL, 1.6GL, 1.6 Ghia.

*April 1984* New models added, 1.3L, 1.6L, 1.6LD, 1.6GLD.

*March 1986* Heavily revised range, new engines and bodywork, but same trim levels.

*September 1987* 1.4LX, 1.6LX.

*September 1988* New 1.3-litre engines, 1.8-litre diesel replaces 1.6-litre.

*July 1990* Range discontinued, replaced by new range.

*September 1990* New range is, 1.3-litre, 1.4 with carburettor or injection, 1.6 with carb or injection, 1.8-litre diesel. Trim levels are LX, GLX, Ghia.

## Fault Finder

This is the booted version of the Ford Escort, so you should check for any of the faults that can afflict Escorts of the same age.

## Verdict

While the Orion can share some of the Escort faults, the fact that it came along later meant that Ford had learnt many of the lessons about quality control that they had faced with the Escort, so the Orion is generally a better car. However, the packaging is better than the driving, and while the Orion is well equipped, on the road it's not the most pleasant car in its class. Best choices are the fuel-injected Ghia versions, which are stuffed with equipment, or the GL which comes along at a good price. As with the Escort, check carefully for illegal clocking. Generally, prices for Orions are much lower than for Escorts, simply because the booted Orion looks older and stodgier than the hatchback.

## FORD SIERRA

Rear-wheel and four-wheel-drive, hatchbacks and estates.

## History

*October 1982* Hatchbacks and estates launched, 1.3-litre, 1.6, 2.0, V6 2.3, 2.3 diesel. Trim levels, L, LX, GL, Ghia, S.

*May 1983* XR4i three-door sports model.

*September 1983* Three-door 1.3, 1.6, 1.6 Economy, 2.3D and 2.3DL, XR 4x4 hatchback.

*October 1984* 1.8L, GL, Ghia, hatchbacks and estates.

*February 1986* 2.0 Ghia EFi hatchback and estate.

*March 1986* 1.6LX, 1.8LX, 2.0LX hatchbacks.

*April 1986* 2.8i 4x4 Ghia estate.

*June 1986* 2.0i GLS hatchback.

*July 1986* RS Cosworth three-door.

*February 1987* Major trim and equipment revisions across the range.

*June 1988* 1.8-litre versions get new lean-burn engine.

*October 1988* 2.9i XR4x4 hatchback and Ghia 4x4 estate, with V6 2.9-litre engine.

*April 1988* 2.9i GLS 4x4 estate.

*June 1989* 2.0-litre versions get new twin-cam engine.

*February 1990* Revised range, 1.6-litre, 1.8 petrol, 1.8 turbo diesel, 2.0-litre petrol. Trim levels are LX, GLX, GLS, Ghia, XR.

## Fault Finder

Engines are tough and capable, well over 100,000 miles is normal, even for hard-driven company cars. Check the service history with a microscope because these cars are often illegally clocked. The other crucial point to remember is that a car which is showing, say 40,000 miles, might have covered 140,000 because the odometer is only a five-number affair. A company car could easily cover 140,000 in four years, when most private drivers will cover around 40,000. No major mechanical problems, but carry out the usual checks for oil leaking from the engine, check the clutch for slipping and listen to the engine on tickover for any undue rumbling. This points to a camshaft problem, usually caused by poor servicing – not changing the oil often enough. A rattling noise usually means the camshaft belt needs replacing as soon as possible. There are plenty of Sierras second-hand so pick one without a camshaft problem. On 2.0-litre engines, valves wear quickly, a smoky exhaust will highlight this fault. Brakes often judder, due to warped discs. Replacing them is the only cure. Check all of the shock absorbers for the correct amount of bounce, but especially the rear pair because they can begin to sag quite quickly – after 35,000 miles. If a tow bar has been fitted, check the car for an excessively smoky exhaust, a sign that engine valves are worn and will need replacing, usually caused by hauling heavy trailers or caravans around for long periods. Bodywork is good, there are few rusty Sierras around, but check for excessive stone chips on the bonnet and around the headlamps. If left, these can quickly turn to quite nasty surface rust. Gearboxes are very tough, so just check for any worn synchromesh and any undue rattling, the latter pointing to gearbox bearing wear. It's worth checking for accident damage because if the Sierra has had a front-end shunt, even a slow speed one, it sends shock waves along the car and they can crease the entire underbody of the car, consequently putting strain on the whole body, and often causing rapid tyre wear and poor handling at high speed. So, beware of accident-damaged Sierras, even if they do look good on the surface.

**Verdict**
A good, solid, reliable workhorse. Engines are mostly uninteresting and rather mundane performers compared with many of the rivals, but you do get virtually unburstable units. Choose carefully, always with an eye on the correct mileage, and the Sierra will prove a loyal friend. Best choices are cars built after 1986 and the best engines are 1.8 and 2.0-litre petrol. Diesel versions are not very pleasant.

**FORD SIERRA SAPPHIRE**
Rear-wheel-drive and four-wheel-drive saloon version of the Ford Sierra.

**History**
*February 1987* Range is 1.6 base, 1.6L, 1.6LX, 1.8L, 1.8LX, 1.8GL, 1.8 Ghia, 2.0LX, 2.0GL, 2.0GLSi, 2.0 Ghia, 2.3D, 2.3LD, 2.3GLD.
*February 1988* RS Cosworth.
*July 1988* New 1.8-litre engine (lean-burn).
*June 1989* All 2.0-litre models get the twin cam engine.
*February 1990* Revised range, 1.6 and 1.8 petrol, 1.8 turbo diesel, 2.0i GLX, 2.0i Ghia, 2000E, 2.0i 4x4, RS Cosworth 4x4.

## Fault Finder

Check out the same areas as with the Ford Sierra hatchback. On the Cosworth 4x4, a full service history is paramount, and check tyres for wear and drive train for any oil leaks. Make sure that the turbo doesn't clatter when winding down, and that power is delivered smoothly right to the limit on the first three gears. Any hiccups here will point to a faulty engine management system, of which there were a number of in early Cosworths, and not all of them will have been replaced.

## Verdict

A good package, and in many ways the Sapphire looks a better balanced design. As with the Sierra, the best models are the 1.8 and 2.0-litre petrol engines, but be prepared for quite a lot of gearbox vibration on the 1.8-litre – this is normal.

## FORD CAPRI

Rear-wheel-drive coupé.

## History

*June 1981* 2.8 Injection.
*March 1983* Range slimmed down to, 1600LS, 2000S, 2.8 Injection.
*October 1984* Range slimmed to special edition Laser 1.6 and 2.0-litre and 2.8 Injection (latter now has leather seats).
*March 1987* Capri 280 limited edition is last Capri.
*June 1987* Range discontinued.

## Fault Finder

On 1.6 and 2.0-litre cars check for oil leaks from the top of the engine, creamy sludge inside the oil cap

which will show that a head gasket has failed and possibly caused engine damage, and listen for rattling camshafts, especially on the 2.0-litre cars. Check for a smoky exhaust, a sign that valve seals or pistons have worn. Check the clutch for slipping, and depress the clutch and listen for rattling, a sign that the gearbox bearings are going. The gearchange should be light, fluid and precise. If there's major resistance getting into any gear there may well be a problem with selector bushes. It is common for synchromesh to fail on second gear. Brake judder is common, as the front discs can warp, so check this carefully when driving. At the back, check underneath the car for oil seeping out of the drive shaft, and when driving, listen for rumbling from the back, a sign that the driveshaft is worn and may not last much longer. Check front suspension turrets for surrounding rust and look in the engine bay for serious rusting alongside the wings, and on the bulkhead between the engine bay and the car's cabin. Check for corrosion on the back wings, especially rust coming through from under the metal near the rear wheel arches.

## Verdict

All Capris are getting old now, but if you can find a good 2.8i with a full service history and with blemish-free bodywork it will reward with good performance. Watch the handling, though, this car is a real brute on a wet road.

## FORD GRANADA (series to 1985)

Rear-wheel-drive saloons and estates.

70

## History

*August 1981* 2.8i saloon and estate.

*October 1981* Heavy revisions to all models, mechanical, trim and equipment.

*April 1982* Vastly improved specifications.

*October 1982* 2.5 diesel saloon and estate.

*September 1983* More improvements to trim and equipment.

*November 1982* 2.0LX, 2.3LX saloons and estates.

*April 1985* Range discontinued, replaced by totally new model.

## Fault Finder

Engines are strong, but look for smoking exhausts due to burnt out valves. On estate models, check for a tow bar, a sign that the car has been pulling heavy loads and that the engine is past its best. On V6 engined cars, check for even running – it's not easy to spot a problem here. Even if one of the cylinders isn't firing properly, it's hard to tell because the car will still pull smoothly, albeit with much slower performance. Make sure that you test drive any 2.8-litre Granada for as long as possible to see if there are any weak spots in the engine's performance. Also watch for a smoking exhaust, especially on the 2.0-litre models, a sign of worn valve seals, or even major piston trouble. If there is a piston problem, you should hear a metallic slap when the engine is ticking over. Listen for rattles from the engine, especially on 2.0-litre versions, a sign that there are camshaft problems. On automatic versions make sure that the gearbox operates smoothly. Auto boxes are slick and smooth, and power

should come on stream smoothly, without any major jerking between gears. Check for gears slipping, and for the gearbox hanging on to gears, both problems which will get steadily worse. On manual versions the V6 gearboxes tend to last longer, the 2.0-litre versions have a slow action and while synchromesh rarely wears out, it can sometimes be beaten by fast changes, so increasing the likelihood of stripping the gears and eventually causing major damage down inside the gearbox. Check the drive shaft for oil leaks, and listen for excessive rumbling from the back axle, both signs that it may need replacing. On cars with power steering, wind the steering right over to each lock and listen for groaning from the steering rack. There will be hissing from the steering on full lock, but this is normal. Corrosion is not normally a problem, except on estates, where the tailgates can rust along their edges. Look also for fading paintwork, especially on metallic gold Granadas.

## Verdict

Good and solid, these square-shaped Granadas have justly built a loyal following. Few things go wrong and with a full service history, and making sure that the mileage is correct, you should not go far wrong. Best choice is a Ghia X with the 2.8 injection engine. These cars are well equipped, have a good ride and provide gutsy performance. Second-hand prices are attractive.

## FORD GRANADA (new shape)

Rear-wheel-drive hatchbacks and saloons.

## History

*May 1985* Range is, 1.8GL, 2.0GL, 2.0iGL, 2.0i Ghia, 2.8i Ghia, 2.8i Scorpio.
*October 1985* 2.8i Ghia 4x4, 2.8i Scorpio 4x4.
*April 1986* 1.8L, 2.0L, 2.5LD.
*January 1987* 2.4iGL, 2.4i Ghia, 2.9i Ghia X.
*November 1988* 2.5LD, GLTD with turbo diesel engine.
*June 1989* All petrol 2.0-litre models get new twin cam engines. 2.0LX and 2.0i Scorpio launched.
*January 1990* Saloon models launched, similar badging and trim to hatchbacks.
*April 1991* Scorpio 2.9i 24-valve saloon and hatchback.

## Fault Finder

Another favourite car with company car drivers, so the first check is to make sure that the mileage is correct, and the car has not been illegally clocked. Make sure that the service record is complete. The 1.8-litre cars should be avoided, due to lack of power, but also because of leaking head gaskets, terrible vibration, and an appetite for valve seals. Gearboxes are also suspect on the 1.8-litre, wearing quickly and suffering from severe vibration, even when they're quite new. On all models check for brake judder caused by warped discs, and also remember that all of these Granadas are fitted with ABS anti-lock brakes. These must be working properly because if not, the car will fail an MOT test. ABS is very expensive to replace. On 2.8 and 2.9-litre versions, check the brake discs for scoring, especially on the front wheels, because these cars quickly get through brake

pads. Check all electrics. The systems are reliable, but only if properly maintained. Any hesitant performance could be a result of blocked air intakes on the fuel injection system. Curing this is fairly easy, but it is a problem which can keep occuring. In serious cases it may have already caused more severe damage to the engine. The fuel-injection system on 2.8-litre cars can become faulty during damp weather, leading to erratic engine performance. If this problem exists, the injection system may need to be replaced. Rust is not a problem, but look carefully for accident damage.

## Verdict

Lacks the style of many of its rivals and prices have dropped accordingly. On the second-hand market, then, value for money is good, and if you choose a 2.8 or 2.9-litre version you receive good performance and an impressive equipment package. 1.8 and 2.0-litre cars are best avoided, their engines are not powerful enough for this big car.

## HONDA CIVIC

Front-wheel-drive hatchback, estate, saloon.

## History

*February 1984* Range is DL three-door hatchback, S three-door hatchback, Shuttle estate.
*March 1985* GT three-door hatchback.
*July 1985* Shuttle 4x4 estate.
*August 1987* Range discontinued, replaced by new range.
*October 1987* New range of front-wheel-drive hatchbacks, saloons,

saloons, estate. Range is 1.3DX
and 1.4GL hatchbacks.
*May 1988* Shuttle and 1.6i Shuttle
4x4 estates.
*July 1990* 1.6VTi three-door
hatchback.
*September 1990* 1.5LSi hatchback
and saloon.
*January 1991* 1.5VEi three-door
hatchback, 1.6VTi saloon,
1.6ESi hatchback.

**Fault Finder**
Check temperature gauge for overheating due to broken head gaskets. Gearboxes should have a
light and very precise change. If
not, and there's a good amount of
crunching, the nylon bushes in the
gearbox may be wearing. If the
lever will not go into a gear, but
there is no crunching, it will
almost certainly be a faulty selector, a fairly common fault on the
first batch of cars in 1984, but
replaced by a better system in
1985. Gearchanges on four-wheel-
drive versions can sometimes be
restrictive, but this is more a
design of the gearbox, rather than
a fault. Carburation on early
models – up to 1987 – sometimes
went off tune, and occasionally
automatic engine chokes would
stay on longer than they should.
Check this on your test drive.
Check the rubber gaiters on the
front drive shafts for splits, and
then turn the steering to each lock
and listen for any clonking sound
caused by faulty CV joints in the
drive shafts. Corrosion is not a
problem, but paintwork is rather
thin, so stone chips will cause
minor surface rusting unless dealt
with quickly. On high performance
versions, check the front wheels
for evidence of kerbing, and the

front tyres for early wear on their
outside edges. If this exists, then
the suspension should be checked
for correct alignment because
regular kerbing can cause the
suspension to move out of line. On
four-wheel-drive models, tyres
which are worn early may be
evidence of hectic four-wheel-drive
use and should set you looking at
the service history and the general
condition of the car, both inside
and out.

**Verdict**
One of the most reliable cars on
the roads, it's rare for a Civic to
pose any serious problems. However, a full service history is
crucial and remember that spare
parts are not cheap. Best versions
are the exciting VEi and VTi
versions, but they may well have
been driven hard.

**HONDA CRX**
Front-wheel-drive coupé.

**History**
*February 1984* CRX launched.
*February 1986* CRXi.
*October 1987* Revised CRXi.

**Fault Finder**
Very strong and reliable engines,
as long as they have been serviced
properly. Check for a full and
complete service history. There
have been a handful of faulty
electronic engine management
systems which caused jerky performance in some cars made in
1986. Most should have been
replaced by now. Check disc
brakes for scoring because these
cars are usually driven hard, and
they have a big appetite for brake

73

pads. Look for accident damage, again because these cars are driven hard.

**Verdict**
Virtually trouble-free, and as long as the service record is correct, and up-to-date, the CRX is a good buy, especially in the later fuel-injected form.

## HONDA INTEGRA
Front-wheel-drive hatchback.

**History**
*March 1986* Range is 1.5DX, 1.5LX, 1.6 Executive.
*September 1989* Range discontinued.

**Fault Finder**
Check for sloppy gearchanges, a sign that the main selector is worn. Check the rubber drive shaft gaiters for splits. Listen for clonks from the front wheels, as this points to defective CV joints. Automatic chokes can get stuck on. Make sure your test drive is long enough to spot this. Seat trim is not too sturdy, check for any rips, and balling of the velour seat covering (small bobbles on the seat material caused by excessive use).

**Verdict**
Very reliable but totally uninspiring Japanese car. Pick the well equipped Executive, if you can find one, but remember that few Integras were sold, so getting spare parts will prove increasingly difficult.

## HONDA CONCERTO
Front-wheel-drive hatchback and saloon.

**History**
*October 1989* Range is 1.4GL, 1.6EX, 1.6i-16.
*October 1991* New range is 1.4i five-door, 1.6i, 1.6i 16-valve, 1.6i 16-valve SE four- and five-door.

**Fault Finder**
A service is essential every 6,000 miles, so first check that these have been carried out. Power steering pumps work erratically on cars built before October 1991. It's best to get the pump replaced if it temporarily stops working, because the problem will reoccur. Check central locking, sometimes it only locks one door, but again, this is a rare and erratic fault. Make sure that camshaft belt chains are replaced at the stipulated service intervals, otherwise engines can be badly damaged.

**Verdict**
A fine car, built in the UK alongside the Rover 200, and incredibly well equipped. Reliability is legendary, as long as the service intervals have been adhered to. Best model in many respects is the incredibly good value 1.5i.

## HONDA PRELUDE (series from 1983)
Front-wheel-drive coupé.

**History**
*March 1983* Range is 1800DL, Executive.
*October 1985* 2.0i-16 coupé.
*October 1987* 2.0i-16 4WS (four-wheel steer).
*March 1989* 2.0iSE.

## Fault Finder

Preludes need a service every 6,000 miles, and owners have a tendency to miss some of them out. First step, then, is to carefully check the service record over. Check that both headlamps pop up when switched on, and retract smoothly when switched off. It is rare for headlamp motors to go in the Prelude, but not unheard of. Engines are very strong and robust, but do look for oil leaks. On a good Prelude there should not be any oil leaks at all. Gearboxes are very strongly built, and they are very light to operate. On hard-driven examples the synchromesh may be wearing, but this is rare. Check the clutch for slipping, especially on Preludes which have been used mostly around town. Corrosion is never a problem, unless stone chips have been left to fester, but even then, the first-class paintwork on the Prelude stands up to quite harsh treatment.

## Verdict

The top range Preludes are rather expensive and in the first year they lose value quite quickly, so for the second-hand buyer they are a good buy. The downside is the high cost of spares and the very short service intervals – factors which will make for relatively high running costs.

## HONDA ACCORD

Front-wheel-drive saloons, hatchbacks, estates.

## History

*February 1984* Range is 1.6DL, 1.8 Executive.
*October 1985* 2.0EX, 2.0EXi saloons.
*January 1986* Aerodeck 2.0EX, EXi three-door hatchbacks.
*September 1989* Range discontinued, replaced by new range.
*November 1989* New range is 2.0, 2.0i, 2.2i, the latter with four-wheel steering.
*April 1991* Aerodeck 2.2i estate.

## Fault Finder

Short service intervals mean that owners sometimes skimp, so check service record fully. Engines are virtually bomb-proof, but check for oil leaks, just in case, and check the oil on the dipstick to see if there is any water mixed in with the oil. If there is, look for another Accord because this signals major engine problems. A bad Accord engine is rare, though. Check for leaks from the power steering pump. As with the Concerto, there have been cases of pumps failing intermittently. The gearchange should be smooth and light, and should slot into gear easily. If there is any problem here it could be something quite costly. Again, though, problems in this area are rare. It's imperative that you check underneath the four-wheel-steer versions for any leaks of fluid from the drive shafts. It's not common, but hard driving can occasionally cause such problems. Also on four-wheel-steer models, check the tyres for any uneven wear, this is a sign that alignment of the wheels is not correct, and it's a correction which can only be carried out by a Honda dealer. Corrosion is not a problem, and as with every other Honda, rust will only start after excessive stone chipping.

## Verdict

The latest Accords have a twenty-four months mechanical warranty, so if you can afford a one year old Accord you will still benefit from a year's cover. But, Accords lose a lot of value in their first year, more than most, because the trade sees them as overpriced, particularly the four-wheel-steer model. This is good news for the second-hand buyer who intends to keep his Accord for some years.

## HONDA LEGEND
Front-wheel-drive saloon and coupé.

### History
*October 1986* Range is 2.5-litre saloon.
*December 1987* 2.7-litre coupé and saloon, previous saloon deleted.
*April 1991* V6 3.2-litre engined saloon and coupé replace previous models.

### Fault Finder
A complex car, and one which demands regular servicing, so the first check is to see that the service record is completely up-to-date. Engines are robust and virtually unbreakable, but check that the engine is clean and free of oil leaks. Check the brake fluid reservoir for any bubbles, a sign that air is getting into the system. This is a problem, but only on a very few early Legends. Check the automatic gearbox for any slipping. Again, a rare fault, but it can be found on early, high mileage Legends. These cars have a multitude of electrical gizmos, so check all electrics. If something does go wrong it can be very hard to track it down, and it can be expensive to repair. Corrosion is unheard of on the Legend, except when stone chips have been left for a long time, and eventually lead to rust. The Legend is a big car, so it tends to get knocked in car parks, and careless drivers often scrape the bumpers. Check the body carefully for any dents or dings, because this seriously affects Legend resale values.

### Verdict
After the initial rather hefty price drop in the first year, Legend prices seem to stabilize, partly because the car is so rare, and also because of its excellent reliability. It is a good buy, but it's crucial that the car comes with a full service history and blemish-free bodywork.

## HYUNDAI PONY (series from 1982 to 1985)
Rear-wheel-drive hatchbacks and saloons.

### History
*March 1983* Range is 1200L, 1200GL, 1200GLS, 1400GLS, in three-, four- and five-door forms.
*July 1985* Range discontinued and replaced by new range.

### Fault Finder
Check the fit and finish of all body panels, many of these early Hyundais were not well made. Check also for peeling paint, and corrosion where the wings meet the sides of the car. Check for any rust caused by stone chips, because this can quickly spread and become a more serious problem. Listen to the engine on tick-over for any undue rattling. This is usually a

sign that the camshaft is ready for replacement. Check for oil leaks, both from the top of the engine and from the sump at the bottom. Check the oil breather pipe for condition, because they sometimes fracture. Check the radiator water. If it's brown and dirty then there could be some corrosion already in the engine, caused by lack of proper anti-freeze and inhibitor. This can sometimes be cured by washing the system through, and putting new inhibitor in. Check for water in the oil, and lift the oil filler cap to see if there is any white gunge on it. If there is, the engine head gasket has failed, and it might already have damaged the engine. Check the brake fluid reservoir, both for the correct level, and also to see if there are any bubbles mixing with the fluid. If there is it means air is getting into the system, and will eventually cause brake failure. Check for brakes pulling to one side. Seized brake calipers will cause this, and they are quite common on Hyundai Ponys made in 1982–4. Check the exhaust with the engine revving, for signs of black smoke. This signals piston or valve seal wear, and sometimes both. Check suspension struts for leaks, especially the front pair. This is quite common on early Ponys. The gearboxes are quite strong, but synchromesh can go on second and third gears within a relatively short time – around 30,000 miles is not uncommon. Inside, check the fit and finish of the trim, it was rather flimsy on Ponys made in 1982–3.

## Verdict

Early Hyundai Ponys were high on showroom appeal, thanks to competitive pricing, but the car was not the best. Poor build quality on early models and engines which simply did not last the course, have kept second-hand prices low. If you can afford it, go for one of the more modern front-wheel-drive models.

## HYUNDAI PONY

Front-wheel-drive hatchbacks and saloons.

## History

*October 1985* Range is 1.3L, 1.3GL, 1.5GLS, all five-door.
*July 1986* 1.3GL, 1.5GLS saloons.
*April 1987* 1.3L, 1.3GL three-door models.
*September 1991* Range discontinued.

## Fault Finder

On high mileage examples – 60,000 miles plus – check for black smoke from the exhaust. This points to valve seal wear. The engines can take high mileages if they are properly serviced, so check for a full service history. Check for oil leaks, particularly from the side of the engine, and dripping down onto the chassis members. This is usually an engine plug replacement job, but if it has been left for too long the car might have been run low on oil and damage caused to the engine. With the engine running, listen for any undue rattling. If it's there it usually means either a rattling timing belt, which can easily be replaced, or if it's a knocking sound it could mean the camshaft is damaged, and this is expensive to replace. Check for brake fluid leaks, usually coming down from under the dashboard and dripping onto the brake pedal. If this has been happening, you should see a light stain on the carpet, because the fluid is very hard to remove. Gearboxes are well made and normally last well, but if the gear-lever does not slot in smoothly and precisely, it will almost certainly be because the automatic selector is worn. Replacement is not expensive. However, if there is a crunching noise when trying to get into gear, and it's hard to get the lever in, it could be the nylon bushes which have worn, or it could be stripping of the gears which has led to loose metal getting into the gear's cogs. If it is the latter problem a new gearbox will be needed. Rust is not normally a problem, but Hyundai paintwork is not as resilient as most of today's mainstream European and Japanese cars, so look for stone chips which could develop into major rust. Finally, check all electrics work properly. There have been no major problems with the Pony, but some owners have reported the occasional malfunctioning electric windows.

**Verdict**

The second generation Pony is worlds better than its forerunner, with high equipment levels and a good build quality. Later versions are rather expensive new, but sensibly priced on the second-hand circuit. Long term residual values are still not looking that impressive.

**HYUNDAI PONY X2 AND COUPÉ**

Front-wheel drive, hatchbacks and saloons.

**History**

*July 1990* S Coupé launched with choice of 1.5LSi or 1.5GSi trim levels.

*September 1990* Range is three-, four- and five-door. Trim levels and engines are, 1.3S, 1.3LS, 1.5GSi.

**Fault Finder**

Although quite a new car, the X2 is essentially a progression from the Pony, so carry out checks for the same potential problems. There is still a question mark over the toughness of the gearbox, so make sure that you use this as much as possible, checking for any harshness when changing gear. If the car has been used around town, check the clutch for slipping by accelerating hard in second and third gears. When braking watch for any pulling, a sign that the brake calipers are seized. If this problem is there the car will usually pull to the left.

**Verdict**

The X2 features more robust trim and improved quality mechanicals compared to the Pony, so longevity is likely to be better. Bought new, the X2 is a little expensive, and on the second-hand market there are still too few of them about to stabilize second-hand prices. If you see a good one, bargain hard. Although this is not a mainstream car, it is quite an attractive proposition.

## HYUNDAI STELLAR
Rear-wheel-drive saloon.

### History
*June 1984* Range is 1600L, 1600SL, 1600GSL.
*April 1987* Mechanical and trim improvements.
*October 1991* Range discontinued.

### Fault Finder
Check for warped brake discs on all versions. A judder through the brake pedal will reveal this. Shock absorbers wear quickly on 1984 and 1985 cars, especially at the back, so check for any undue floatiness during cornering, and any crashing noises when going over bumpy surfaces. Listen to the engine for any serious rattling. Early versions of the Stellar – those made in 1984 and until March 1985 – had poor crankshaft design which often led to early failure. Check the water pump on 1986 models. If there is a knocking sound on tick-over, the pump could soon fail. On all models, check the drive shaft differential at the rear for leaks, and listen for any rumbling when driving. When driving off from rest, make sure that there is no delayed jolt from the back, a sure sign that the drive shaft joints are worn and will soon fail. On most Stellars, the gear-change becomes sloppy with age, and there have been cases of the gear-lever parting company with the gear box. Check this carefully by waggling the gear-lever once it's in a gear – there should be virtually no sideways movement. Corrosion can be a problem, especially on the tops of the front wings and where the wing meets the front door. Check for this carefully, because if there is corrosion there it is probably coming through from under the wing, and rotting right through. Look for water leaks into the boot, although this is a fairly uncommon occurence on this car. Seat trim is not the toughest, so look for any rips, because they can spread quite easily, and look for bobbling of the velour seating material because this soon gets grubby and shaves lots of value off when the time comes to resell.

### Verdict
The Stellar was old fashioned when it appeared and although it's a big car for low cost it's even more old fashioned now. Second-hand prices are low, and so will be the residuals when it's your turn to sell. If you need a cheap, big saloon the Stellar is worth a look, but if you can put up with something a little smaller, and much more modern, take a look at major European rivals.

## HYUNDAI SONATA
Front-wheel-drive saloons.

### History
*June 1989* Range is 1.8GLi, 2.0i, 2.0GLi, 2.4GLSi.

### Fault Finder
Engines are strong and capable, but they always sound tinny. Listen for rattling timing chains, and look for oil leaks, but there are no real horror stories here. Check for brake judder from warped brake discs at the front. Make sure that all electrics are working properly, there were a batch of early cars – made from June 1989

to March 1990 – with faulty electric window control panels. Check alloy wheels for pitting. This makes them look tatty quite quickly, and takes value off. Check all interior trim for fit and finish. Most Sonatas are well screwed together, but there are also some early ones – some of those produced during 1989 – which were less than perfect.

## Verdict

Reliable but totally unremarkable mid-range saloon. Prices are dropping quite quickly, so there are bargains to be had second-hand. Best choice is the 1.8-litre, as both the 2.0 and 2.4-litre cars plummet in value. If you like some character in your motoring look elsewhere.

## ISUZU PIAZZA

Rear-wheel-drive sports coupé.

## History

*February 1986* Piazza Turbo.
*September 1986* Four-speed automatic option.
*February 1988* Major suspension modification carried out by Lotus, plus trim and equipment improvements.

## Fault Finder

Engines need careful examination, partly because these cars have usually been driven hard. Oil leaks must be thoroughly checked out, and the oil level and condition of the oil should be examined closely. The oil should be clean, and not black with bits of brown in it; dirty oil is a sign of corrosion inside the engine. Check the inside of the oil filler cap for the white gunge which is one important pointer to a failed head gasket. Check the drive shaft housing on the rear axle for any signs of oil leaks, and inspect the rubber gaiters where they meet the rear wheels, the gaiters should be intact and not leaking fluid. If there is a clattering sound for a few seconds after the car has stopped it's almost certainly a problem with the turbo's blades, and the only sensible cure is to replace the turbocharger, a fairly costly exercise. Gearboxes that crunch when changing gear are near to failure, but when synchromesh wears on either second or third gears, this is rarely a major problem, and the gearbox may last for several more years. On early Piazzas, built before February 1988, the suspension was dreadful, making the car very wallowy around corners, and bad damping caused a lot of crashing noise over bumpy roads surfaces. These suspension systems should be checked for leaking shock absorbers. Any clonking noises from the suspension when turning hard to the left or right point to worn bottom ball joints. On Piazzas made after February 1988 Lotus took charge of suspension design, and the result is a car which handles very well indeed, cornering virtually flat, and although giving a taut ride, digesting most bumps. If the Piazza you are looking at is one of these cars and the suspension is soggy then there is a problem with the shock absorbers, although it can usually be cured simply by replacing them. As a first check, look for leaks from the front struts. Inside the car there are two bean-can type control pods either side of the steering wheel. On cars made prior to 1988 these vibrated terribly, even on fairly smooth road surfaces, with the result that some of the control wires inside become loose, or totally disconnected. So, check that all switches and all electrical items are working properly.

## Verdict

After February 1988 the Piazza became a fine car to drive, before that it was quite unpleasant, due to its soggy handling. A comprehensive service record is vital with this car, because if the turbocharger is not looked after properly it can fail, and repair can be quite costly.

## ISUZU TROOPER

Four-wheel-drive multi-purpose vehicle.

## History

*February 1987* Range is short and long wheelbase models (three- and five-door). Engines are 2.3-litre petrol, 2.2-litre turbo diesel.

*June 1987* Duty Special, with higher equipment list.

*January 1988* Heavily revised range, 2.6i petrol, 2.8 turbo diesel, both in choice of short or long wheelbase, and with Standard, Duty or Citation equipment levels; Citation includes air conditioning, cruise control.

*January 1989* Heavy equipment revision.

*February 1992* Heavily revised range with new engines, a V6 3.2-litre petrol and 3.1-litre turbo diesel. Three trim levels, Standard, Duty, Citation, and

choice of three- and five-door versions.

## Fault Finder

Engines are near unbreakable, but they do need regular attention, otherwise the petrol engine in particular can go off-tune, and run ragged. Check for an even tick-over on the 1987–8 petrol versions and rev the engine hard, looking for any black exhaust smoke, a sign of worn valve seals, and expensive engine repair work ahead. This check is especially important if the Trooper has a tow-bar fitted, because this will mean the vehicle has been strained, at least some of the time. Diesel versions will be smoky, but on the test drive check for smooth performance, there should be no jerkiness, and the turbo should boost in smoothly. A slight whistle from the turbocharger is normal, but there should not be any clattering when it boosts, this is a sign of broken or misaligned turbine blades. The gearchange is notchy, but it shouldn't be hard to get into gear. There is no history of faulty gearboxes, or of worn synchromesh, so if either of these do exist then the Trooper you are looking at has probably not had an easy life, and should be avoided at all costs. On the earliest Troopers, those that came here during the first year, 1987–8, the umbrella handbrakes had a habit of unlatching themselves. All of these should have been rectified by now, but Isuzu would not admit to the problem, so it's always wise to leave the Trooper in gear, as well as leaving the handbrake on. Check the free-wheeling front hubs to make sure that they engage properly when four-wheel drive is selected. There is no substantial history of failing hubs, but if the Trooper has been used off-road they can become dirty and sometimes corrode inside, and that can cause them to stop working properly. Look very carefully at the underside, to see if there has been any damage caused by hectic off-road use. While down there, check the shock absorbers for leaks, and check the two drive axles for leaks of transmission fluid. Rust has not been a major problem with the Trooper, but quality control was not good during the first year, and it's only Troopers produced in the last two years which have been of really high quality. This means you should look carefully at the fit and finish of the interior trim, the condition of the seats, and check that all of the electrics are working, especially electric windows. Outside, examine the paintwork carefully for any peeling or bubbling, and also check for accident damage, although few Troopers seem to have been driven recklessly. However, try and avoid any Trooper which looks like it has been used on a farm, these vehicles are traditionally treated rather harshly, and their interior trim is not as robust as that of a Land Rover.

## Verdict

Prices for second-hand Troopers are very attractive, the problem is, finding a good second-hand one. There are not many about, due to import controls on Japanese vehicles, and owners, tend to hold on to them as well. Best choice is the turbo diesel which provides sprightly performance coupled with economical motoring.

## JAGUAR XJ6/XJ12/DAIMLER

Rear-wheel-drive saloons.

## History

*July 1981* XJ12 HE.

*September 1983* Range is 4.2-litre saloon. Sovereign 4.2-litre launched with higher equipment level than ordinary 4.2-litre. XJ12 Sovereign, Daimler 4.2-litre, revised Double-Six (V12 engine).

*October 1986* Range discontinued and replaced by new range. Straight-six cylinder engines; 2.9-litre, 3.6-litre, Daimler 3.6-litre.

*October 1988* XJR 3.6-litre with sportier suspension and sporting embellishments.

*September 1989* 4.0-litre and Sovereign. XJ12 Sovereign rebadged Jaguar V12. Daimler 4.0-litre.

*June 1990* Jaguar Sport XJR 4.0-litre.

*September 1990* 3.2-litre XJ6.

## Fault Finder

First, check for a full and complete service history, this is a must with this car. Many Jaguars are used as company cars, so they should have been well looked after, but they usually cover high mileages, so check the service history with a microscope to make sure the car has covered no more than its stated mileage. Engines are very quiet, so if there is any rattling on tick-over there is a problem. Jaguar have not had any major problems with engines, apart from faulty oil pumps on some 1985 4.2-litre models. Affected pumps would usually fail around 15,000 miles, so by now they should all have been replaced. Lucas fuel injection systems on 3.6-litre cars should be viewed with some suspicion, they do not have a good reputation. The Bosch fuel injection on later cars has proved very reliable. Electronic engine management systems on 3.6-litre cars made in the 1987 model year would sometimes give erratic running, causing stalling in heavy traffic. Again, most of these should have been replaced by now, but just in case, check for smooth running, especially at low speeds once the engine has warmed up. Check for any slipping from the automatic gearbox, it should change gears very smoothly. If there is any lurching when the car goes into its next gear, or hesitation between moving the gear-lever and the gearbox selecting a gear, there is too much wear in the system. Manual gearboxes on 2.9-litre cars are not the best, often losing their synchromesh in second gear, and sometimes proving hard to get into gear. There has also been a problem with the clutch action on 2.9-litre manual cars. On 2.9-litre cars built from October 1986 to July 1987, clutch take-up was too snatchy, which meant masses of revs had to be used when changing gear. This makes town driving a nightmare. This problems also affected 3.6-litre manual cars, and as with the 2.9-litre, it did not disappear until a new clutch routing was designed towards the end of 1987. On 4.2-litre models the twin rear brake cylinders often rust and

then leak fluid. Look under the rear of the car to check for leaks. Rear axles were a problem for some time, and even on the latest versions you should listen for excessive whine. Some noise is normal, but if it's intrusive, or there's a deep rumbling from the back, there is a problem and the axle may need to be replaced, a hideously expensive job. Try and get a friend to sit in the back of the car while you are taking your test drive. They should place their feet either side of the transmission tunnel. If there is movement clearly felt under the floor when the gearbox is changing gear then there is a problem with the transmission link to the rear axle, an expensive problem. On all models, but especially 2.9 and 3.6-litre cars, check the suspension shock absorbers at the front for leaks, and make sure that they are telescoping correctly. These are heavy cars, so the suspension system has to work hard. At the rear, check the suspension for any sagging, or crashing over bumpy roads. There should not be any noise from the rear suspension. If self-levelling suspension is fitted, make sure that it keeps the car level when a load is placed on board. Make sure it doesn't sit lower on one side than the other. Any problems here are truly expensive to rectify. Brakes should be progressive and very powerful. Any pulling to left or right will point to seized brake calipers, a problem on some 1985 cars. Check the all-round discs on all versions for any scoring as the XJ6 has a large appetite for brake pads. Under the bonnet, look at the brake fluid reservoir to check the level is correct. If it is too low there is a leak somewhere, a problem with some XJs built up to 1984, and mainly caused by leaking master cylinders at the back. While looking under the bonnet, check for any accident damage, which should be revealed by any twisting of the chassis members – under the engine – or creasing of the insides of the wings. Part digital dashboards on mid-1980s cars are not generally liked and have often proved unreliable. Try and avoid these. Corrosion is a problem on 4.2-litre cars, and it most often appears on the rear valance, under the rear bumper. If caught early this can be stopped, but when the valance is already rotting, rust could also have spread inside the rear wings, and by then corrosion will be widespread. On the front wings, check the area around the headlamps and along the tops of the wings for corrosion. Once it takes hold here it will spread like wildfire. The quality of interior trim should be checked closely. On cars with velour seat coverings the material can ball-up – small balls of material all over the seat cushion – and this seriously detracts from the value. On hide trimmed cars, check for serious cracks in the leather. Many Jaguars have had car phones fitted and when these are taken out it often leaves ugly screw holes. If you can find a Jaguar without these it retains a better value.

**Verdict**
Choose carefully and you can find first-class Jaguars at sensible prices. It's a lot of car for the money. But, beware of clocked cars, noisy rear axles, rust on earlier models and slipping auto gearboxes. Best choice is a 3.6, 4.0 or 3.2-litre car, the later the better. Avoid underpowered 2.9-litre versions.

## JAGUAR XJ-S, XJ-SC CABRIOLET, XJ-S CONVERTIBLE
Rear-wheel-drive sports coupés and convertibles.

**History**
*June 1983* 3.6-litre coupé, XJ-SC 3.6-litre Cabriolet.
*July 1985* XJSC-HE Cabriolet.
*April 1988* V12 Convertible.
*September 1988* XJR-S coupé.
*September 1989* Jaguar Sport XJR-S 6.0-litre.
*May 1991* 4.0-litre coupé replaces 3.6-litre and all models have major bodywork revisions and restyled interiors.

**Fault Finder**
As with all Jaguars, a full service history, and verification of mileage are all-important. On early manual 3.6-litre cars, check for smooth clutch operation. The clutch cable routing design on early manual convertibles and original manual saloons was not good, and led to jerky driving in town, unless the car was given an inordinate amount of revs, making for very stressful driving. Avoid these cars. A good manual gearbox on a 3.6-litre car – those built after January 1986 – is the one to aim for, because it gives good performance and reasonable fuel economy. On automatic models, check for any slipping from the gears, although it must be said that these

autos are very reliable. Any misfiring or less than smooth running at medium to high speeds usually points to a defective engine management system, common on 1986–7 3.6-litre cars. On V12 engined cars the best versions are the HE, the earlier cars drank even more fuel and were susceptible to worn valve seals. Check for black smoke from the exhaust, a sign of worn seals. The V12 should tick-over smoothly and evenly, if there is an uneven engine beat then the fuel-injection system is most likely at fault, a problem which afflicted some 1982–3 V12s. Check the rear brake cylinders for leaks, as well as looking for any brake fluid seeping on to the rear disc brakes. Check the discs for scoring, as the V12 in particular is very heavy on its brakes. Check all cars for suspension problems, especially at the back. The car should sit squarely, with no sag at the rear. On 3.6-litre cars in particular, listen for creaking or clonking from the rear axle. It is not common on these cars, but there have been some faulty axles. Normal axles should be virtually silent. Electrics are normally good, but check electric door mirrors because these sometimes fail, and replacing them is quite expensive. Check the interior for badly cracked leather seats, or velour-covered seats whose material has balled-up. Both these traits badly affect resale values.

### Verdict
The V12 is a very thirsty car and servicing and repairs are very expensive, but it does provide some of the smoothest grand touring motoring you could hope

for. A better choice from the costs point of view is the 3.6-litre which keeps its value better and in manual form is really pleasing to drive. If you can afford it, the very best XJ-S is the new 4.0-litre, but so far there are few on the second-hand market.

### LADA RIVA
Rear-wheel-drive saloons and estates.

### History
*April 1984* Range is 1200, 1200L, 1300, 1500GLS.
*October 1985* 1300 and 1500 estates, 1300GL Special saloon.
*June 1986* 1300SL saloon, replaces 1300GL Special.
*August 1986* 1600SLX saloon.
*April 1991* New range, 1300E, 1300L, 1600L saloons; 1300, 1500 estates.

### Fault Finder
Look for oil leaking from the top of the engine, usually a result of a worn head gasket. On all versions, on tick-over listen for any rattling from the engine, a sign that the crankshaft is not getting enough oil, and also listen for any mechanical slapping, a sign that the pistons are slapping. Check the exhaust for excessive smoke when the engine is revved hard, a sign of worn valves. Gearboxes are generally quite good, but if the gear-lever crunches when you're trying to put it into gear, it could be the gearbox bushes, or it could mean the gearbox has loose metal floating around inside it. The latter is an expensive fault to rectify. Check brakes for any pulling to one side or other. This is

usually the result of a seized caliper, quite common on these cars. The brakes should work very effectively, and they need very little pressure before they bite. If the pedal feels spongy then you should also look in the brake fluid reservoir, under the bonnet, for small bubbles. These will point to a leak somewhere in the system. If the wheels lock too easily when braking – try braking normally at a junction – then the calipers are seizing on, usually as a result of corrosion, and usually on the back wheels. This can be sorted out quite easily, but may reoccur. Check the suspension struts at the front for any leaks, and also check that there is no fluid leaking from the tops of the suspension turrets inside the engine bay. While you are looking under the bonnet, check along the insides of the wings and the engine supports for any signs of corrosion because this can eat its way right through the wings. Corrosion can be a problem outside, again on the wings, but also on the back wings, although this is more of a problem on the estate versions than on the saloon. On saloons, look inside the boot for sitting water, and look under the floor matting in the boot for any signs of rust in the corners. Check all gauges and switches for proper working because electrical connections have not always been the best. Window winders can often become hard to wind down, a problem which can only be solved by taking the door panel off and readjusting the runners. Check all exterior paintwork over carefully for a good finish – many of these cars suffered from poor paint application, so look for patches of bubbled paint.

## Verdict
The Lada is essentially quite a tough car, although lacking in the social graces expected of most of today's European cars. If you want a very inexpensive and mostly reliable runabout that is also quite practical, then take a look at the estate. Best engines are 1.5 and 1.6-litre, the 1.3-litre is too slow.

## LADA SAMARA
Front-wheel-drive hatchbacks, estates.

### History
*October 1987* Range is 1300L, 1300SL, 1300SLX, all in three-door form.
*October 1988* 1300L, 1300SL five-door, 1500SL, 1500SX five-door.
*February 1989* 1500SL, 1500SLX five-door.
*July 1990* 1100 Select, 1100L three-door.
*April 1991* New range, 1100E three-door, 1100L, 1300GL, 1500GL three- and five-door.

### Fault Finder
Check doors for proper fit, especially the driver's door which often hangs badly. Engines are mostly reliable, so carry out the usual checks for oil leaks and check the quality of the oil by looking for any black or brown speckles on the oil on the dipstick (a sign of corrosion inside the engine). If none of these faults exist then the engine is quite sound. Gearboxes vary from quite precise to very rubbery in their action, but unless there is lot of crunching, or it's very hard to get into any gear, there should not be a serious problem. Brakes can seize their calipers, usually on one

side of the car, but this is rarer than in the older Lada saloon. Still, check for any pulling to left or right. Water leaks through the front windscreen surround should be checked for, because this is quite a common problem on pre-1988 models. check the carpet by the brake pedal for any leaking fluid from the brake cylinder. Again, only a few of these cases have been reported. Check the front tyres for excessive or uneven wear, as front suspension geometry can be fairly easily upset by regular kerbing of the front tyres. Corrosion is, so far, not a problem with the Samara, so you just need to check the bodywork over carefully for any flaking paint or paint defects, although these are rare, so far, the Samara's paintwork has been quite impressive.

## LADA NIVA
Four-wheel-drive multi-purpose vehicle.

### History
*April 1984* First right-hand-drive versions.
*January 1988* Cossack launched.

### Fault Finder
Many Lada Nivas are bought for off-road use, so look carefully underneath for any damage to the sump guard, and for any evidence of oil leaks. While you're down there, check the front and rear drive axles for any leaks from the differentials. This is rare on the Niva, but excessive high speed use, or hectic off-road use, can cause the drive shafts to 'dry-up' and once that happens they soon become damaged. Gearboxes are

not the strongest, so check for any crunching or resistance when slotting into gears. However, getting into reverse gear is an acquired art, and if you cannot get it right the first or second try, that doesn't mean the gearbox is not working properly, it's simply a poor design. The high- and low-ratio four-wheel-drive lever is not very smooth, requiring a hefty push to activate the four-wheel-drive. Check it does move, as many become locked due to poor or infrequent servicing. Alternators are renowned for failing, especially on Nivas built during 1985, so check that the red electric warning light is not coming on, a pointer to this problem. Check also for engine overheating due to a failed engine fan, another common problem. The dashboard is rather flimsy, so check that it's still firmly attached to the bulkhead – some have come right away. Seats are not made of the strongest material, so they can suffer rips, which can soon spread; try and avoid a Niva with less than pristine seat covering. Corrosion is not normally a problem, but if the Niva has been used off-road check for any rust bubbling through from the underside of the front wings, and check the bottoms of the doors because water can get inside and then cause rot to come through. The rear door should also be examined closely for any corrosion, and make sure you give it a hefty slam closed so that you can see if any rust granules drop out of it.

### Verdict
A solid but very unrefined workhorse which has often been used by a farmer or construction company, so care is needed when buying

second-hand. But, if you can put
up with the rather rudimentary
mechanicals and heavy fuel consumption this vehicle is worth a
look. It must be said, though, most
rivals are more refined, although
they do cost more.

## LANCIA Y10
Front-wheel-drive hatchback.

### History
*June 1985* Range is Fire, Touring,
  Turbo.
*July 1989* LXie, GTie.
*June 1990* Selectronic (automatic
  transmission model).
*February 1991* Range trimmed to
  Selectronic and GTie.

### Fault Finder
Check all electrics very carefully.
Make sure that the red electric
warning light is not on, because this
points to a failing alternator, fairly
common on Y10s made in 1985 to
early 1986. Selectronic versions are
sometimes quite jerky, although
gears rarely slip. Best choice is a
manual model. Engines are tough
and really only need to be checked
for oil leaks and rattling timing
chains. On turbo versions listen for
any clattering when the turbo
boosts, a sign that the turbocharger's blades are damaged. On
turbos look for engine overheating,
often caused by a faulty oil breather
pipe. Check interior trim over carefully, especially the fit of the dashboard. Listen for any squeaks or
rattles, these are very common on
Y10s before 1988. Corrosion is not a
problem, but make sure that the
tail-gate closes properly, quite a
number of these have fallen out of
line after regular use.

### Verdict
Not much goes wrong with the Y10
but it is a very small car, and
therefore its appeal is limited. The
best choice is a Y10 with the Fiat
designed FIRE engine because it's
smooth and reliable, and it returns
good fuel economy. The Turbo
model is not really recommended
because the engine soon becomes
tired, and it's always noisy.

## LANCIA DELTA
Front-wheel-drive and four-wheel-
drive hatchbacks.

### History
*September 1982* 1.5LX joins the
  range.
*June 1983* 1300, 1600GT.
*June 1984* 1600 HF Turbo.
*July 1986* Heavy revisions for all
  models. Range is 1300, 1300LX,
  1600GTie, 1600 HF Turbo IE.
*May 1987* HF Turbo 4x4.
*February 1988* HF Integrale 4x4.
*October 1989* Revised HF Inte-
  grale, more powerful engine,
  uprated brakes, suspension.
*July 1991* Even more powerful HF
  Integrale, with modified body,
  brakes and suspension.

### Fault Finder
Electrics are suspect on all models,
even the latest versions. The most
common fault is for all of the dials
to fail, the rear wash/wipe, and the
heated rear window. Quite often,
the central locking partially fails,
so that only one of the doors will
lock or unlock. Electric door mirrors are another regular failure.
Engines are strong and lusty, even
the small 1.3-litre, but on the GT
and Turbo it's very important that
the camshaft belts are changed

every 36,000 miles. If they aren't, they can snap and cause serious damage to the engine, usually quickly leading to a complete engine seizure. If there is any noisy rattling from the engine on tick-over it may well be the crankshaft which isn't being fed enough oil. By the time you hear this rattle the crankshaft may need replacing. Gearboxes are strong, but the lever can become disconnected from the gearbox itself when a bolt down in the gearbox works loose. Regular servicing should stop this happening. Brakes are mostly trouble-free but on GT and Turbo models check the brake fluid reservoir to make sure it's filled to its correct level. Also check the front disc brakes to see if there is any brake fluid on the discs, a sign of a small leak. You may also notice this when braking, because any fluid leak onto the discs can lead to serious pulling to one side. Rust is seldom a problem, except as a result of stone chips or accident damage. Interior trim is rather flimsy, so check it all fits properly and that all switches work well. The plastic guard under the steering-wheel column on cars up to 1986 can sometimes work loose and begin clattering.

**Verdict**
Thoroughly likeable car offering terrific performance, safe handling and a first-class ride. But electrics are always suspect and the fit of interior trim can be disappointing. Best all-round model is the GT but the Turbo adds more power and, if you have the money, the Integrale's performance will make you smile. A must is a full service record coupled with no accident damage.

**LANCIA PRISMA**
Front-wheel-drive saloon (saloon version of the Delta).

**History**
*August 1983* Range is 1500, 1600ie.
*July 1986* Modified models, 1600ie, LXie.
*May 1988* 1600 Symbol (high level of equipment).
*September 1990* Range discontinued.

**Fault Finder**
This is the booted version of the Lancia Delta, so the same potential problem areas exist with the Prisma.

**Verdict**
Prisma prices are usually lower than equivalent engined and equipped Deltas, simply because the Prisma shape is not so desirable and the car is traditionally driven by older drivers than the Delta. Best choice is the 1.6ie which blends good performance with perfectly adequate equipment and sensible second-hand pricing.

**LANCIA DEDRA**
Front-wheel-drive saloons.

**History**
*February 1990* Range is 1.6ie, 1.8ie, 1.8ieSE, 2.0ie, 2.0ieSE.
*October 1990* Dedra Turbo.

**Fault Finder**
Very few problems have reared their heads since this car's launch, but check that the camshaft belt has been changed at the recommended service interval, especially on the 2.0-litre engine. Look for

any engine oil leaks, though so far this does not seem like a Dedra problem. Gearboxes also appear to be tough, but on hard driven examples there is always the possibility that synchromesh can go, and when it does it will usually be on second gear. Brakes should always be checked for scoring of discs, and the rubber drive shaft gaiters should be checked for any splits, and replaced if they are damaged. There are no recorded examples of rusty Dedras, thanks to galvanized body panels and thorough anti-corrosion treatments. Check the body over for any accident damage. Electrics must always be checked, especially electric windows and sun-roof. One minor annoyance; after around 15,000 miles the driver's seatbelt often fails to retract back smoothly, often hanging out of the car's door when the driver gets out.

**Verdict**
The Dedra has so far not sold in the numbers its makers hoped for, so it's always hard to judge what is a good second-hand value. Certainly, it seems to have been a very reliable car so far. Best choice is the 1.8ie, a good package of performance and price. The Turbo is fiendishly quick, but quite expensive.

**LANCIA THEMA**
Front-wheel-drive saloon.

**History**
*October 1985* Range is 2.0ie, 2.0ie Turbo, 2.0ie Turbo LX, V6 2.8-litre.
*March 1988* 8.32 launched, using V8 Ferrari engine.

*June 1989* Modified range with new multi-valve 2.0-litre engine and launch of SE special equipment models.

**Fault Finder**
Camshaft belts must be replaced on 2.0-litre engines, preferably at 36,000 miles, but sooner on cars which have been driven hard. Listen for timing chain rattle from the engine. Check for oil leaks from the bottom of the engine, and lift the oil filler cap to check for the creamy white sludge deposit which points to cylinder head gasket wear. Manual gearboxes can become rather hard to slot into first gear, and synchromesh can wear on hard-driven cars – in the Thema's case, mostly on third gear. Check the drive shafts for clonking noises, a sign that the CV joints are wearing, and check for brake squeal, usually only caused by a build-up of brake dust, but sometimes the result of the brake pads wearing down too quickly. Check all electrics, the Thema is not a good advertisement for Italian electrics. Interior trim on Themas up to 1987 was not always well put together, in particular examine the dashboard which often rattles and squeaks, and the door panels, which can come away from the door.

**Verdict**
In many ways the Thema is a lot of car for the money, and if you can find one which has been regularly serviced and is free of rattles or squeaks, you've found a good one. Beware, though, resale values will never be great.

## LAND ROVER COUNTY
Four-wheel-drive multi-purpose vehicle.

### History
The County is the well trimmed version of the vehicle which has been in constant production since 1948.

*March 1983* New generation Land Rover 110 long wheelbase launched. Choice of 2.3-litre diesel, 2.3-litre petrol, V8 petrol engines.

*January 1984* New 2.5-litre diesel engine replaces 2.3-litre.

*June 1984* Land Rover 90 short wheelbase version of the 110 launched. Only available with 2.2-litre petrol engine.

*May 1985* 90 gets option of V8 petrol engine.

*July 1985* 90 gets option of 2.5-litre four cylinder diesel.

*November 1986* 2.5-litre turbo diesel available on 90 and 110. V8 engine power uprated.

*February 1991* Defender badged models launched with choice of 90 and 110 bodies, 2.5-litre diesel and turbo diesel and V8 petrol engines.

### Fault Finder
Many people believe that a Land Rover will just go on and on. The problem with this perception is that servicing is often neglected, and although the Land Rover is undoubtedly strong it does need regular 6,000 mile servicing. The first check, then, should be for a full service history. On older models this is unlikely, but it is most definitely a bonus to have a full history. Gearboxes and engines both need several checks. The gearboxes on all Land Rovers built before 1984 need careful scrutiny. Remember, firstly, that even a very good Land Rover gearbox whines a lot, but if the gearbox changes gear a little while after the gear-lever has been slotted into gear – there could be a lurching movement when you're on the move – then there is a problem, and this particular vehicle should be avoided. Likewise, drive the Land Rover hard in each gear because there have been cases of Land Rovers dropping out of gear. This usually applies to those built up to 1985 and is often a direct result of poor or irregular servicing. However, it could be a more serious problem; if it's hard to get into gear, coupled with jumping out of gear on the move, there is a problem with the gear selectors, and this can be quite expensive to rectify. The heavy duty suspension is tough, but it should always be checked over carefully, especially if the vehicle has been used off-road. The springs should be firm, both on- and off-road, and the Land Rover should sit the road squarely and levelly. If there is any sogginess or soft bounce from the springs, or any lean, it will usually mean the entire spring set on the affected wheel will need replacing. Look under the vehicle for broken coil springs. These were fitted in place of the leaf springs which were standard on all Land Rovers previous to the 90/110. Look also for leaks of fluid from the shock absorbers. Replacements are not horrendously expensive but such a problem is often a pointer to a hard life, doubly so if the surrounding coil springs are heavily corroded or broken. Check under the vehicle for any transmission fluid leaks. This is often a sign of serious problems

91

because the fluid may already be dangerously low. This check is vitally important, all the more so if the gearchange is awkward. On the engine front, the diesel and petrol four-cylinder engines are generally quite reliable, though the diesel must have proper, regular servicing. If it doesn't, then the engine oil often sludges, causing blockages which can lead to overheating and prematurely worn bearings. Although all Land Rover engines are quite noisy, listen for any severe rattling from the engine when idling, usually a sign that bearings are worn. This problem is more commonly found with the four-cylinder petrol engine than with either the V8 or the diesel. On all engines look for excessive exhaust smoke when revving the engine hard. The diesel models will always smoke a little, but if there is a lot it points to worn valves and valve seals. Both the petrol and diesel four-cylinder engines suffer from cracked cylinder heads, a problem which most often occurs when servicing has been neglected. The diesel engines, both turbo and naturally aspirated, must have regular oil changes. Surprisingly, the V8 engine is not as tough as might be thought. There have been a number of cases of blown cylinder heads leading to engine overheating. Again, servicing is often the key to keeping this fault at bay. Beware high mileage V8 Land Rovers with rough sounding engines. This can signal imminent problems with worn valves, but it can also point to a broken exhaust manifold, altogether less serious a problem. On all versions, the four-wheel-drive differential lock

can suffer from leaks and corrosion inside the differential box, placed underneath the Land Rover. If it's hard to move the differential lock lever – next to the gear-lever – then corrosion may well be the reason. Underneath the Land Rover, look carefully at the steering box for any signs of leaks or damage. It's placed behind the front radiator grille. The Land Rover 90 doesn't have the same heavy duty rear axle as its longer wheelbase 110 brother, and this can lead to worn rear half-shafts, which will eventually stop the rear axle providing drive. The only way to check for this is to see if there is any undue hesitation from the back end when moving off from rest. Any loud clunking from back there could point to this problem. The wheels are subject to lots of movement on most Land Rovers, simply because these vehicles are very often driven on bumpy, irregular surfaces, and this can affect the wheel hubs. The only proper way to check for such wear is to get the vehicle jacked-up off the ground and then to move each wheel to see if there's too much play. If there is it's usually best to look for another Land Rover, because repairs in this area are expensive. Corrosion of the body work is not a problem, simply because almost all panels are rust-free aluminium. But don't let this give you a false sense of security about rust in general. The backbone chassis can rust. Check this very carefully. Least serious is corrosion of the arms which come out from the central chassis member. These can rust at their ends – nearest the wings of the Land Rover – but if this has happened replacement is not too expensive. More serious is rusting of the back chassis members, and this can often be started by heavy towing because this places lots of strain on the rear chassis members. Most serious is any rusting of the main backbone of the chassis. If you see this, leave that particular Land Rover alone. Body rust can take place, but the main areas are under the bonnet where the steel bulkhead – between the engine and the passenger compartment – can become corroded. It's also wise to check along the insides of the engine bay, they can be affected by rust.

## Verdict

Land Rovers keep their value exceptionally well, so if you see one which is cheap there is most definitely a problem with it. The best choices are the turbo diesel – though this is expensive new and keeps a relatively high second-hand value – and the ordinary diesel. The four-cylinder petrol model is short on performance, not as tough as the diesel, and noisier at high speeds. The V8 is a good performer with tremendous pulling ability but its 15mpg average fuel returns will only make petrol company owners smile.

## LAND ROVER DISCOVERY
Four-wheel-drive multi-purpose vehicle.

## History
*November 1989* 200 Tdi (turbo diesel), V8 petrol in three-door form.
*September 1990* Five-door versions launched.

## Fault Finder
Engines are robust and reliable. As long as servicing has been carried out regularly and by a Land Rover dealer there should be no major engine problems. So far, none have been reported. Do make sure that on turbo diesel versions the turbocharger is boosting, because on motorway journeys the turbo is boosting almost all of the time, so there is a good deal of wear and tear on this unit. Electrics must be carefully checked over. There have been a number of failures of electric door mirrors in particular, and some electric windows failing. Gearboxes can be troublesome, usually as a result of gearbox bearings wearing too quickly. Check for any undue rattling when trying to gently push the gear-lever into a gear, and when the clutch is pressed down, listen for rattling, a sign that the clutch bearings are also wearing. These faults are not common, but they have been experienced by a fair number of Discovery owners. Trim quality is good, but check that it is all screwed together properly, especially in the front – the dashboard and door panels. If a tow hitch is fitted, check the exhaust for blue smoke, (remember that there will always be some smoke from the turbo diesel) a sign that valve seals are wearing. Again, an uncommon fault, simply because the engines are so strong, but if the Discovery has been subjected to too much strain the engine will become weakened. Door locks should all be checked to make sure they are working properly.

## Verdict

Early Discoverys, those built during the first six to eight months of production, were not terribly well put together, and they suffered from a multitude of niggling little faults, most of which will now have been put right. The best Discovery to buy is a turbo diesel with around 20,000 miles on the clock, long enough for any problems to have been sorted, not too long that the engine will have become tired through heavy use. The V8 is a real barnstormer but its fuel thirst makes even strong men weep.

## LOTUS ELAN

Front-wheel-drive sports convertible.

## History

*October 1989* 1.6, 1.6SE (SE is a turbo).

## Fault Finder

The major check here is for any clonking from the front drive shafts when turning the steering wheel over to full lock. Also, listen for any bump as the car is moved away from rest. Both of these problems point to wear on the front CV joints. As an additional check, look under the car to see if the rubber gaiters by the front wheels are intact. If they aren't, grit will almost certainly have got in, and the lubricant will have got out, causing the CV joint to wear prematurely. Engines demand regular servicing to keep them in top-top condition, so make sure that the service history is complete. Check the front tyres for wear as hard driving puts them under a lot of pressure, and they are not cheap to replace. Any uneven tyre wear should make you ask questions about front suspension wear. Listen for clonking noises when driving over bumps, this will usually be as a result of wear of the suspension's lower ball joints. The convertible hoods are well made, but look inside for any evidence of water leaks. This is not a common problem, though. Make sure that there are no rips in the material, caused by careless use, or vandals. The GRP – glass reinforced plastic – body is well made, but check for any starring of the body, caused by any dents. Even a slight bump can cause this, and once the paint stars and cracks it makes the car look tatty, and it's very hard to repair. Check for proper door fit. Again, this is seldom a problem, but some bodyshells on early cars, those made from October 1989 to April 1990, have been known to lose some rigidity, so making it harder to close doors properly. Interior trim is good and solid, so an Elan with less than perfect trim has not been well looked after, and should be avoided.

## Verdict

Wonderful engines give these cars terrific performance and they have also proved very reliable, so far. Build quality is better than most previous Lotuses. Never buy an Elan without a full service history, and be prepared to pay top rates, as these cars are rare and much sought after.

## LOTUS EXCEL

Rear-wheel-drive sports coupé.

## History

*October 1982* Excel launched.
*October 1985* Excel SE.
*November 1986* Excel SA (automatic gearbox).

## Fault Finder

The early Excel was renowned for its engine going off-tune, so make sure that the car you are looking at has an engine that is running sweetly. An Excel which has an engine that's less than smooth on tick-over could be a problem later. Check for a full and comprehensive service history, with all the work carried out by a Lotus dealer. The engines can suffer from oil leaks from both the top and bottom of the engine. If these are coupled with a low oil level, then leave the car well alone. On tick-over the engine should not be noisy, it should sound very sweet. Severe rattles are sometimes pistons beginning to slap, or, more commonly, timing chains which need tightening or replacing. If there is a raucous sound from the engine when revving it hard, along with puffs of black smoke from the exhaust, then valves may be seriously worn. All of these problems are usually only there if the car has not been properly looked after. If it's been regularly serviced, these sort of problems rarely arise. Check shock absorbers on all Excels for leaking, and also for proper damper control. Engine mounts regularly wear, no matter the age of the car, so watch out for any lurching from the engine as you pull forwards from rest. If this exists, take a look at the exhaust manifold as well, because engine movement may have caused the manifold to snap. Brakes are very efficient, so look out for any grabbing or, alternatively, any sponginess through the pedal, these signs point to worn brake pads and low brake fluid pressure. On older cars, say those over six years old, check underneath to make sure that the main chassis is not rusting. There is an eight-year anti-rust warranty on the chassis, but a check is always worthwhile, and particularly revealing if the car has been in an accident. It is very common for the gearbox to lose synchromesh, even after as little as 30,000 miles, and sometimes it goes on third gear, as well as more commonly on second. Major gearbox break-ups are rare. Check inside the car for flimsy trim, especially on cars built more than two years ago. Also, check that all switches work properly, electrics on pre-1987 cars were never impressive. On all Excels, check carefully for any accident damage that might have caused the paintwork to star. As with any fibreglass-bodied car, paint starring is very hard to correct and can soon spread. Look very carefully at the different panels on the Excel to see if the paintwork is all the same colour. Fading paintwork was a problem on cars produced between 1982 and 1984, and it seriously affects resale values.

## Verdict

An exciting car to drive, with a truly smooth engine and excellent road manners. Prices are still rather high, partly because of the fact that new prices have crept up so much, but also because the Excel is relatively rare. Best model is a manual version made in the last three years, but don't dismiss the rivals, they are tough acts.

## LOTUS ESPRIT
Rear-wheel-drive sports coupé.

### History
*April 1981* S3.
*October 1986* Turbo HC.
*October 1987* HC, Turbo HC with new body.
*May 1989* Turbo SE with modified body.
*July 1991* New Turbo HC.

### Fault Finder
The major problem is that the Esprit is always driven hard, and they usually cover high mileages. This means that the mechanicals can become quite tired. Listen for any rattling from the engine on tick-over, a sign that the timing chain is in need of replacement. Rev the engine hard and listen for any tinkling sounds from the engine, it should rev smoothly and sweetly. On turbo models, the turbo boosts strongly from around 2500rpm. If it comes in any later, then there is a problem, if it emits anything other than a faint whistle, there is a problem, and when the turbo is coming off-boost you should not hear it at all. If there is any clattering from the engine when throttling-off it may well be the turbo blades out of line, a problem on 1986 and early 1987 models. Oil leaks should be looked for, and any evidence of engine fires. On Esprits built before 1984 fires were quite common, and some insurance companies refused to insure the car. On the test drive keep checking the temperature gauge for any signs of overheating, especially when the car is dawd-ling in traffic, because the electric fans had a habit of cutting out when they were most needed, especially on Esprits up to 1987. Carefully check all electrics. The faults range from fairly minor – the door mirrors refusing to work – to the potentially dangerous – all of the lights failing. Check also for an efficient heater. On cars built up to 1988 the system was not very efficient, and on some cars it barely seemed to work at all. The main problem is lack of heat to the feet. Often the body of the car could be pumped with hot air but the drivers' feet would be freezing cold. Esprit air conditioning is not the most effective system, and check for fluid leaking out and on to the floor near the passenger's feet. Look very carefully for any accident damage which could have bent the separate chassis, and also check for rust on the chassis. On cars built in the last six or seven years this should not be a problem, but on an Esprit any older, check this over carefully. The paintwork should be looked at very carefully, both from the point of view of faded paint, and also to see if any of the paintwork has starred, the result of even a minor bump. Rectifying this is not easy.

### Verdict
High performance motoring, but the risk of getting a bad Esprit is high as well, unless you really check it over carefully. Running costs are high but this is an exciting car, and one which will always be rare. As with the Excel, there are some powerful rivals.

## MAZDA 121
Front-wheel-drive hatchback.

### History
*January 1988* Range is 1.1L, 1.3LX, 1.3LX Sun Top.
*August 1989* 1.3LX SR.
*December 1991* Range discontinued, new model launched, the GLX with 1.3-litre engine.

### Fault Finder
Check for tired engines, especially on the 1.1-litre because this tends to be used mostly around town. Check the clutch for slipping in second and third gears, a very important test when the car has been used in town. Check automatic chokes for proper operation, sometimes they do not switch off when they should. On Sun Top models check that the large sunshine roof rolls back without snagging in its rails, and check that it is in good condition. Look for water leaks around its edges.

### Verdict
A very reliable little car which is well equipped. The only drawback for many potential owners will be its small size. Nippy around town, but not the most practical from a carrying point of view. Opinions are divided about the looks of the new 121, and so far there is no news on reliability.

## MAZDA 323
Front-wheel-drive hatchbacks, saloons, estates.

### History
*March 1981* Range is 1100 (three-door) 1300 (three- and five-door)

1500 Auto (five-door), 1500GT (three-door).
*July 1982* 1500 estate.
*March 1983* 1500GT saloon, plus modifications across the range, and new trim.
*September 1985* Totally new range replaces previous line-up. Range is 1.1LX, 1.3LX, 1.5GLX, 1.5GLX saloon.
*November 1985* 1.6i hatchback.
*May 1986* 1.5GLX estate.
*September 1986* 4x4 Lux hatchback, Rallye hatchback, both with turbo petrol engines.
*July 1987* Revised and rationalized range, changes to equipment.
*October 1989* Totally new range replaces previous range. 1.3SE, 1.6SE, 1.6 Executive, 1.8GT.
*May 1991* Revised range, 1.3LXi, 1.6GLXi, 1.8GTi.

### Fault Finder
On all 323s built up to October 1989 – and in particular the 1.3-litre – check for a properly functioning automatic choke. The choke often either cuts off too soon, or, more commonly, stays on for too long. This seriously affects fuel consumption, sometimes making it drop as low as 22mpg, and it can only be cured by replacing the choke, not tinkering with it as some Mazda dealers tried to do when the problem first became known. Listen for rattles from inside the gearbox. This is a sign of gearbox bearings wearing and though not a common fault, it occasionally rears its head on 1.3-litre models produced in the mid 1980s. Check the clutch because they didn't last long on any 323 produced up to 1989, and replacement is relatively expensive. Check the rubber gaiters on

the front drive shafts. On 323s produced during the first three years of front-wheel-drive production the gaiters did not last well. Listen out for clonking from the front when turning, this is a sign of worn CV joints, and also listen for any clanging when driving over rough roads, a sign that the bottom joints of the suspension may be worn. Corrosion is rarely a problem, but when it does occur it often starts in the roof channels where paint can flake off. On metallic painted cars, check for the same colour all over, as 323s made during the first three years of production did not have the most resilient finish. The 323 built after 1989 is better than its forerunner in just about every respect, so aside from checking the major mechanical parts there is little to worry about.

**Verdict**
Early 323s were not as reliable as people liked to believe. The automatic choke problem undoubtedly put many people off buying another 323. However, the latest versions – those produced during the past three years – are very good indeed and provide some of the most reliable motoring you could find anywhere. Do remember, though, that the 323 needs a service every 6,000 miles, and that can begin to get rather expensive.

**MAZDA MX-5**
Rear-wheel-drive convertible.

**History**
*March 1990* MX-5 launched.

**Fault Finder**
Look for leaks from the convertible top, although this is only mentioned because it's a sensible check, the hood fits well and so far there have been no stories about badly leaking roofs. Check that the roof catches at the top of the windscreen work properly. Mechanically the MX-5 is, so far, very reliable and as long as you carry out the usual checks to engine and transmission there should be few problems here. A full service history is a must, and it's imperative that you check for accident damage. An MX-5 which has been in a serious accident is a car best avoided.

**Verdict**
This car is likely to become a future classic. It's good to drive, so far it's proved exceptionally reliable, and it doesn't cost a fortune to run. Disadvantages are lack of cabin space and the fact that there are few of them on the secondhand market. There is no such thing as a cheap MX-5. If the price is low, then something is wrong.

**MAZDA 626**
Front-wheel-drive          hatchbacks, saloons, coupés, estates.

**History**
*May 1983* Range is 1600LX saloon and         hatchback,        2000GLX saloon, hatchback, coupé.
*November 1985* 2.0i coupé.
*October 1987* Completely new 626 . Range is 1.8LX saloon and hatchback,     2.0GLX,     2.0GLX Executive        saloon        and hatchback, 2000i GT hatchback and coupé.

*March 1988* 2.0iGT 4WS (four-wheel-steer) hatchback.
*June 1988* 2.0GLX, GLX Executive estates.
*October 1988* 2.0iGT estate.
*January 1990* Heavily revised range, 1.8GLX, 2.2iGLX 4x4, 2.0iGT, 2.0GLX.
*February 1991* 2.2iGLX 4x4 estate.

## Fault Finder

On cars from 1983–5 check the engine on tick-over for any rattling. The timing chains on these cars should have all been replaced at least once by now, but it's worth checking that this has been done by looking carefully at the service history. On 2.0i engines built up to 1987 the camshafts have been known to fail, partly because the camshaft belts have not been replaced soon enough. Again, check on the service record that this work has been carried out, and listen for any severe rattling from the engine, especially when revving it hard. On four-wheel-steer versions check the tyres for any uneven wear, a sign that the geometry of the system may be out of alignment. This is a rare occurrence, but because the system is complex this check is a must. Surface rust on pre-1986 cars is not unheard of because the paintwork was rather thin and stone chips could easily lead to surface corrosion. Check the bodywork over carefully. On cars built during the past five years there should be no signs of corrosion. On estate versions, check the general condition of the cargo area for any damage caused by carelessly stowed loads.

## Verdict

The 626 is a capable car which has suffered few reliability problems, but it's never been a car which has excited, even in its four-wheel-steer and four-wheel-drive forms. Second-hand prices vary a lot, depending on mileage and the condition of the bodywork. 4WS and 4WD versions lose a lot of value during the first year to eighteen months, so for a second-hand purchaser, this is the time to buy.

## MAZDA RX-7

Rear-wheel-drive coupé and convertible with unique Rotary engine.

## History

*February 1986* RX-7 coupé.
*July 1989* Series II Turbo coupé and convertible.

## Fault Finder

The unique Rotary engine really needs an expert to assess its condition, but there are checks you can carry out to see if it's essentially sound. The engine should be virtually silent on tick-over and should show between 500 and 1000rpm on the rev counter. If there's an uneven tick-over and the revs show over 1000rpm then the engine has problems. Rev the engine gently, but right to the top of its rev range, and a warning buzzer should sound. The engine should rev cleanly with no hesitation and it should be so smooth that the buzzer – plus the rev limiter on later models – is the only sign that the unit is at its limit. When you lift your foot back off the throttle the engine should settle back down without backfiring. However, if there is a burbling sound from the exhaust, don't worry, this is normal. Get someone else to rev the engine and watch for smoke from the exhaust. Some smoke is acceptable – and the exhaust pipe will almost certainly be black inside – but any puffs of black smoke can mean the engine is damaged. To make matters more complicated, a solid stream of black smoke when revving hard, plus uneven running, could just mean that the spark plugs are oiled up. This is less of a problem on post-89 models than on earlier Mk 1 versions. To check if this is the problem, get a plug wrench and take one of the plugs out, checking for an oily ignition point. If this is the problem, and the car has not been serviced for some time, then this may be all it is. Clearly, a full service record is vital, buying an RX-7 without one is a real gamble. Gearboxes are very tough, but there's the usual problem of losing synchromesh on second gear, especially on cars which have been used in town a lot. Check the clutch for slippage, this is quite a common problem on pre-1989 models, cars which also suffer from quite early clutch failure, the clutch plates can wear out after as little as 25,000 miles. On turbo models there is little evidence of premature turbocharger wear, but listen carefully for any clattering from the engine when the turbo is going off-boost. So quiet is the RX-7 engine that you will easily hear this. Brakes should be examined, both for scored front discs and also for glazed brake pads. Check the discs with a finger to find if they are damaged, and make sure that the brake pedal is progressive. Good RX-7 brakes are excellent, but where the pads have glazed they will feel rather wooden. The pop-up headlamps normally work very well, it's rare for one of them to fail, but make sure you check them carefully. Look also for water inside the headlamp lens, there have been a few cases of this. On convertible models, check the roof for wear, and check the interior over carefully for any water leaks. As with the MX-5, this is not usually a problem area, but it should always be thoroughly checked. Make sure that the catches for the convertible roof at the top of the windscreen surround work easily. Corrosion is not a problem on the RX-7, but do check carefully for any stone chipping, especially around the headlamps, because this can lead to unattractive surface rust, and if left this can creep down behind the headlamp covers.

### Verdict

The Rotary engine gives the RX-7 super-smooth performance, but it is also its weak spot if it has not been serviced correctly and regularly. The Rotary has traditionally had a bad name, due to problems with the unit in the long deceased RO80, but today it is a reliable engine and it can last 200,000 miles without major problems. Best versions are the post-1989 RX7s, but beware of tail-happiness in the wet, a trait common to the latest cars.

### MERCEDES-BENZ 190

Rear-wheel-drive executive saloons.

## History
*September 1983* 190, 190E (E denotes fuel injection).
*October 1984* 190D diesel.
*July 1985* High performance 2.3-16.
*August 1986* 2.5-litre diesel.
*January 1987* 2.6-litre 190E.
*October 1988* 2.5-16 high performance model.
*June 1990* 1.8-litre injection model launched.

## Fault Finder
High mileage is quite normal, but not a problem, these engines are good for around 200,000 miles. Most important is a full and proper service record, and all of the work must have been carried out by Mercedes-Benz authorized dealers. Front brake discs have been known to warp, but this is not a common problem, and it can easily be spotted. When braking, even lightly, there will be a strong judder through the steering. This can only be remedied by fitting new brake pads. On cars with ABS anti-lock brakes, check that this is working. Failure has been known at 80,000 miles plus, and it's a very expensive system to replace. Manual gearboxes are rather clonky, with a long shift between changes, but mechanical problems are rare. If the gearchange is not smooth and light, do not buy. Rear axles are strong but on the most powerful versions there have been cases of excessive whine and on a few occasions this has developed into major axle wear. On the test drive listen carefully for any rumbling from the rear. Corrosion is unheard of, so if there is any it is a sign of a car which has not been well looked after. Check also for accident damage, usually spotted because of uneven tyre wear.

## Verdict
So little goes wrong with these cars, it's no wonder that they keep terrific second-hand values. Although the 190 is quite a small car, and in 1.8-litre form it's an indifferent performer, the build quality is always impressive. Buy to keep for many years.

## MERCEDES-BENZ W124
Range of rear-wheel drive saloons, estates (TE versions) and coupés (CE versions). E badge on saloons and coupés denotes fuel injection. D badge for diesels.

## History
*October 1985* Brand new range launched. Models are 200, 230E, 250D, 260E, 300D, 300E.
*April 1988* 300E 4-Matic saloon and 300TE 4-Matic with automatically operating four-wheel-drive system.
*Steptember 1988* 200E and TE with new injection 2.0-litre engine, plus trim and equipment changes to all other models.
*October 1989* 300E-24 valve and 300TE-24.

## Fault Finder
There are seldom problems with any of these cars, but it is vital to check the mileage, as many of them cover high mileage, and some are clocked by unscrupulous owners. Servicing at an authorized Mercedes-Benz dealer is a must. Check the engine for oil leaks, though these are rare. Listen for any whine from the rear axle.

Again, this is rare, but if it is there, avoid that car, because it will almost certainly mean a new drive differential is needed. On 2.0-litre versions, look for smoke from the exhaust because there have been cases of worn valves. You should also hear this as a faint rattle from the engine. This check is very important in 2.0-litre estate versions. On cars with automatic gearboxes check for any slipping between gears, this is a very important check on estate versions which have been fitted with a tow bar. On 4-Matic four-wheel-drive models, make sure that there are no oil leaks from the drive shafts. Check also that the system comes into operation smoothly. Any jolting when the front axle cuts in should ring warning bells in your mind – there is a very expensive problem. Brakes can sometimes suffer from brake judder caused by warped front discs. Check this by braking quite hard and lifting your hands off the steering wheel for a second or two. Any shake through the steering points to either brake judder or bad tracking, the latter problem spotted by uneven tyre wear. On automatic versions where there is the choice of Sport and Economy modes, make sure that the switch between the two modes works properly. There have been cases where the electronic sensor has failed. Manual gearboxes are rather ponderous in operation but they are smooth and light, so if there is any restrictiveness, or crunching, from the gearbox, there is a problem, and that car should be avoided. Diesel cars are at least as reliable as the petrol versions, but they do become noisier with age as engine bearings wear. Check for

undue noise – inside the car the diesel Mercedes is very quiet – and look also for leaks of diesel fuel under the car, due to worn pipes. The latter fault is fairly common on diesel models around seven or eight years old.

### Verdict
Very expensive second-hand, and with good reason, these cars are just so reliable. Buying privately can save you some money, but for a cast-iron certainty, go to a Mercedes-Benz dealer. Best versions are 230 and 260 models fitted with lots of optional equipment. The 200 is refined, but it's slow and tends to be abused by hard driving owners.

## MERCEDES-BENZ 230 AND 300 COUPÉS
Range of two-door rear-wheel-drive coupés based on the floorpan of the W124 range.

### History
*October 1987* 230CE and 300CE launched.
*June 1988* 230CE gets ABS anti-lock brakes.
*October 1989* 300CE-24 valve.

### Fault Finder
As with every other Mercedes-Benz, very little goes wrong with the coupés. Look at the same areas on these cars as on the W124 saloons and estates. One fault which occasionally occurs on automatic versions built in October 1987 and early 1988 is the failure of the electronic selector in the gearbox, making it impossible to shift gears. This is rare, and because it's a fault which occurs

without warning, it's not possible
to spot. In theory, most of these
selectors will have been replaced
by now, so the best way to check
this is to go through the service
history, looking for such a
replacement. Brakes always need
checking on a Mercedes, not
usually because of major problems,
but because the pads get heavy
use, and therefore wear quite
quickly. If not replaced soon
enough the discs can be ruined,
and then they need replacing. The
coupé versions do not seem to have
the same brake judder problem as
the saloons, so if there is shake
through the steering it's usually
bad wheel tracking, a fault underlined by uneven tyre wear. Always
check the tyres at the rear,
because these suffer heavy use and
can wear quite quickly. They are
expensive to replace. Corrosion is
not a problem, and there should
not be any areas where the
paintwork is poor, these cars are
amongst the best finished in the
world. As with any Mercedes,
check the service history carefully,
make sure that the mileage is
genuine, and that the car has been
serviced by a Mercedes dealer.

## Verdict
Prestige never comes cheap, and
neither does the ultimate in reliability, which explains the high
second-hand prices of these cars.
But if you want a car which you
can eventually hand to your grand-
son, the CE is it.

## MERCEDES-BENZ SPORTS COUPÉS/CONVERTIBLES
Range of two-door coupés and
convertibles.

## History
*March 1986* New range is 280SL,
300SL, 380SL, 380SEC, 420SL,
420SEC, 500SL, 500SEC,
560SEC.
*October 1989* New 300SL, 300SL-
24 valve, 500SL two-door convertibles.

## Fault Finder
Look for a full service history, and
carefully examine the bodywork.
While corrosion is not generally a
problem, many SL and SEC
models suffer from rippled sides,
due to neglectful treatment and
parking dents. Once the bodies are
dented they are hard to put right.
If rust has taken hold, again,
usually as a result of poor care, it
usually starts under the rear
bumper and the rear wing, and can
become quite nasty unless taken
care of quickly. Mechanically there
really are few problems. The
engines are good for 200,000 miles,
there are rarely oil leaks, and
gearboxes seem virtually bomb-
proof. Do check the automatic
gearboxes for excessive whine, and
make sure there is no slipping in
the gears. Manual gearboxes are
reliable, but they are less sought
after than the autos, partly
because the manual gearboxes are
rather heavy to operate. If there is
excessive smoke from the exhaust
when revving the engine hard it's
usually as a result of worn piston
rings, rarely is it anything more
serious. Check for water getting
into the front headlamps, a
common problem with 1984–5
cars. Check the operation of the
windscreen wipers, because one or
other can become lazy, sweeping
across the screen slightly slower
than the other. Eventually one will

fail. This is a fairly common problem on SL models produced from 1980 to 1983. Look for sagging rear suspension, especially on the SL models produced in the early to mid 1980s. Alloy wheels can become pitted, so check this carefully because they are very expensive to replace, and there are a good number of SLs with non-standard alloy wheels, some of which can detract from long-term value.

## Verdict
These cars are so sought after that even an 11- or 12-year-old 350SL can command around £12,000. Indeed, the SL in particular is one car which is increasing in value, rather than dropping. The SEC is less popular, but it still retains an amazingly healthy resale value. Best models are the 300SL because it's relatively inexpensive to run, or the 500SL which is quite quick, but rather costly.

## MERCEDES-BENZ S-CLASS
Range of rear-wheel-drive four-door saloons.

## History
*October 1980* Range is 280SE, 380SE, 380SEL, 500SE, 500SEL.
*March 1986* New range is 300SE, 300SEL, 420SE, 420SEL, 500SE, 500SEL, 560SEL. SEL denotes long wheelbase version.

## Fault Finder
No major engine problems here. Like all other Mercedes, these cars are good for 200,000 miles without major problems, provided regular servicing has been carried out by an authorized Mercedes-Benz dealer. Make sure that the mileage is correct by cross-referencing with the service book. Do check brakes for any juddering caused by warped discs, although this is a rare fault. Gearboxes are very tough, but make the usual check for slipping automatic selectors. Corrosion is not a problem, but check carefully for any accident damage.

## Verdict
The ultimate Mercedes-Benz saloon, with ultimate pricing to match. These cars simply do not date and they are virtually trouble-free. Do make sure that the mileage is correct and that the car has not been involved in a major accident. If the S-Class car you are looking at is way below the expected price there is something wrong with it.

## MERCEDES-BENZ G-WAGEN
Four-wheel-drive multi-purpose vehicle in short and long wheelbase forms.

## History
*March 1984* Range is 230GE, 280GE, 300GD.
*February 1991* New range is 300GD, 300GE.

## Fault Finder
Sturdy engines which stand up to a lot of abuse, just check them over for any oil leaks. On 230GE models there were some faulty engine mounts which should all have been replaced by now. To check, look at the service record, but also drive the G-Wagen forwards fairly quickly and watch out for a lurch

or clonk from the engine, pointers to worn engine mounts. Check that the differential lock levers are working smoothly. These can become locked in position, especially if the G-Wagen has often been used off-road and not cleaned underneath properly. Check for any oil leaks from either the front or rear axle. Although this is rare, it can happen if the underside of the G-Wagen is badly knocked, or if regular servicing has not been carried out. Steering is a little vague, in line with the design of most vehicles which can be used off-road, but it should not make a clacking sound. If it does it's usually because of worn track rod ends. Also, listen for groaning from G-Wagens fitted with power steering. This is usually a sign that the fluid has leaked out. If this is happening, after time you will also notice the steering getting heavier. New power steering systems are expensive. Listen for clanking from the suspension, especially when travelling over bumpy surfaces, a sign that the ball joints in the bottom of the suspension have worn and need replacing. Brakes are efficient, with plenty of progression. The only problem you might find is that they sometimes pull to the left, a sign of a seized brake caliper. This is a rare fault, but it is one which can appear if the vehicle has been used off-road very regularly. Corrosion should not be a problem, these vehicles are very well protected, but you should look for any accident damage, as well as bad repairs. Interior trim is solid but on those G-Wagens made in 1985 and early 1986 the driver's seat belt would not always retract cleanly when it

was taken off.

### Verdict
Lacks the panache and style of the Range Rover, perhaps, but the G-Wagen is a formidable machine with an enviable reliability record. Used values hold up, but relatively speaking not as well as all other Mercedes-Benz. Best choice for a blend of performance and economy is the six cylinder 300GD diesel.

## MITSUBISHI LANCER
Front-wheel-drive saloon and hatchback.

### History
*May 1984* Range is 1200GL, 1500GLX, 1800GL Diesel.
*August 1986* Revisions to trim, plus new, more efficient engines.
*July 1988* New range is, 1300GL, 1500GLX, 1600GTi 16-valve.
*September 1989* Liftback models, 1500GLX, 1800iGLX four-wheel-drive.
*March 1990* 1800GTi 16-valve saloon and Liftback with new twin-cam engines.
*August 1990* 1200 and 1500 engines become 12-valve units.

### Fault Finder
Early Lancers, those built between 1984 and 1986, had rather weak petrol engines. They were fine for around 50,000–60,000 miles, but after that they often suffered bad oil leaks and warped cylinder heads due to engine overheating. This was remedied in 1986 with the launch of the new engines, a range of much tougher units. Check for timing chain rattle, especially on the 1.5-litre unit, and

listen for any undue clattering from the GTi 16-valve. This is usually a faulty camshaft, a problem which sometimes occurs if the car has been run low on oil, typically because it's not been serviced regularly. This problem can also be caused because the cam belt has not been replaced regularly enough. Have a really good look at the service record to see when the belt was last changed. The diesel models are rather noisy, both on tick-over and out on the road. But listen for serious rattling, and look for dense clouds of black smoke when accelerating hard, both signs of a seriously worn engine. Corrosion is not normally a problem on the Lancer, but on early versions – 1984–6 – paintwork was rather thin, so any scratches could quickly turn to rust. On metallic paint versions check that the paint all matches, some models have suffered from paint fade on bonnets.

## Verdict

The Lancer is a good second-hand car because little goes wrong and as long as it's been looked after it should give many years faithful service. In many ways it's best to avoid the GTi versions because while they are fine cars, they do tend to have been treated less than sympathetically by previous owners.

## MITSUBISHI COLT

Range of front-wheel-drive three- and five-door hatchbacks.

## History

*March 1981* 1200GL three-door.
*February 1982* 1200EL three-door.

*July 1982* 1400 Turbo three-door.
*February 1983* Name change, all models known as Mirage.
*March 1984* Range discontinued, replaced with new range consisting of 1200GL three-door, 1500GLX three- and five-door, 1600 Turbo, three-door, 1800GL diesel five-door.
*August 1986* Heavy restyling with new front grille, bonnet and bumpers, better suspension and better performing engines.
*June 1988* Range discontinued, replaced with new range consisting of 1300GL, 1500GLX, 1600GTi-16 valve.
*September 1990* 1300 and 1500 versions get new 12-valve engines.
*April 1992* Range discontinued, replaced with new range. Models are, 1600GLXi, 1800GTi, both with 16-valve engines, 1300GLi with 12-valve engine. All models in three-door form.

## Fault Finder

This is another very reliable car with few faults to report. The early engines, as with the Lancer, were not very strong, so those built in the early to mid 1980s should be examined closely, both for engine and water leaks. You should also listen for any undue rattling from the petrol engines on tickover, often a sign that camshafts are wearing. Make sure you also keep an eye on the engine temperature gauge, looking for any signs of overheating, a pointer to a broken cylinder head gasket. And make sure that you look at the inside of the oil filler cap for any creamy white gunge, another sign that the cylinder head gasket has failed, and is letting water into the engine. On cars produced between 1983 and 1984 you should check the gearboxes carefully for any signs of wear, because they were not very strong. All Colt gearchanges should be very light and smooth, if not, there is a problem. On all models produced before August 1986 check the suspension struts for any leaks, and make sure that the car sits the road squarely. On the road there should not be any undue bounce over bumpy road surfaces, if there is, it means that the shock absorbers need replacing. Corrosion is not generally a problem, but on cars made prior to 1985 check the bodywork over really carefully for any stone chipping which has either been badly touched up, or which is turning to corrosion. This sort of surface rust can soon litter the sides of a Colt. It's also possible that there will be rust around the headlamps, especially on cars made prior to August 1986. Check this carefully because rust here can eat right through the headlamp surrounds. Paintwork was quite thin for the first five years of Colt production and metallic paint has been known to dull and fade. Check this carefully because the metallics are fiendishly hard to match. The final point is that spare parts for the cars built from 1981 to 1984 are not that easy to come by.

## Verdict

In terms of design the Colt has improved dramatically over the years, so that today it can truly be said to have grown up. Running costs are not so bad on cars

produced during the last five years because of Mitsubishi's three year mechanical warranty, but on early models parts are increasingly hard to get hold of and engines are not the strongest. Best models are those from August 1986 – and the newer the better.

## MITSUBISHI GALANT

Rear-wheel-drive saloons and estates.

### History

*March 1982* Estates (1600 and 2000) launched, along with 2000 Turbo saloon. Trim levels are GL, GLS saloon, GL and GLX estates.

*July 1984* Range discontinued, new range of front-wheel-drive saloons launched. Range is 1600GL, 1800GL Turbo diesel, 2000GLS.

*September 1986* Changes to suspension and engines to make them more efficient.

*March 1988* Range discontinued, new range of front-wheel-drive and four-wheel-drive saloons and hatchbacks launched. Range is 1800GLS, 2000GLSi.

*July 1988* 1800GLS Turbo diesel and 2.0GTi 16-valve.

*May 1989* 2.0i 16-valve four-wheel-drive and four-wheel-steer model. 2.0GLSi five-door hatchback.

### Fault Finder

On early rear-wheel-drive Galants check for worn rear differentials. You will hear a rumbling from the back when driving at slow speeds, and a whine at higher speeds. Listen also for any clonking when changing gear. Look under the car

107

at the rear and check to see if oil is seeping from the differential. If it is, problems are on their way. Gearchanges should be smooth and light. Any crunching noises mean the gearbox is worn. When putting the clutch in, listen for any rattling, a sign that clutch bearings are worn. This test should also apply to the front-wheel-drive Galants. On the first generation Galants check the bodywork over carefully, especially for rust along the tops of the front wings, and at the back of the car, under the rear bumper. Make sure that all electrics are working. Generally, these are reliable but the top range Galant is packed with electrically operated items, and windows in particular have been known to fail. Check the early Galant for water pump failure by listening for a knocking sound when the engine is ticking over. The front-wheel-drive Galant is very reliable, but on the models produced from mid 1984 to the end of 1985 check the power-steering system on 2000GLS models. It is very light but it also suffers from leaks from worn seals. If the steering is at all heavy at parking speeds, or if it is slow to operate, or makes a knocking noise when the steering wheel is turned hard over, then there is a problem. Heavy brake servo assistance on cars made between 1984 and 1988 means brake pads can wear quickly and on cars which have covered a high mileage it's possible that the brake discs have been scored. Check for this by running a finger over the disc. If the brakes feel spongy, or if they are slow to operate, there could be a leak in the system. Check inside the brake fluid reservoir for any bubbles, a

sign that air is getting in. This is a rare problem on the Galant, but not unheard of. Check for suspension leaks on all Galants older than six years because there were a few 1985 models where this was a problem. On front wheel drive Galants, corrosion is generally not a problem, and even stone chipping rarely produces serious rusting. On 2000GLS models made in 1984-5 check the front and rear colour-coded bumpers for signs of scuffing due to careless parking. This is not a real problem but it can make the car look tatty and is often a sign of a careless owner. It will also knock some value off the car.

### Verdict
The Galant is best in front-wheel-drive form, and in any case, the rear wheel drive models are few and far between now. A 2000GLS is an excellent choice if you can find a good one because it's stuffed with equipment and has mostly proved reliable. The 1988 models are also impressive, but try and go for the 2.0-litre engine, the 1.8-litre is not so smooth or refined.

## MITSUBISHI SPACEWAGON
Front-wheel-drive estate car with two rows of rear seats.

### History
*April 1984* Five-door Spacewagon 1800GLX launched.

*October 1985* 1800 turbo diesel.

*September 1986* Number of changes to trim and equipment, including fitting fold-flat rear seats for improved cargo space.

*January 1992* Restyled Spacewagon GLXi with high equipment level and 2.8-litre 16-valve engine.

## Fault Finder

Very reliable, but carry out the usual checks to the engine for oil leaks, and cylinder head gasket damage. There have been cases of the gearchange selector cable snapping after as little as 20,000 miles, but this is not a fault you can spot, it just happens. If the Spacewagon has a tow bar fitted it may have been hauling heavy loads, so check the exhaust for excessive smoke, a sign that the engine valve seals have worn due to heavy use. On models with power steering there is always some hissing when the steering is turned hard to right or left, but if there is groaning and the wheel is relatively hard to turn, there may be a leak in the system. This has occasionally happened. Check the rubber drive shaft gaiters at the front wheels for any splits, and if there is a knocking sound when you turn the steering hard to left or right there could be CV joint problems. This problem will usually only arise if the rubber gaiters are split, but on hard-driven Spacewagons the CV joints can wear prematurely. Corrosion is not a problem, just look for rust caused by stones hitting the bodywork.

## Verdict

One of the most reliable cars on the market, and not that many of them available, so second-hand prices are quite high. Pick as new a model as possible because by its very nature, the Spacewagon tends to be used by big families and they can take their toll on interior trim.

## MITSUBISHI STARION TURBO

Rear-wheel-drive sports hatchback with coupé styling.

## History

*April 1982* 2000 Turbo launched.

*September 1986* Heavy revisions which include a wider body, uprated suspension, gearbox, rear axle and drive differential, plus addition of anti-lock brakes and anti-skid system.

*September 1987* Revisions to suspension for better roadholding, front and rear track increased.

*March 1989* 2.6-litre turbo replaces 2000 Turbo.

*November 1990* Discontinued.

## Fault Finder

Rear differentials are the main problem area. Due to the high power of this car, the rear differential can fail at a relatively low mileage – 40,000 miles is not unheard of. Check under the car for leaks from the differential, and when driving listen for any undue rumbling from the rear. The gearbox is tough, but hard use can make the synchromesh on second and third gears fail after as little as 20,000 miles. More seriously, gearbox bearings may need replacing after 50,000–60,000 miles. Listen for rattling from the gearbox when the engine is ticking-over. Turbocharger failure is the major engine problem, especially on the 1982–4 cars. When the turbo boosts it will whistle, but if there is any clattering there is almost certainly a problem with the turbo blades. Likewise, when the turbo boosts it should do so smoothly. If there is any hesitation, or hiccuping, the turbo may need replacing. If there is a backfire, it's more likely it's the fuel injection system which is not working properly. Check the brakes for scored discs, and also check for leaks, both from the brake master cylinder, and leaks of fluid near the brake pedal. This can fairly easily be spotted because any fluid will probably have leaked on to the carpet, and it's not easy to get rid of the stain. Check for accident damage. Corrosion should not be a problem, the Starion's paintwork was always good.

### Verdict

An underrated sports coupé, the Starion provides stunning performance, even if the lag before the turbo boosts is annoying. Good examples are few and far between, but if you can find a good one, buy it. This car could become a minor classic. Best colour is red, try and avoid white, it never looks as good, and residual values are lower.

### MITSUBISHI SHOGUN

Four-wheel-drive multi-purpose vehicle, available in short wheelbase (three-door) or five-door long wheelbase.

### History

*July 1983* Three-door soft-top and hard-top estate models with 2.6-litre petrol engines.
*January 1984* 2.3-litre turbo diesel in hard-top form.
*November 1984* Five-door 2.3-litre Turbo diesel.
*March 1985* Five-door 2.6-litre petrol.
*September 1986* Turbo diesel versions get new 2.5-litre engine, the five-door models get an improved rear axle differential,

as well as larger tyres.
*March 1989* 3.0-litre V6 petrol model, plus new intercooled 2.5-litre turbo diesel engine.
*February 1990* New model introduced with bulkier body styling, increased equipment.

### Fault Finder

Another very reliable vehicle, the Shogun should first be checked for mileage accuracy, as many have covered high mileage. Engines are tough, so there should be few problems here, but check for blue exhaust smoke from hard-worked petrol engines, especially on those Shoguns with a tow bar fitted. There have been problems with the freewheeling front hubs on Shoguns built between July 1983 and November 1984, due to corrosion. This has normally only affected those relatively few Shoguns regularly used off-road, and it's simply cured by freeing the hubs from corrosion. Gearboxes are strong, but with the clutch depressed listen for any rattling. Some rattling is normal, but excessive rattling means the gearbox bearings are worn and will soon need replacing – a job which usually needs to be carried out on Shoguns which have covered over 80,000 miles. The lever for switching from rear-wheel-drive to four-wheel-drive can sometimes prove hard to move, but only on those models which have been subjected to heavy off-road use. On early Shoguns, those built between July 1983 and December 1984, there were some poor paintwork finishes, leading to flaking paint around the roof channels. Check for this, because it can spread. Check underneath for any leaks from the front or rear axles, although this is very rare indeed, usually only occuring when the underside has been damaged on rough ground. Tyres should all be checked for any uneven wear because heavy off-road use can affect the suspension alignment at the front.

## Verdict

Little goes wrong, making the Shogun one of the best second-hand buys. Demand will always be strong but in many ways the most desirable versions are the pre-1991 models which don't have the bulky bodywork. Always try and buy a Shogun which hasn't been used off-road.

## NISSAN MICRA

Front-wheel-drive hatchback.

## History

*June 1983* Range is DX, GL, GL Automatic, all with 1.0-litre engine.

*January 1984* 1.0L.

*June 1985* 1.0SGL, plus trim and mechanical improvements to all models, including new gear ratios.

*April 1987* Five-door versions launched. They are Colette, SGL, SGL Automatic.

*April 1988* LS, Colette, GSX models unveiled with more powerful engines and better equipment.

*March 1989* Heavily revised range. Line-up is three-door 1.0LS, three- and five-door 1.0GS, 1.2GS, 1.2GSX.

*April 1990* 1.0S three-door with low equipment level.

## Fault Finder

1985-7 Micras were recalled by the manufacturer to correct a fault which caused oil to leak on to the speedometer cable and then to drip down onto the accelerator pedal. A large number of these cars did not go back into dealers for the recall, so check your car has not still got this potentially dangerous fault. Not built to take excessively high mileages, a Micra is generally past its best at 70,000 miles. When driving, listen carefully for any rattles from the engine, it should be running smoothly and quietly. If there are untoward noises it will most likely mean the water pump is on the way out. This can be a potentially serious problem because if it seizes it can cause the Micra's all-alloy engine block to quickly overheat. If this happens you could be looking at a new engine. When driving, carefully watch the engine temperature gauge. If it quickly climbs up near the red sector then the cylinder head could be warped, due to previous overheating. Overheating can also be caused by a blocked radiator. As with some other Nissans, the Micra has to have a special anti-freeze, and its radiator must be regularly flushed through. If this hasn't been done then overheating may already have occured, with consequent damage to the engine. Spotting a leaking cylinder head gasket is easiest by taking the radiator cap off and looking for a creamy white, sludgy gung around the top of the radiator cap. If it's there, there's almost certainly a head gasket leak. Check the constant velocity joints on each front wheel. The rubber boots which cover them should be intact, and not suffering from any leaking. This is quite a common fault on Micras which have been used around town – the common territory for this small Nissan. Exhaust systems are not especially expensive, which is good news, for the average Micra gets through one of these every 24,000 miles, again a result of mostly town driving when the system doesn't get a chance to dry out properly, so leading to excessive corrosion. Bodywork can become tatty because the metal and paintwork are both thin, and therefore susceptible to knocks, especially in town car parks. Micras with damaged paint can rust quite quickly and quite badly.

## Verdict
As an around-town car the Micra makes a lot of sense, but only if you get one with relatively low mileage. If you can find such a Micra you should be rewarded with a car which will give unflustered and faithful service. Best choice is a 1.2-litre model because they have the extra power you need for those occasional out-of-town trips. But this car doesn't last as long as a Rover Metro, VW Polo or Peugeot 205.

## NISSAN CHERRY
Front-wheel-drive three- and five-door hatchbacks.

## History
*September 1982* New range replaces old Cherry. Range is 1.0DX, 1.3DX, 1.3GL, 1.5GL Automatic.
*November 1983* 1.5-litre Turbo three-door.
*February 1984* Heavily revised range. 1.0L three-door, 1.3GS three- and five-door, 1.3SGL three- and five-door, 1.5 Turbo.
*October 1984* 1.3L is launched. All models get new styling, revised suspension.
*September 1986* Range discontinued.

## Fault Finder
The previous Cherry range had a bad reputation for corrosion and while this later range was better, they still need examining carefully for rust, especially around the tail-gate and the bottoms of the doors. 1.0 and 1.3-litre engines are not very strong and can suffer warped blocks if they have ever been allowed to overheat. Check for oil leaks, and look inside the oil filler cap for the creamy gunge which points to a cylinder head problem, a common fault on Cherrys made in 1982–3. Suspension should be checked for leaks, especially at the front where fluid can leak down on to the disc brakes. Check this carefully because it can seriously affect braking ability. Window winders often fall off and windows themselves sometimes drop inside the door panels. A stiff window winder is a pointer to a future problem. The Turbo model should be checked for premature exhaust wear. Also, check Turbo versions for soggy suspension caused by worn shock absorbers, they never last long.

## Verdict
Not much goes wrong with the Cherry, but it's not a very desirable car, even in Turbo form where its soggy handling does

little to inspire confidence. If you must have one, go for as late a model as possible, that way there's less risk of rust. Many of the rivals are better cars.

## NISSAN CHERRY EUROPE
Front-wheel-drive hatchback using Nissan body and Alfa Romeo engines.

### History
*August 1983* 1.2-litre and 1.5-litre GTi launched.
*November 1985* Range discontinued.

### Fault Finder
For potential faults on this model please refer to the Alfa Romeo Arna. The only difference between the Arna and the Cherry Europe are their different badges.

## NISSAN SUNNY
Front-wheel-drive saloons, coupés and estates.

### History
*April 1982* Range is 1.3DX, two- and four-door saloons, 1.5DX and DX Auto four-door, 1.5DX, 1.5GL and GL Auto estates, 1.5GL coupé.
*October 1983* 1.3DX estate.
*January 1984* Heavily revised range, 1.3L two-door, 1.3GS, 1.5GSL four-door, 1.5SGL coupé, 1.3DX, 1.5SGL estates.
*October 1984* 1.3L four-door.
*September 1986* New Sunny range of hatchbacks, saloons, coupés, estates. Range is 1.3L, 1.3LX three-door hatchbacks, 1.3LX, 1.3SLX, 1.6LX, 1.6SLX, 1.6SGX, 1.7LX diesel, all avail-

able in saloon and hatchback form. Coupé and estate are badged 1.6LX.
*March 1987* 1.6LX saloon and hatchback.
*September 1987* 1.6ZX coupé 16-valve.
*May 1988* LS, GS, GSX models replace L, LX, SLX, SGX.
*August 1988* Saloons rebadged as Pulsar.
*April 1989* New range consists of, 1.4LS, 1.6GS, 1.6GSX, 1.7D – all in saloon and hatchback form. Coupés are 1.6GSX, 1.8ZX. Estates have choice of either 1.6-litre petrol or 1.7-litre diesel, same badging as hatchbacks.
*June 1989* 1.8ZX hatchbacks in three- and five-door.
*February 1991* New generation. Range is 1.4LS in three- and five-door hatchback, and four-door saloon, 1.6GS saloon and five-door hatchback, 1.6GSX coupé.

### Fault Finder
Models built in the early 1980s, up to 1984, had weak gearboxes. A common fault is for the gearbox main selector to fail, making it impossible to get into most gears. This problem begins with a stiff gearchange and then it suddenly proves impossible to get into any gear. Usually, there's little time between the initial stiffness and the total failure. The easiest check here is to see what the quality of the gearchange is like – on all Sunny models it should be smooth and very light. Brakes on cars built before 1986 have a tendency to seize their calipers when braking. This usually pulls the car to the left, but occasionally to the

right. Suspension on pre-1987 cars is soft and not well sorted out. Leaks are common from front suspension shock absorbers on pre-1985 cars. Look for fluid leaking down the sides of the struts.

## Verdicts
Reasonably reliable cars but often with dubious bodywork and paintwork. The best models are those made after March 1987 when handling and performance were improved.

## NISSAN BLUEBIRD
Front-wheel-drive saloons, hatchbacks and estates.

## History
*April 1984* Range is 1.8DX, 1.8 Turbo, 2.0GL, 2.0SGL saloons. Estate model is 2.0GL.

*August 1984* ZX Turbo 1.8-litre saloon.

*March 1986* Range discontinued. New range is, 1.6L, 1.6LX, 1.8ZX Turbo, 2.0LX diesel saloons and hatchbacks.

*March 1987* 1.8ZX Turbo hatchback.

*November 1987* 1.8 Turbo Executive saloon.

*January 1988* Revised range, 1.6LS, 1.8GS, 2.0GSX, while 1.8ZX, 1.8 Executive, 2.0 estate are unchanged.

*April 1990* 1.6S saloon and hatchback.

*August 1990* Range discontinued.

## Fault Finder
Mechanically this is quite a reliable car, but there were problems with bodywork and poor engine running on early models. On Bluebirds built in the early 1980s – up to 1985 – there was very little underbody anti-corrosion protection, so this needs to be checked carefully, both for rust on the sills, but also on the underbelly. These early models also had problems with poor engine carburettor design so that there were flat spots throughout the rev range. The only remedy for this is to fit another type of carburettor. From 1984 the anti-corrosion protection became better but the carburettor problem got even worse, making the Bluebird difficult to start and making for very poor fuel economy. Again, the only answer is to replace the carburettor. Bluebirds built up to 1986 had poor suspension design and also suffered from leaking suspension at the front and sagging rear suspension. Check that the car you are looking at sits the road properly. Pre-1986 Bluebirds also suffered from poor cooling systems, with the radiators often getting blocked by corrosion. Check the radiator water. If it's rusty brown there is almost certainly serious corrosion which could already have led to engine overheating. Cars built from 1986 did not have the carburettor problem, and the suspension system was better designed, so giving better handling, and few cases of leaking. Brakes need checking on all versions because on pre-1986 models they could often seize, sometimes locking one wheel, and on post-1986 models the pads often wear quickly, especially on Turbo versions, and this often means the discs are damaged. Check for scored discs.

## Verdict
Early versions of the Bluebird, certainly those up to 1986, are not

a good buy. Post-1986 cars are better but the Bluebird is not a very impressive car overall. Best choices are the Turbo, which is fairly quick, and the estates, which are reasonably roomy.

## NISSAN PRIMERA
Front-wheel-drive saloons, hatchbacks, estates.

### History
*September 1990* Range is L, LS, LSX, GS, GSX, ZX, available in saloon and hatchback forms.
*December 1991* Revised range. 1.6L, 1.6LX, 1.6SLX, 2.0LX, 2.0SLX, 2.0SGX, 2.0GT in four-door saloon and five-door hatchback. In five-door estate form the range is 1.6LX, 2.0LX, 1.6SLX, 2.0SLX.

### Fault Finder
Still a relatively new car, so few problems have surfaced yet. On cars with metallic paint look for chipping and flaking, especially around the roof. Electric windows sometimes stick, and if this happens the problem gets progressively worse until the motor will not power them up or down. Listen for clonks from the front of the car. This is usually the brake discs moving slightly when the car hits a bumpy road surface. Replacement of the discs usually cures this problem. Some of the earliest Primeras had dripping underseal which made the car look tatty. Electrics mostly seem good, but there have been a number of cases of heated rear window switches not working properly. Check the tyres, particularly those at the front. They seem to wear quite

quickly – between 15,000–25,000 miles – and that's even on the fairly basic, average performance Primeras.

### Verdict
After a somewhat shaky start due to poor paintwork finish this British-built Nissan seems to be proving mostly reliable. Best choice is a 1.6-litre Primera built in the last two years.

## NISSAN STANZA
Front-wheel-drive hatchback and saloon.

### History
*February 1982* Range is 1.6GL saloon, 1.6GL, 1.6SGL, 1.8SGL hatchbacks.
*November 1984* 1.6L saloon.
*September 1985* Revisions to 1.6SGL, 1.8SGL.
*September 1986* Range discontinued.

### Fault Finder
Paintwork problems were common on Stanzas from 1982 to mid 1983. They included flaking and peeling paint, badly applied paint with differing thicknesses on different body panels, and lack of underbody anti-corrosion protection. So, check the bodywork over carefully, and look under the car to examine the underside of the sills, and also to look for corrosion on the underbelly of the car. A rattle from the engine which increases in severity as you push the throttle down will almost certainly be a camshaft problem, a fault most usually found on Stanzas produced from 1982 to 1984 which have covered over 40,000 miles. Check the

engine temperature gauge on all models for any signs of overheating, because the alloy engines in the Stanza had a habit of blowing their cylinder head gaskets at low mileage, often around 30,000 miles. Check the exhaust for blue smoke, a sign of worn valve seals, a problem on 1.6-litre models. Engine hesitation when accelerating is due to poor carburettor design, a problem with most 1.6-litre Stanzas. Check steering for undue play due to worn track rod ends. This should also become apparent because of a clacking sound when the car goes over a slightly bumpy road surface. Check the brakes for any pulling, usually to the left, a sign of seized brake calipers. Handling is dreadful, with a combination of excessive oversteer and understeer, making the vehicle unpredictable on fast corners. This is a design fault and little can be done about it.

## Verdict
Not a good car to buy, the Stanza had one of the worst suspension designs developed by man. The only advantage to buying a Stanza is that it will not be expensive, but truly there are better cars.

## NISSAN PRAIRIE
Front-wheel-drive and 4wd multipurpose estate.

## History
*June 1983* Prairie launched in single version using 1.5-litre petrol engine.
*May 1985* Revised and expanded range. 1.5SGL, 1.8SGL, 1.8 Anniversary.

*May 1989* Range discontinued, replaced by new range, consisting of, 2.0SLX, 2.0SLX four-wheel-drive.

## Fault Finder
Check gearboxes on the original 1.5-litre cars because the bearings tend to wear within 40,000 miles. To check for this, run the engine then put the clutch down and listen for any undue rattling. 1.8-litre versions can suffer from worn camshafts if the engines have not been serviced regularly. Listen for rattling from the engine which gets louder as you press the accelerator pedal down. Watch the temperature gauge on all models to see if it climbs into the red, and check the inside of the oil filler cap for creamy white gunge. If you find any, and if the temperature gauge gets too near the red line, then the cylinder head gasket has failed and the engine block may already be warped. If the engine is overheating but the oil filler cap is clear, then the problem may well be corrosion in the cooling system, a common problem with early 1.5-litre cars. Check the water inside the radiator to see if it's rust coloured. Such a problem is not always fatal, as long as the system is flushed through and new rust inhibitor is added to new water. Check the engine for any undue movement when moving away from rest. On 1.8-litre models the engine mounts are not the best, soon wearing and causing engine movement which can be felt as a slight lurch when moving away from rest. Repair is not expensive but it needs to be carried out quickly or pressure on the exhaust manifold may cause it to snap. On

four-wheel-drive models check the state of the tyres. If they are badly worn this can point to previous owners using the four-wheel-drive system too regularly on the road. It's a basic system which is meant to be used only part-time, so if it is used regularly it can place undue strain on the drive train. So, check underneath the 4x4 Prairie for any leaks from either front or rear axles. Surface rust can be a problem on Prairies produced during 1983 and 1984, due mainly to thin paintwork, but it rarely becomes a serious problem. Do look carefully for rust on the bottom of the tail-gate, this is fairly common on Prairies. It's also a good idea to slam the tail-gate closed to see if any rust comes falling out, a sign that corrosion has taken hold inside the tail-gate. Check the sliding side door. This doesn't usually cause any problems, but any lack of servicing can mean it doesn't get any proper attention, and therefore becomes hard to close smoothly.

## Verdict
Prairies produced during the last three years are the best bet because they have good quality paintwork and few reliability problems. Earlier Prairies do not stand the test of time very well, quickly looking untidy and sounding wheezy.

## NISSAN 200/300ZX

Rear-wheel-drive coupés.

## History
*June 1981* 280ZX Targa.
*May 1984* 300ZX, 300ZX Turbo.

*July 1987* Major trim and equipment changes. Revised suspension and better steering system.
*May 1990* Completely new 300ZX with 3.0-litre engine powered by twin turbochargers.

## Fault Finder
A very reliable car, the most important check to make here is for a full service history containing evidence of regular servicing. On Targa-Top cars check for a good fit and make sure there is no evidence of water leaking in, though these faults are rare. The rails which the Targa-Top fits into can become rusty, and this can creep onto the surrounding paintwork, making it flake and blister. On cars produced prior to July 1987 the steering racks sometimes leaked, causing groaning from the steering and too much heaviness. Power steering pumps failed on some cars produced in late 1986 but all of these should have been replaced by now. On single turbocharged models there is little evidence of turbo failure, but some produced in late 1986 suffered from loose piping from the exhaust which caused hesitant running at full boost. If the car doesn't run smoothly at high speed, this could be the problem. Bodywork has always been good, aside from the problem mentioned earlier with Targa-Topped cars, but check carefully for any accident damage, and examine metallic colours for any fading. The latest 300ZX Twin Turbo has not been on the market for long enough, or in sufficient numbers, to be properly assessed, but so far the omens look good.

## Verdict

Nissan's sports car changed from an out and out muscle car to a too big and rather stodgy handling American-style cruiser, before it changed into the exotic looking 300ZX Twin Turbo. The best models are those produced before 1987, unless you can afford a Twin Turbo, a car which should keep its value well.

## NISSAN PATROL

Four-wheel-drive multi-purpose vehicle.

## History

*February 1982* 2.8-litre petrol and 3.3-litre diesel engines in three- and five-door bodies.

*August 1986* Trim and mechanical improvements.

*October 1989* New engines replace previous units, they are 3.0-litre petrol, 2.8-litre turbo diesel, 2.8-litre diesel, plus major body and trim revisions.

*December 1991* Range discontinued.

## Fault Finder

As far as reliability and desirability are concerned, the versions produced after October 1989 are the best. On models prior to that, look carefully for corrosion, especially around the rear tail-gate and under the front and rear wings. Underbody anti-corrosion measures were not good and this, combined with relatively thin metal and thin paintwork, made it all too easy for rust to take hold. Engines are all robust, but most are very noisy. Check for crankshaft rattle on early petrol models, (1982–4) clearly heard when the engine is ticking over. On early diesel models, check for any fuel leaks, usually found at the back of the vehicle where the piping runs from the fuel tank. Gearboxes are strong, but very notchy, and quite heavy to operate. Check there is no crunching when trying to get in gear, but it must be said that this problem is very rare. Less rare is a sticking four-wheel-drive differential lock, caused by corrosion which has usually taken hold after the Patrol has been used off-road for long periods. Make the usual check for leaking front and rear axles, but again, this is rare.

## Verdict

Until the launch of the latest generation Patrol, this 4x4 followed some way behind its nearest competitors, remaining relatively agricultural compared to the likes of the Mitsubishi Shogun and Isuzu Trooper. The advantage is that the Nissan is not too expensive second-hand. The hard part is finding a Patrol which has good, clean bodywork. Choose the lastest model you can find.

## OPEL MANTA

Rear-wheel-drive coupé and hatchback. Confusingly, the saloon version was called a coupé by Opel.

## History

*September 1982* Range is high trim Berlinetta coupé, Manta hatchback, GT/J coupé. 1.8S engine replaces 2.0S unit.

*July 1983* GTE hatchback and

coupé with 2.0-litre injection engine.

*August 1983* GT hatchback with 1.8-litre engine replaces GT/J. Trim similar to Berlinetta.

*November 1984* Revised suspension, improved trim and equipment for all models.

*October 1986* Special edition Manta Exclusive in coupé and hatchback form. This car is distinguished by its four round headlamps.

*July 1988* Range discontinued.

### Fault Finder

The Manta engines are mechanically straightforward but they tend to become ragged performers once they are over around 70,000 miles. This is usually down to worn cylinders and pistons and can be spotted by a rattling noise when the engine is revved hard. Look also for oil leaks from the engine and around the steering box. In the latter's case this is often first noticed when the steering becomes very heavy and then begins to creak when turned. Re-lubricating the steering rack is often all that is needed. The gearchange is light but notchy. However, these gearboxes have not got a good reputation for long life. Listen carefully for any rattling when the clutch is depressed and the gear-lever slotted into gear, a sign of worn gearbox bearings which often means the gearbox is on its last legs. Check front suspension struts for leaks – quite a common problem on the Manta. Brakes should be checked for any pulling to one or other side, often caused by brake fluid leaking down onto the front discs. Like-

wise, any sponginess through the brake pedal will also point to this; Manta brakes are normally light but rather wooden in operation. Check the brake fluid reservoir, both for the correct level of brake fluid, but also for any air bubbles, a sign that there's a leak and that air is getting into the system. There have been cases of some of the brake fluid evaporating, particularly on Mantas made after November 1984 when a bigger brake servo system was used. So, if the brake fluid is low, but there are no bubbles in the fluid, this could be the problem, and it can be cured by topping up the fluid. When this problem does occur it takes a long time for the fluid to go back down, and in some cases it appears to stabilize completely. Obviously, as with anything to do with brakes, any problems here should be carefully checked over by a professional. Bodywork was generally good on the Manta, but all these cars should be examined closely for accident damage. Rust can take a hold, but it's rarely serious. The most prone area is the front apron, under the front bumper. This collects stone chips and these can quickly turn to surface corrosion. The sides of this spoiler are quite low to the ground and therefore they're often scraped against kerbs when parking. Again, rust is often the result, and if it is not treated fairly quickly it can spread.

### Verdict

Mechanically very simple, some would say crude, by today's standards, second-hand Mantas are inexpensive, but for good reason; they are old fashioned compared with most of today's sporting coupés. Nevertheless, a good GTE version will provide inexpensive motoring.

## OPEL SENATOR/MONZA
Rear-wheel-drive saloon (Senator) and coupé (Monza).

### History
*February 1983* New range, consisting of Senator 2.5E, 2.5C, 3.0E, 3.0C, 3.0CZDE, Monza 3.0E.
*March 1984* Monza 3.0GSE.
*October 1984* Monza 3.0E gets option of new four-speed automatic transmission. Opel now becomes Vauxhall Senator.

### Fault Finder
These are good, sturdy cars with long-lasting engines, but check the mileage because most of these cars will have been used as company cars, and consequently will have covered high mileages. On 3.0-litre models in particularly, check for an exhaust which is black inside, and look for excessive bluey-black smoke, because once over about 70,000 miles these cars use a lot of oil, and these are two of the most obvious signs of this. The same problem can exist with 2.5-litre versions, but usually it's not as serious. Brakes need a careful check on all of these cars. Because they are so heavy they tend to get through brake pads very quickly, and many owners do not get them replaced quickly enough, so causing scoring of the discs. Check the discs for smoothness by running a finger over them. Look at the wheels for evidence of excessive kerbing because if this has happened it can loosen the steering

rack. To check for this, listen for any clonking from the front when the wheels are being turned at low speed. On 3.0-litre cars there have been a number of defective power steering pumps which leaked and made for increasingly hard steering effort. Most should have been replaced by now, but to check, listen for a groaning noise when the steering wheel is turned hard over. Paintwork is usually good and there are few problems with corrosion. Check under the rear wheel arches on all Monzas and Senators for leaks from the suspension struts. Check electrics on all cars – the Monzas made in early 1984 did have a problem with faulty electric window switches.

### Verdict
The Monza, in particular, is a much sought after car today, and if you can find a good one it will provide smooth and potent transport. The Senator can be good, too, but high mileage is the norm and it often leads to excessive valve wear and high oil consumption. Best versions are those with 2.5-litre engines.

## PEUGEOT 205
Front-wheel-drive three- and five-door hatchbacks, and convertible.

### History
*October 1983* Five-door range launched, consisting of, 1.0-litre 205, GL, GR, GT, GLD diesel, GRD diesel.
*April 1984* GTi three-door.
*September 1984* 205GE becomes entry model, and other models get trim and equipment improvements.
*February 1985* XE, XL, XR, XLD

three-door models.

*September 1985* XT 1.4-litre three-door.

*June 1986* 1.6CTi convertible.

*August 1986* XS 1.4-litre three-door.

*November 1986* Junior 1.0-litre three-door.

*January 1987* GTi 1.9-litre three-door.

*December 1987* Number of changes, most important being uprating of engines to give more power.

*June 1988* Junior Cabriolet 1.4-litre.

*August 1990* CTi 1.6-litre gets power operated hood.

*January 1991* Style 1.1-litre, Style 1.8-litre, 1.8-litre diesel turbo.

**Fault Finder**

On petrol engines, check the top of the engine for oil leaks from worn engine gaskets. This is most common on cars made in 1984. Later designs of head gasket are better. On the smallest petrol engines produced during 1983 and 1984 there were problems with oil feed to the main part of the engine, resulting in worn rocker shafts. On the 1.6-litre engines the camshaft belt is the main worry. It really should be replaced around every 38,000 miles, but Peugeot dealers do not always do this as a matter of course, and if it does fail, which they often do if left for much longer than 38,000 miles, then serious engine damage will result. Check the service history for this replacement, and if it has not been done, negotiate the price down and get it replaced as soon as possible. The 1.6-litre engine can also suffer crankshaft problems if engine oil is not changed regularly. This means

at least every 6000 miles, so check for a full service record, with work carried out by a Peugeot dealer. On the GTi models, both 1.6 and 1.9-litre, the oil can become contaminated even earlier, and many experts believe the oil should be changed every 3,000 miles. It's unlikely that most previous owners will have done this, so it's important to listen out for any undue rattling from the engine on tick-over, often a pointer to imminent problems caused by poor oil quality. The 1.4-litre engines in particular can suffer from poor running, due to the carburettor design. The petrol vaporizes, especially when the engine has been warmed up and then left for a while. Restarting can be a problem. There's little that can be done about this, although a Peugeot dealer can alter the fuel/air mix a little, and this can help. Petrol-injected engines are hard to drive smoothly in town because of a too-quick fuel cut-off system. This can usually be helped, if not cured, by advancing the engine idling speed slightly. Gearboxes on all versions, but especially the 1.6-litre engined cars, are not very strong, so synchromesh fails quite early on, sometimes fading on second and third gears from 25,000 miles onwards. Check this out, because a sub-standard gearbox will get steadily worse. Check electrics, especially electric window winders, and warning lights, they sometimes come on for no reason. On diesel cars there are few engine problems but, again, regular servicing should have been carried out and the timing belt should have been replaced at around 36,000 miles.

## Verdict

A popular car, some would say a cult-car, the 205 is a good buy as long as it's had regular servicing. On the 1.6-litre cars the condition of the cam belt is of paramount importance. Good buys are the GTi models, and for most the 1.6-litre will be best, and any of the diesel versions because they can cover very high mileage without major mechanical problems, and they are as good to drive as a petrol-engined car.

## PEUGEOT 305

Front-wheel-drive four-door saloons and five-door estates.

## History

*February 1983* Revised range is GL, GR, GRD diesel, SR, each available in saloon and estate forms.

*August 1983* GT saloon. GR saloon and estate get higher power 1.5-litre engine.

*December 1983* GT estate.

*September 1984* GLD saloon and estate get new 1.8-litre diesel engine. 1.9-litre diesel still fitted to GRD, but new 1.8-litre is an option.

*October 1984* GTX saloon and estate, Automatic saloon and estate launched.

*May 1985* SRD diesel saloon with 1.8-litre engine.

*October 1985* New SR saloon and estate with 1.6-litre petrol engine. SRD diesel estate.

*August 1986* GL models get 1.5-litre petrol engine.

*July 1987* GRD Executive estate.

*September 1988* Range discontinued.

## Fault Finder

On all 305s, it's very important that there is a full service record because if the oil is not changed regularly these cars can quickly develop serious engine problems, including oil blockages, causing the top of the engine to stop working properly, worn valves and incorrect valve clearance. All of these engines are overhead camshaft units and they must be checked for cambelt wear. This will usually reveal itself by a noisy rattle from the engine on tickover. But it's far better to know that the cam belt has been changed – you will see this on the service receipts – because a good many garages do not change the cam belt until there is a problem, and by then it can be too late. In spite of all this, the 305 engine is generally pretty robust, but do check for oil leaks. When they do appear it's often from the top of the engine and it's rarely serious, it's usually a result of a worn gasket and provided it's spotted early enough and replaced no serious damage should have been caused. The gearchange is one of the lightest and most precise there is, and the gearbox itself is reliable and sturdy, so if there is any crunching, or a reluctance to go into gear, there is a serious problem looming, so you should look for another, better model. Shock absorbers need checking over, especially at the front where they are prone to leaks. This problem is more common on the diesel-engined cars, partly because of the extra weight of these engines compared to the petrol units. On all versions the front driveshafts should be carefully examined because the driveshafts' rubber gaiters can easily split. Once dirt gets inside it can damage the CV joints. If there is a clunking sound when turning the wheel at low speeds, or a grinding noise at any speed when turning, then this is usually the problem. On some petrol 305s made during 1984 and 1985 there were a number of rogue starter motors which caused intermittent starting problems. They will almost certainly have all been replaced by now. Rust is seldom a problem, but when it does occur it's usually on saloon models where it appears along the bottom of the boot lip. Watch for this because it can spread to the main areas of the boot or the rear valance quite easily. It's also wise to look for any resprays in this area because unless all of the rust has been taken out it will soon recur.

## Verdict

The 305 was never the most exciting of cars but it can still provide good, roomy transport and it doesn't cost a fortune to run. If you can find a diesel with a full service history, and evidence that the cam belt has been changed – assuming the car has covered over 50,000 miles – then you could become the owner of a rather uninteresting but nevertheless faithful car.

## PEUGEOT 309

Front-wheel-drive three- and five-door hatchback.

## History

*January 1986* Range is 1.1GE, 1.3GE, 1.3GL, 1.3GR Profile, 1.6GL, 1.6GR, 1.6SR.
*October 1986* 1.6SRi, 1.9GLD diesel, 1.9GRD diesel.
*May 1987* Three-door versions,

1.1XE, 1.3XL, 1.9XLD, 1.6XSi, 1.9GTi.
*September 1988* GTi 1.9-litre five-door. More powerful engine for five-speed 1.6-litre petrol models.
*March 1989* Special Equipment versions of all models.
*October 1989* Heavily revised 309, plus, GL and GR automatics get the more powerful 1.6-litre petrol engine.
*January 1990* 1.8GRDT turbo diesel.
*June 1991* New fuel-injection models launched. 1.1i Style, 1.5iGL, 1.4iGLX, 1.6iGR. Carburettor versions continue as before.

## Fault Finder

Many of the potential problem areas which exist with the 205 also apply to the 309, simply because they share broadly the same engines. So, make sure the car has been serviced regularly, check whether the camshaft belt has been changed on any engines above 1.1-litre – except the 1.3 which uses an overhead valve engine – and on the smaller engined cars listen out for crankshaft rattling from the engine on tick-over. Additionally, any 309s with power assistance should be checked for any groaning from the steering which can point to a leak from the steering box. This check is very important on a car which looks like its wheels have been kerbed regularly as this sort of bad driving can affect the condition of the steering box. On all 309s, check underneath the car for split driveshaft rubbers, and listen for any clonking noises from the front, a sign that the CV joints are worn.

## Verdict

The 309 is not an attractive car but it's a very practical machine which is usually inexpensive to run. You have to make sure that it has been regularly serviced, this really is a vital check, and on high performance versions you have to look for signs of hooligan driving – worn front tyres, crunching gearboxes and accident damage. Best choices are any of the diesels, they really are superb cars, and the GTi which combines high performance with practicality.

## PEUGEOT 405

Front-wheel-drive and four-wheel-drive four-door saloon and five-door estate.

## History

*January 1988* Range is launched, 1.6GE, 1.6GL, 1.6GR, 1.9GL, 1.9GR, 1.9GRi, 1.9SRi, 1.9GTX.

*April 1988* 1.9GLD, 1.9GRD diesels.

*July 1988* High performance Mi-16, 1.9GTD turbo diesel.

*October 1988* Estate model range launched. Engines, trim and equipment the same as the saloon range.

*February 1989* Major trim and equipment revision.

*May 1989* Four wheel drive 1.9-litre GLx4 saloon.

*October 1989* Mi-16x4 saloon.

*January 1990* Standard power steering for 1.9GR petrol and diesel models.

*August 1990* Heavy revisions to dashboard design, plus equipment uprating. Launch of 1.8GRDT diesel turbo saloons and estates.

## Fault Finder

On models made during 1988-9 there were problems with carburettor petrol engines. The engines stall regularly in cold weather, even when the engine itself is warmed up. Carburettor-engined 405s made during 1988–9 are not economical. Both of these faults are due to the engines running too hot and not receiving enough fuel. Most of these early cars will by now have had the main jet on the carburettor changed to give better fuel flow. Changing the engine fan sensor so that it cuts in sooner and stays on for a longer time usually makes the engines run cooler. Check which carburettor is fitted to any carb-powered 405. There have been a large number of different types, but the best is a Weber. Older Solex carburettors suffer from worn spindle ends which cause jerky performance, and sometimes even cause the engine to stop altogether. Fuel-injection models also run on quite a lean fuel mix and this means they can sometimes cut out, especially in stop-start town traffic. This can be corrected quite easily by turning the screw on the inlet manifold and making the car run richer, and with a slightly higher idling speed. Make sure that the engine is running smoothly and quietly. Any undue rattling may mean that the main bearings need replacing. This is a problem on 405s which have not had regular oil changes, so check the service record carefully. The camshaft belt needs changing at 36,000 miles. It is imperative that this is done, otherwise the engine may seize and you'll need a new one. Some specialists recommend replacement of the belt even sooner, say around 20,000 miles, but the best advice is simply to make sure it is definitely replaced at 36,000 miles. Rust is not usually a problem but stone chips do appear on the bonnet and this can be a troublesome area if the chips are not touched-up soon after appearing. Electrics should be checked carefully as water often gets into the electric window motors and can cause them to short, either sending the windows down by themselves or stopping them closing. Check the quality of the interior trim, it's still on the flimsy side, especially on estate cars which tend to be most abused by owners. It's a must to check the windscreen washers because they operate through the windscreen wiper arm and often become blocked. Finally, look for evidence of 'clocking', as many 405s are used as fleet cars (one in seven company cars is now said to be a 405) and many will have covered high mileages, often at the hands of less than careful owners.

## Verdict

Choose carefully and there's no reason why a 405 should not give many trouble-free miles. Regular servicing is a must, check the cam belt has been replaced if mileage is over 36,000, and check the quality of the trim. Best choice has to be one of the diesel models because they have fewer reliability problems and Peugeot's diesels are still the best for performance, refinement and economy.

## PEUGEOT 505

Rear-wheel-drive saloons and estates.

## History

*February 1982* Estate versions of the saloon launched. They are, 2.0GL, 2.0GR, 2.0 Family, 2.5GRD diesel, and Family diesel.

*October 1982* SRD turbo diesel saloon, plus trim and equipment improvements to other models.

*October 1983* GL, GLD, GTi saloons, GLD estate.

*December 1983* GTD turbo diesel saloon.

*August 1984* Equipment uprate for most models, including tail-gate wash/wipe for GL and GLD estates.

*October 1985* SX saloon, SX Family estate.

*January 1986* Major trim and equipment changes, plus new models; 1.8GR, 1.8SR saloons. GTi and GTi Family get new 2.2-litre injected petrol engine.

*August 1986* GTD turbo diesel automatic estate.

*October 1986* V6 saloon.

*July 1987* Equipment changes for GR and GRD saloons and Family estates.

*September 1991* Range discontinued.

## Fault Finder

On all versions, but particularly on the GTi models, check the rear driveshaft over carefully, looking for oil leaks and listening for any rumbling at low speeds. The GTi models made from January 1986 are especially prone to worn driveshaft teeth, causing some loss of friction, and eventually loss of power to the driving wheels. Another check here is to see if there is any delay, and a clonking noise from the rear when dropping the clutch and driving off, again, a pointer to driveshaft wear. The V6 engined cars are real oil gulpers when they've covered high mileages, around 70,000 plus, so check for bluey-black smoke when the engine is revved. Valve wear is common on 2.0-litre cars, especially when they've been used for towing, so check for rattles from the engine when revving hard, and look for clouds of exhaust smoke. On 2.0-litre cars you also need to check the gearboxes over carefully, especially the manual ones. Gear selectors can wear, initially leading to a sloppy gear-lever, but eventually making it very hard to get into gear at all. Front suspension struts wear relatively quickly – most need replacing every 30,000 miles, and they also leak, so check under the wheelarches for any dribbles of fluid running down the struts. On all estate cars check for rust around the bottom edge of the tail-gate, and slam the tail-gate closed to check for any corrosion inside the door skins – if there is any you'll see rust dust drop out. Check the electrics over, especially where electric windows and door mirrors are fitted. On 505s built in 1986 check the operation of the door mirrors, because sometimes they would turn back towards you, but not away. On all models, listen for rumbling from the front wheels, a sign that the wheel bearings need to be replaced. Also, ease the hub-caps off and look at the centre of the front wheels to see if oil is leaking out, another sign that bearings may need replacing.

**Verdict**
The 505 was an underrated car. It's reasonably solid, quite roomy in saloon form, and as an estate, it's simply cavernous. Diesel versions are excellent, and the engines last a long time. The petrol models are less successful because the 2.0-litre is not too strong and its manual gearbox does not have an enviable reliability record. Best model is a V6, and as new as possible.

**PEUGEOT 605**
Front-wheel-drive executive four-door saloon.

**History**
*September 1990* Range is 2.0SLi, 2.0SRi, 2.0SVi, 3.0SV, 3.0SVE, 3.0SVE-24.
*January 1991* 2.1-litre SRdt turbo diesel.
*July 1991* Automatic gearbox optional on SRdt.

**Fault Finder**
Check for a full service history because almost all of these cars have been used as company cars, and they soon clock up the miles. On the 2.0-litre engined cars, check for rattle from the crankshaft when the engine is gently revved. This should not be a problem, but if the car has not been serviced regularly, and it's covered a high mileage, wear is possible. On automatic gearbox cars, check for any slipping in the gears, though there have been few cases of this reported so far.

**Verdict**
Still quite early for any conclusive reports of reliability problems, but by and large the 605 seems a very

well designed and well built car. Not such an expensive feel inside as a Jaguar or a Rover, but the 605 is certainly a good driver's car. Best models are the 3.0SV, and the SRdt diesel.

## PORSCHE 924
Rear-wheel-drive 2+2 sports coupé.

### History
*August 1981* Range continues with 2.0-litre 924 and Turbo. Sports suspension package now available as an option on 924.
*October 1985* 924S launched with 2.5-litre engine.
*September 1986* Revisions to trim and equipment, including standard electric door mirrors.
*September 1988* Range discontinued.

### Fault Finder
Engines can wear quite quickly, especially the valve seals, so look for excessive smoke from the exhaust, and engine hiccups at high speeds. Turbos are not good. The turbochargers fail with monotonous regularity. The first obvious check here is to make sure that it is still boosting. If there's a clattering sound from the engine on deceleration, then the turbo is faulty, and soon to fail completely. During 1984 there were a few faulty water pumps. Most will have been replaced by now, but listen for a knocking sound when the engine is ticking-over, just in case. Gearboxes are strong, but the linkage is not. Check for any hesitation between lifting the clutch and the rear wheels biting. If there is a clonking sound from

the rear of the car when shifting gear, and a rumbling sound at higher speeds, then the drive shaft may well need replacing. On 924s produced during 1982 there were a batch of less than perfect driveshafts. Brakes are usually good, but if the 924 has been kerbed regularly it can affect the front left brake pipes. Check for any leaks and any pulling to the left. Also, run your finger over the brake discs to check for any scoring. Check for leaks from the fuel tank feeder pipe. If this problem exists you will see small droplets of petrol on the ground, underneath the tank. Electrics need examining because windows sometimes failed. The pop-up headlamps rarely fail, but check them to make sure they both work properly. If one of them is lazy it means it's soon going to stop working. Corrosion is not normally a problem, but check the headlamps in their up position to see if rust has taken a hold around their edges. If it has it should be treated quickly, otherwise it can soon spread. Metallic gold models need to be looked over carefully, preferably not in direct sunlight, so that you can see if the panels all match. There were cases of fading paintwork on models producing during 1986.

### Verdict
Often scorned as the hairdresser's Porsche, the 924 is actually not a bad car. A good Turbo is the model to go for because they are now becoming near classics. Don't expect fireball performance from any of these cars, rather revel in the first-class handling.

## PORSCHE 944
Rear-wheel-drive 2+2 sports coupé
and convertible.

## History
*April 1982* 944Lux with 2.5-litre
engine.
*September 1985* 944 Turbo with
2.5-litre engine, 944 gets
uprated suspension, flush-
fitting windscreen, new design
alloy wheels.
*September 1986* 944S with more
powerful 2.5-litre engine.
*August 1988* 944 gets new 2.7-litre
engine, 944S2 launched with
3.0-litre engine. Turbo engine
remains at 2.5-litres but power
is upped to 250bhp.
*January 1989* 944 Convertible.
*January 1991* 944 Turbo convertible in limited numbers.

## Fault Finder
The major requirement is for a full
and complete service history,
preferably carried out by a franchised Porsche dealer. Study service documents carefully – there
have been several forged histories,
relating to crash-damaged or
stolen 944s. On cars made between
1982–5 there were problems with
the engine timing belt. If the car
has not been properly serviced,
and the timing belt tension not
checked every 24,000 miles, and
changed completely at 48,000
miles, the engine can be seriously
damaged. This problem can be
heard as a deathly rattle when the
engine is softly revved, the result
of the valves hitting the pistons.
An expensive repair. Also during
1982–5, the hydraulic engine
mounts often leak, making the car
vibrate badly and tick-over
becomes harsh and uneven. This
can be checked for definite by
looking for any leaks around the
engine mounts. On cars made
between 1983–91 the power steering rack can leak and if it does it
has to be completely replaced. If
this fault is there, expect a low
groan from the steering when it's
on full lock. Repair is very expensive, it can be as much as £1,000.
On all 944s, look for blown cylinder
head gaskets, as this is quite
common, especially on 944s which
have not been well looked after,
and this is a seriously expensive
problem. Replacement runs into
thousands of pounds because the
oil mixes with the water and soon
causes the aluminium cylinder
bores to become scored. Check the
oil dipstick to see if there is any
water on it – if there is there'll be
water bubbles on the oil. This
problem almost always heralds
serious cylinder head problems.
Rust is rarely a problem. Check for
accident damage, as many 944s
have been involved in accidents,
some of which will have been
serious. Go around the car carefully, comparing the gaps between
doors and frame, and bonnet and
body to check they are all equal.

## Verdict
Justifiably retains a high second-
hand value. Good examples can be
found but it's imperative that
there is a full service record. High
mileage is not a problem, as long
as they are looked after, these cars
are good for 150,000 miles without
major problems.

## PORSCHE 911
Rear-wheel-drive and four-wheel-
drive 2+2 sports coupé, targa and
convertible.

## History

*September 1983* 911 Carrera coupé and cabriolet with new 3.2-litre engine. Optional Sport package of extra equipment available.

*September 1989* New 911 launched. Choice of rear-wheel drive (Carrera 2) or four-wheel drive (Carrera 4) in coupé, convertible and targa form with new 3.6-litre engine.

*September 1990* Tiptronic automatic gearbox as extra cost option.

*December 1990* 911 Turbo coupé with 3.3-litre engine.

## Fault Finder

These engines can drink oil, even when they are running properly. A litre per 2,000 miles is fairly normal. Heater control panels often fail and have to be replaced, and at around £500 a go this is not cheap. The heater sensor inside the cab keeps failing, even on cars built during the last two years. Replacement is not expensive, but it means the heater system doesn't work properly. Electrics are not normally a problem, but on 911s built during the late 1970s-early 1980s, there is a tendency for the sun-roof and the electric windows to stick. The only way of curing this is to keep putting talcum powder on the rubbers! Tyres last around 25,000 miles on the rear, around 35,000 miles on the front, and they are very expensive to replace. Bodywork is good, with the exception of the bonnet which seems to attract stones. Rusting always occurs around the headlamps where stones usually hit the bodywork. Door handles often become stiff and sometimes impossible to open. Brake calipers can seize, especially on the nearside left. You'll notice this when braking, as the car will pull to the left.

## Verdict

Fiendishly expensive second-hand – although prices have begun to fall a little recently – and something of a handful to drive, due to the weight of the engine at the back. But the rewards are stunning outright performance and potent image. Turbo versions are terribly overpriced, and not that much faster than normal 911s. Choose one with a full service history, and beware, there are many dodgy 911s on the market.

## PORSCHE 928

Rear-wheel-drive 2+2 sports coupé.

## History

*September 1983* S series 2 launched with more powerful 4.7-litre engine.

*September 1986* Series 4 launched with slightly restyled body and new 5.0-litre engine.

*March 1988* Sports Equipment model with more powerful engine.

*March 1989* GT coupé with further uprated engine, stiffer suspension, sports seats.

## Fault Finder

The most reliable Porsche, but also the most expensive to service, so check that the 928 has a full service history, and that all work has been carried out at a Porsche dealership. Brakes are a weak spot because this car gets through brake pads very quickly. So check for any grinding noises from the front, and run a finger over the discs to check if they are scored. Gearboxes are very strong but on early 928s, the first Series 2 cars in 1983, high mileage – around 70,000 – could lead to slipping gears. The gearchange on the 928 is barely noticeable, it's so smooth, so if there is any lurching or hesitation here, there is a serious problem. On 1983 and early 1984 cars there were a number of faulty fuel injection systems which made the car run rather roughly, especially around town. There are still some of those cars out there on the second-hand market. The front of the 928 often gets knocked or scuffed when parking and this can make it look very tatty. Try and avoid such a car. Corrosion rarely takes hold, but the bonnet can get hit by stones and that occasionally leads to messy corrosion. On metallic gold and silver 928s look carefully for any mis-matched paintwork because if part of the car has been resprayed it's very hard to get a good colour match.

**Verdict**
Glorious grand tourer, with amazingly good performance and safe handling, coupled with first-class reliability. But running costs – mostly servicing – are astronomic.

**PROTON**
Front-wheel-drive saloons and hatchbacks.

**History**
*March 1989* Range is 1.3GL, 1.3GLS, 1.5GL, 1.5GLS, 1.5SE, each available in saloon or hatchback form.
*January 1991* All versions get new

12-valve engines.
*June 1991* 1.3GE saloon and hatchback, while 1.3GL and GLS get trim and equipment improvements.

**Fault Finder**
On the 1.5-litre engines check for camshaft wear by listening for a rattling engine, and look for oil leaks from the top of the engine. Faulty water pumps were found on early 1.3-litre cars – those made in 1989 – but most should have been replaced by now. Check the top radiator hose because this can chafe through against the engine. Gearboxes are fairly sound but the synchromesh on second and third can fail very early – sometimes in as little as 20,000 miles on cars built before 1991. Steering geometry can easily go out of alignment if the wheels have been incessantly kerbed. Check this by looking for scarred front wheel rims and checking if the car wanders when being driven in a straight line. Examine the front tyres for uneven wear. Check all water pipes for leaks, especially where they join the engine and the radiator. Most early Protons, those built from mid to end of 1989, suffered from poor hose clips and poorly fitting pipes. If you hear what sounds like rushing water when you accelerate it almost always means the engine thermostat is about to fail. On all Proton saloons, and in particular those built before mid 1991, check the boot for water leaks, especially in the corners. Interior trim is a touch flimsy, so make sure that it all fits properly and that all switches work.

## Verdict

The first Protons to reach these shores were not well finished, the chief complaint being poor paintwork and badly fitting trim. Engines and transmissions are an old Mitsubishi design, but made in Malaysia, so the design is good, the manufacture sometimes less successful. Second-hand prices vary tremendously, and the best choice has to be one of the cars produced from around September 1991 onwards, and choose a hatchback if you can, they hold their value better.

## RANGE ROVER

Four-wheel-drive     multi-purpose vehicle.

## History

*September 1981* New 3-speed automatic gearbox for the five-door model.

*July 1983* New five-speed manual gearbox in place of previous four-speed.

*April 1986* Five-door turbo diesel.

*November 1987* High specification Vogue turbo diesel.

*March 1988* Vogue SE.

*October 1988* All models get new four-wheel-drive transfer box and uprated centre differential.

*October 1989* Bigger engined diesel turbo (2.5-litre) and 3.9-litre V8, plus modified gearboxes.

*January 1991* Major suspension changes.

## Fault Finder

Petrol V8 engines should rumble gently on tick-over. If there is any rattling it usually means either the camshaft or the tappets are worn, and this could herald major repair expense. It's vital that a Range Rover has been serviced regularly, in line with stipulated service intervals because it means regular oil changes will have been carried out – vital to the long life of the engine. Engine tappets are self adjusting, so if there is a noticeable ticking when the engine is idling it will mean the oil has not been changed regularly enough and that the tappets are sticking because of sludge. Such an engine requires major work. Engine head gaskets are prone to failure, especially if the RR has not been regularly serviced, or it's been subjected to hard towing. On your test drive check the temperature gauge carefully, if it quickly goes near the red line a head gasket may need replacing. Care also needs to be taken with the aluminium block; it needs special anti-freeze in all year round. The water should be green or blue, if it's a rusty colour there could be potentially disastrous internal corrosion. If the RR is fitted with a tow bar look for thick blue smoke when pulling away, it could signal serious wear to the engine's pistons. On all gearboxes, manual and auto, check for oil leaks underneath the RR, and also see that the centre differential lock works. If the lever will not engage smoothly, there is a serious problem. On automatic gearboxes there is a dipstick to check the fluid level. This must be checked, and if the level is low or, more importantly, if the colour is anything other than red, then the torque converter is almost certainly breaking up, and will soon fail. Such a RR must be left well alone. Off-road use may well have damaged the underside of the RR. Check that the fins on the gearbox housing are not flattened. If they are it could have been thumped down on hard ground, and there may be other damage. Off-road use may also have caused damage to the suspension and steering, although generally speaking the RR is very tough. Check that all four corners sit evenly, badly listing Range Rovers are quite common and this points to broken shock absorbers. The Range Rover's ride is soft, and very wallowy on pre-1986 models, but when driving on-road there should be a high level of stability, with no bouncing or vagueness. If the steering has noticeable play in it there may well be problems with the steering rack. It's a good idea to check the tyres for uneven wear, this will signal suspension or steering problems. Because this is a very heavy vehicle the brake pads wear quickly, and a less than scrupulous previous owner will soon damage the discs by letting the pads get too low. Good RR brakes are excellent, anything less than positive and precise braking means the pads, and possibly the discs, will need to be replaced. Range Rovers do rust, in spite of the major body panels being made of aluminium alloy. Door hinges can rust right through, causing the doors to drop, and the tail-gate is notorious for corroding. However, structurally Range Rovers are very good, as long as they haven't been damaged underneath. The best way of checking if there is rust inside a RR tailgate is to slam it down and watch for specs of rust falling out. Electrics need looking at. Check everything works properly, particularly the lights which have a tendency to short

and cause bizarre lighting sequences – switch on the headlight and sometimes only the rear fog lights come on. This type of fault is especially prevalent on Range Rovers used off-road.

## Verdict
The shape has barely changed in over twenty years, and many of the earliest Range Rovers are still going strong. A good second-hand buy if you buy wisely and if you can afford the 16mpg, and less, fuel returns. One of the best is the Vogue turbo diesel with the 2.5-litre engine which is slightly more economical (22mpg) and which keeps its value well. Of the petrol models, the best choice is a Vogue with automatic gearbox.

## RELIANT SCIMITAR SS1/SST
Rear-wheel-drive, two-seater convertible.

## History
*February 1985* Choice of two engines, 1.3 or 1.6-litre Ford units.

*June 1986* 1800 Ti using Nissan turbocharged engine.

*October 1987* 1.4-litre, using Ford engine.

*April 1990* SST models with restyled body, plus trim and equipment uprate.

## Fault Finder
Engines are mostly reliable, being Ford and Nissan units, but it's imperative that you check all water cooling hoses and hoses to and from the engine, because they often expand too much when hot, and then begin to leak. On the turbocharged Nissan 1.8-litre

engined cars check for a tired turbo, listen for a clattering sound when slowing down – this means the turbo is damaged, usually due to poor heat dispersal, a common fault on Ti versions built between June 1986 and February 1987. Listen for a clonking rear axle and any loud whining from the axle, pointers to a worn back axle. This problem is not so common on the Ford-engined cars as on the Nissan-engined models, mostly because of the extra power which the Ti produces. Any crunching from the gearbox when trying to change gear must be viewed with suspicion. The turbocharged cars have the weakest gearboxes, so you are most likely to find problems there. Rear suspension must be examined for any leaks from the shock absorbers, especially on the earliest cars, those made during the first six months of production. Later, a modified system was fitted which is much more reliable. On all Scimitars you should check the condition of the bodywork and the paintwork. While the body is generally of good quality, even a small knock can make the paintwork star and crack. This can then spread, making largish areas of bodywork crack and splinter, and it's not easy to repair. Look also for any badly fitting panels. This is not common, but on SS1s produced from February 1985 to November 1985 the fit of the doors was not always ideal, and often worsened the more the car was used. Check the condition of the hood carefully. On cars made before April 1990 there were leaks from the top of the winsdscreen surround. Make sure that all of the door locks and the boot lock work

properly and are not stiff. Inside, it's important to check the fit of the trim. Again, those cars produced in the first six months do not have a good reputation for fit and finish.

## Verdict
The SS1 is an ugly looking car with the roof in place, slightly less so with it down, so the best choice is the slightly prettier SST. The turbo is very powerful but not as tough as the 1.6 and 1.4-litre cars. Avoid 1.3-litre models, they do not provide the best performance.

## RENAULT 5
Front-wheel-drive hatchback.

## History
*January 1982* GTL gains five-speed gearbox.
*April 1982* Gordini Turbo.
*October 1982* TX luxury specification model.
*May 1984* Major trim and equipment revision.
*February 1985* New Renault 5 replaces previous range. New three-door range is 1.0TC, 1.1TL, 1.4GTL, 1.4TS, 1.4TSE, 1.4 Auto.
*June 1985* Five-door models, TL, GTL, Auto.
*February 1986* 5GT Turbo.
*June 1986* GTD diesel.
*July 1987* Heavily revised range, 1.1 Campus, 1.1TL, 1.3TR, 1.4GTS, 1.4 Auto, 1.8GTX, 1.6TD diesel, 1.6GTD diesel, GT Turbo.
*August 1989* New Prima versions with high equipment levels, plus trim additions across the range.
*September 1990* Campus 1.4-litre.

133

## Fault Finder

Engines are not the strongest, and rockers and camshafts wear after as little as 50,000 miles if oil changes and regular servicing are not faithfully carried out. Check for a full and comprehensive service history. Look for oil leaks from the top of the engine on all versions. Look for excessive exhaust smoke, a sign of worn valves, a problem common to all 5s which have covered high mileage. On GT Turbo models made between 1987 and 1989 look in the service history to see if the steering system has been repaired. Some of the casting on the steering was not of high quality and often broke, causing total loss of steering. There is no way of knowing when this is going to happen, and Renault did not recall cars, saying there was no major fault, so make sure you check for evidence of this part being replaced. Gearboxes last fairly well, but much depends on how the car has been driven. On Turbo models the gearbox bearings can wear in as little as 40,000 miles. Check for this with the engine on, by putting the clutch down and listening for rattling. Worn synchromesh is not uncommon on all versions, and on automatic models check for any gear slipping, although this is not a common problem with the R5. Engine overheating on GT Turbo models is common, but is usually dealt with by the automatic engine fan. However, there have been failures of these fans, so make sure that it is working. If it isn't the car will almost certainly have overheated already, usually causing severe engine damage. Look on the oil dipstick for any globules of water – a sign that the head gasket has failed. Restarting a Turbo when the engine is already warm can be a problem on cars made from February 1986, and retuning the carburettors can solve some of the problem, but not always completely cure it. On all versions made before 1986, check the suspension, especially at the rear, for any sagging, or leaking from the shock absorbers. This is a common problem. On R5s fitted with electric windows, make sure these work smoothly and effortlessly. Many become too stiff, defeating the motors. Bodywork corrosion is a problem, and the older the car, and therefore the worse the anti-corrosion measures, the worse the problem. Common areas for rust are the back of the rear wheelarches – look under the rear arches here – and anywhere along the wings. The wings are usually worst affected, but it's also possible to find rust on the bottom of the tail-gate and bottom of the doors. Check this over carefully, because a lot of the rust on the 5 eats through from under the metal, so by the time it's got to the surface it's a major problem. Having said that, even a badly rusting wing rarely affects the essential structure of the car and replacing the offending wing can solve the problem, at least for a while. Brakes squeal badly on cars over two years old and is usually due to a build-up of brake dust, but seized calipers can also make a noise when braking heavily. Check this by seeing if the car pulls to one side when braking. It's also a good idea to check for any brake fluid leaks. These can usually be spotted because the fluid drips down on to the brake pedal. Look for stains on the carpet, because these are hard to remove. Interior trim on all Renault 5s is flimsy, although it steadily improved as the years passed. On all versions, check for good interior fit and finish, and make sure that all switches are working.

**Verdict**
The 5's cult status has been snatched away by the Peugeot 205, but the Renault is still a good second-hand buy because it's cheap to buy and fairly inexpensive to run. The secret is to get a good one, and that means low mileage, no rust, and no turbo. Best model is the 1.4GTS.

**RENAULT CLIO**
Front-wheel-drive hatchback.

**History**
*March 1991* Range is three- and five-door, 1.2RL, 1.2RN, 1.4RT.
*December 1991* 1.8-litre RT five-door, 1.4RN, 1.4S, 1.9RL diesel, 1.9RN diesel.
*January 1992* Clio 16-valve.

**Fault Finder**
So new that few problems, and certainly no major ones, have yet occurred. Check the rear windscreen wiper, though, there have been faulty motors which make them turn on when they are switched off. Most should have been replaced by the time the Clio gets on to the second-hand market.

**Verdict**
Essentially the replacement for the 5, the Clio is selling fairly well, and so far it looks to be quite

reliable. New prices are not being discounted very much so prices should remain quite high on the second-hand market.

**RENAULT 9**
Front-wheel-drive saloon.

**History**
*March 1982* Range is 1.1C, 1.1TC, 1.4TL, 1.4GTL, 1.4TLE, 1.4GTS, 1.4TSE, 1.4 Auto.
*March 1983* 1.6-litre TD diesel.
*April 1984* 1.7-litre GTX.
*August 1985* Trim, equipment and mechanical uprating, including more powerful engine for GTL.
*February 1986* 1.4-litre Turbo.
*October 1986* Revised range is 1.2TC, 1.4TL, 1.4GTL, 1.4 Auto, 1.4 Turbo, 1.6 TD diesel.
*September 1989* Range discontinued.

**Fault Finder**
The 1.1-litre engine is prone to oil leaks, usually caused by poor seals, rather than failing cylinder heads. Check under the car for any evidence of large-scale leaks, and be suspicious if the underside of the car is coated with oil, because this will have flowed from the engine. Check the oil level a couple of times. On 1.4-litre engines in particular, look for excessive bluey-black exhaust smoke, a sign that the valve seals have worn. This is most common on cars built between March 1982 and August 1984. Gearboxes are not strong on any of these cars and should be checked carefully for crunching when going into gear – usually the nylon bushes have worn – or difficulty getting into gear – most often a result of the gear selector

wearing. Also, listen for worn gearbox bearings, a fairly common fault on 1.1-litre cars which have covered over 60,000 miles. On 1.7-litre versions check for timing chain rattle from the engine, and for excessive oil thirst. The only way to check for this is to watch the exhaust for lots of smoke. On Turbo versions built between February and October 1986 restarting the engine again when warm is often very difficult, due to fuel evaporation in the carburettor. The carburettor can be adjusted and this sometimes solves the problem. Like the Renault 5, the 9 Turbo engine gets hot very quickly, although it doesn't suffer the same chronic overheating as its smaller brother. Nevertheless, on any turbo, watch the temperature gauge to see if it gets too near the red line, a sign that previous engine overheating has caused damage. Water leaks through the bulkhead near the floor on the driver's side are common on many 9s built in the first year of production and is often not spotted until it's caused corrosion. Lift the carpets on both sides of the floorwell to check for dampness and corrosion. Brakes can squeal annoyingly after only 10,000 miles, but this is usually due to dust build-up, rather than any serious fault. But make sure that you check the front disc brakes for any scoring, in case a previous owner has run the brake pads too low. Electric windows and central locking should be checked because both were prone to failure. Also, check all switches to make sure they work properly. On 9s built from October 1986 to May 1987 there were a batch of faulty heated rear screen switches. On Turbo versions in particular, check the front drive shaft gaiters to see if the rubbers are split. And listen for any clonking when turning the steering wheel fully to the left or right. From August 1985 the GTL received a power increase and a new twin-choke carburettor. This system is much more reliable than the lower power engine previously placed in the 9, a unit which would often stray off-tune. Turbo models after October 1986 have a more powerful engine, and disc brakes all round. These are the best versions to look for. The previous Turbo was very heavy on front brake pads, wearing them down very quickly and often damaging the discs. Corrosion can be a problem because on the early cars the paintwork was not well applied. It was a full year after the launch of the car that the paintwork improved, and water leaks into the body of the car were mostly cured. On the outside, the rear of the wheelarches can rust, but the tail-gate is also a favourite spot, as well as under the rear bumper.

### Verdict

The 9 was never as successful as Renault had hoped, but in many ways it's a very good buy second-hand because the mechanicals are quite sound. The problem is, finding a good 9, without serious rust and with low mileage and a full service history.

### RENAULT 11

Front-wheel-drive        hatchback based on Renault 9.

## History

*June 1983* Range is three- and five-door, 1.1TC, 1.4GTL, 1.4 Auto, 1.4TSE.

*September 1983* 1.8GTS, 1.8TXE.

*May 1984* 1.6TD diesel, 1.4 Turbo.

*September 1984* TXE, Electronic.

*August 1985* GTL gets more powerful engine.

*October 1986* Heavily revised range launched. 1.2TC, 1.4TL, 1.4GTL, 1.4 Auto, 1.4 Turbo, 1.6GTD diesel, 1.7TXE.

*September 1989* Range discontinued.

## Fault Finder

The same faults and potential problem areas are found on the 11 as on its booted brother, the 9. One additional area to examine is the fit of the rear tail-gate. After being slammed closed lots of times the latches can wear, so it's often hard to close the hatch completely. Also, look for leaks around the window rubbers on the hatchback, and for any staining of the boot carpet which might point to this happening.

## Verdict

Slightly more popular than the 9, the 11 nevertheless failed to make its mark in the highly competitive mid-range hatchback market. There are better cars – cars which last longer and which look better, too.

## RENAULT 19/CHAMADE

Front-wheel drive saloon (Chamade) and hatchback (19).

## History

*February 1989* Hatchback range is launched. 1.4TR, 1.4GTS, 1.4TS, 1.4TSE, 1.8GTX, 1.8TXE, 1.9GTD diesel.

*December 1989* Chamade range launched. Range is 1.4TS, 1.4GTS, 1.4TSE, 1.7GTX, 1.7TXE, 1.9GTD diesel.

*September 1990* Extra equipment for TXE. 1.4-litre Prima three- and five-door hatchbacks and Chamade four-door.

*February 1991* 1.4GTS-X.

*May 1991* 1.8-litre 16-valve hatchback and Chamade.

## Fault Finder

So far, this seems to have been a very reliable car. The body work should be examined for any accident damage, or even dents caused by careless parking, because the metal is very thin and it can soon look tatty if the car hasn't been well looked after. On all versions check for any rattling timing chains. So far there don't seem to have been any problems in this area, but it's worth a listen when the engine is ticking over. Check the condition of the rear bumper, because even a fairly low speed bang can make it crack, or even shatter. Gearboxes seem strong, but the gear-lever is not robust, and with heavy-handed use it can become sloppy, and eventually come loose. Regular servicing should stop this happening. Front brake pads do wear down rather quickly, due mostly to quite heavy servo assistance, so check the condition of the pads and the front brake discs.

## Verdict

The 19 is a deservedly popular car which seems to be holding quite high second-hand values. The 1.4-litre cars are the best, providing a good blend of performance, fuel economy and low servicing costs.

## RENAULT 21
Front-wheel-drive saloons, hatchbacks and estates, and four-wheel-drive estate and saloon.

### History
*June 1986* Range is 1.7TL, 1.7TS, 1.7RS, 1.7GTS, 2.0RX, 2.0TXE.
*October 1986* GTD diesel, TD turbo diesel. Savanna estate range launched, 1.7TL, 1.7GTS, 2.0GTX, GTD diesel.
*April 1987* 2.0TXE Auto.
*May 1988* 2.0 Turbo.
*September 1989* Hatchback range launched. Range is 1.7TS, 1.7GTS, 1.9TD diesel, 1.9GTD diesel, 2.0GTX, 2.0TXE Auto, 2.0TXi.
*August 1990* Savanna 2.0GTX 4WD. 2.0 Quadra Turbo 4WD.

### Fault Finder
Check the 1.7-litre engine in particular for timing problems giving erratic engine running, especially when warm, and listen for timing chain rattle. After high mileage, around 70,000 plus, the 1.7 can use a lot of oil, and you can usually spot this trait by looking for black smoke when the engine is revved hard. Diesel models are very reliable but rather noisy, but check for diesel leaks from the engine. These will usually be spotted as globules on the ground under the back of the engine, but it's usually only a fault which afflicts the first 21s, and then only when they've covered a high mileage – in excess of 80,000 miles. Water pipes chafing through against the engine are quite

normal on all versions up to November 1989, due to bad siting of pipes. Check for leaks, and worn pipes which might soon leak. Manual gearboxes are not very strong and bearings inside the gearbox wear quite rapidly. Check this with the engine on by listening for rattling when the clutch is pushed down. On Turbo models the gearboxes usually get harsh treatment from drivers and they are not much stronger than on the normal cars, so make sure the lever is not too sloppy. Another problem with the Turbo gearbox is the loss of reverse gear, this even happens on quite new models. The 21 should shift into reverse easily, if there is any resistance it can mean further gearbox problems later. On Savanna estates check for a tow bar because the 1.7-litre engine is not strong enough to haul heavy loads around, and damage may have been caused to the engine. Again, look for bluey-black smoke from the exhaust, a sign that valves or their seals have worn. Four-wheel-drive versions seem mostly reliable but check the tyres over for any uneven tyre wear, a sign that the 4x4 system might not be working properly, or that a wheel or wheels might be out of alignment. This alignment problem can occur when the front wheels have been regularly kerbed, so check for damage to the wheel trims. Regular kerbing can also affect the power steering system, causing it to leak and lose pressure. If the steering is groaning when you take the steering wheel right over to full lock, a leaking system will almost certainly be the problem. Look at the rubber gaiters over the front drive shafts, by the front wheels. They can split quite easily and must be repaired as soon as possible, before permanant damage is caused to the driveshafts. On the first Turbo versions – built during the latter half of 1988 – the gaiters were not of the best quality and the driveshafts found it hard to stand up to the Turbo's power, so check these over carefully. Interior trim should be examined carefully, the 21 is not the most solidly built car inside and bits of trim do fall off. Electrics can be bad, with electric windows and roof failing, and erratic central locking, sometimes working, sometimes not.

## Verdict

The 21 is a fine car, especially in 2.0-litre form, and preferably in Savanna estate guise, but the 1.7-litre is not as successful and the hatchback models have failed to catch the UK public's attention. This means there are bargains to be had, and this is one of those cars which you can usually shave even more money off, simply because they are not in great demand.

## RENAULT 25

Front-wheel-drive hatchback.

## History

*July 1984* Range launched, 2.0TS, 2.0GTS, 2.2GTX, 2.7-litre V6.

*July 1985* Turbo, with 2.5-litre V6 engine.

*July 1989* 2.0TXE, 2.0TXi, V6 2.9-litre.

*May 1990* Heavily revised range, 2.0GTS, 2.0TX, 2.0TXE, 2.0TXi, 2.9-litre V6, V6 Baccara.

## Fault Finder

Check for noisy camshaft belts in the 2.2-litre models and rattling timing chains on the V6 cars. On V6 cars look for evidence of oil leaks from the bottom of the engine, because the sump plugs sometimes work loose. On Turbo models check for water leaks through the cylinder head gasket, and for fouled spark plugs which can cause uneven engine running and occasional backfires. The turbocharger itself is quite strong, but check that the car has been serviced regularly by a Renault dealer becuase if not, the turbocharger can wear quite quickly. On automatic gearbox versions, gears can slip but a worse problem, especially on the V6 models, is that the gearboxes sometimes will not change up a gear when they should, then all of a sudden they surge up a gear. Check this out because such a gearbox has not got long left. Suspension should be checked over carefully, especially at the rear where it can sometimes sag on one side. Make sure that the car sits on the road squarely. Brake pads on V6 cars do not last long, and the discs become scored very easily. Check for squealing from the front of the car when braking, and make sure there are no grinding noises. Power-steering systems are mostly quite robust, but lack of service can mean contamination of the steering system fluid which leads to gradual loss of power assistance. If the steering feels rather heavy, or there's a high pitched whine when the wheel is turned, this could be the problem. It's most common on TXE and TXi models built from mid to end of 1989. Interior trim is

A

RENAULT    RENAULT

fussily styled but also very flimsy, so look out for badly fitting dashboards, and switches which don't fit their mountings very well.

**Verdict**

The 25 has only proved really popular in France, and so second-hand prices here are very low, making the 25 good value. The newer the better, and you must have a full service history. The 2.0-litre injection cars are best value, the V6 and Turbo are heavy on fuel and costly to service, but they are relatively cheaper second-hand than the 2.0-litre cars.

**RENAULT ESPACE**

Front-wheel-drive and four-wheel-drive multi-purpose vehicle.

**History**

*July 1985* Range is 2.0GTS, 2.0TSE.

*April 1988* Heavily restyled body and new range 2.0GTS, 2.0TXE, 2000-1.

*March 1989* TXE Quadra 4WD and 2000-1 Quadra 4WD.

*June 1991* New Espace replaces previous model. New range is 2.0RN, 2.0RT, 2.0RXE, 2.9RT, 2.9RXE.

**Fault Finder**

The 2.0-litre engined models should be checked for timing chain rattle, and leaks from the sump plugs at the bottom of the engine. Look under the Espace for evidence of oil leaking back along the length of the underside. Make sure you also check the oil dipstick before you drive off to check the engine is full of oil. The body is plastic, fitted over a steel chassis.

If the body is gently bumped it usually re-forms, so there is little problem with the starring of paintwork which occurs on some fibre glass cars. However, look carefully for evidence of accident damage, especially at the front, because even a fairly slow speed shunt can cause the chassis to de-form. This is not easy to spot, but check for any uneven tyre wear, the result of the wheels having been knocked out of alignment because of a damaged chassis. Look also for any corrosion on the chassis, although this is rare it can occur; if the underside has been badly knocked, or the vehicle has been involved in an accident. The remote control linkage from the gear-lever to the gearbox can fail on Espaces made from the end of 1985 to the middle of 1986. The only warning of this is an increasingly sloppy gearchange, just before the remote fails. On 4x4 versions it's wise to check for any damage to the driving axles, and in particular, oil leaks from the driveshaft differentials. So far there haven't been any major problems here, but if regular maintenance is missed, or the vehicle is used off-road, then damage can occur. Likewise, on all Espaces, check the driveshaft gaiters to make sure they are not split. This is sometimes a problem on the in-board drive gaiters on the front-wheel-drive models once they've covered around 80,000 miles plus. Interior trim is quite hard wearing, and this is one of the few Renaults to be truly well finished, and properly screwed together. Never buy an Espace which hasn't got a full service history because these vehicles usually cover high mileages, and it's vital that servicing has been carried out routinely to keep this vehicle in good condition.

### Verdict

Much sought after, the Espace retains a high second-hand value. If you see one which looks cheaply priced there will be something wrong with it. Try and get a version made after 1988, the models before will be very tatty by now. Best models are those with the 2.0-litre petrol-injection engine.

## RENAULT GTA V6

Rear-wheel-drive coupé.

### History

*August 1986* Range launched, V6, V6 Turbo.

*January 1992* Range discontinued, to be replaced by the Alpine A610.

### Fault Finder

Engines are tough, but on those cars made prior to 1990 there were problems with engine cooling, and some cars even suffered small engine fires. Check for overheating not just by looking at the temperature gauge, but also listening to see how often the engine fan comes on. If it starts cooling when you are out on the open road then there is a problem. Usually it's blocked cooling ducts caused by pipes collapsing. In town driving the fan will come on often, even in a GTA in tip-top condition. Check the plastic body panels for any accident damage, because these cars are virtually impossible to repair properly if they've had a major

shunt. Gearboxes are strong, there should be few problems, but synchromesh can fail on third gear. The turbocharged cars are mostly reliable but on some of the early versions – those made from August 1986 to April 1987 – there were a number of faulty engine management systems which could cause engine misfiring and jerky performance when accelerating hard. Check for petrol leaks under the cars because the fuel tank is at the front and leaks can occur in the piping between the tank and the rear engine. This is only a problem with GTAs made between August 1986 and December 1986. Check for any accident damage at the front of the car because even if it looks to have been mended properly, an accident may well have damaged the chassis. A good way to check for this is to examine the tyres for any uneven wear. Make sure that the tyres are examined in any case, because the rear ones wear quickly, and they are a different size from the front pair so they cannot be swapped around. Replacement tyres are hideously expensive. The rear drive axles are very strong, and there have been few problems. But if there is any clonking when moving off from rest, or groaning at high speed, then the differential is almost certainly badly worn. Dashboard gauges should be looked at very closely. They are mostly digital, and they are very unreliable. The usual fault is a malfunctioning fuel gauge. It can show Full when it's empty, and it may not re-register when the tank is filled up. The easiest way to check this is to turn the engine on and off a few times to see if you get the same readings. Trim can be badly fitted and it is also flimsy, so a GTA with high mileage is unlikely to have a pristine cabin. Check everything fits correctly, and that all of the switches work. Windscreen wiper motors on cars made in early 1987 often failed to work correctly. One of the blades would become increasingly lazy and eventually stop working. This, in turn would stop the remaining blade from making a complete sweep. The windscreen wipers' motor always whirrs very noisily, but one which is about to cause problems will usually makes a clacking sound, as well.

## Verdict
Very cheap to buy second-hand, mostly because of their reputation for poor build quality. But a good GTA is a stunning performer, with head-turning looks. Buy carefully and you will not regret it.

## ROVER 200
Front-wheel-drive saloons and hatchbacks.

## History
*June 1984* Range launched, consisting of 213, 213S, 213SE, Vanden Plas.
*April 1985* Heavily revised range, plus addition of new 1.6-litre cars. Range is 213, 213S, 213SE Auto, 216S, 216SE, 216 Vanden Plas EFI, 216 Vitesse.
*October 1988* 216SE gets fuel-injected engine.
*October 1989* Range discontinued, replaced by completely new range of front-wheel-drive hatchbacks, 214Si, 214SLi, 214GSi, 216GSi.

*July 1990* 216GTi 16-valve.
*September 1990* Three-door models launched. 214S, 214SI, 216GTi, 216GTi Twin Cam.
*March 1991* 218SD diesel, 218SLD Turbo diesel.
*June 1991* 220GTi 16-valve three-door.

## Fault Finder
1984–9 Best buys are cars with mileage below 50,000, above that there can be camshaft and oil leak problems. Look closely at service records to see when the camshaft belt has been replaced, it should be renewed every 40,000 miles. Check these cars for rust problems along the front wings and at the bottoms of the front doors. Check the rubber gaiters on the front driveshafts for any splits. On the new range of Rovers made after October 1989 check Twin Cam models for worn camshaft belts, especially if the belts have not been replaced by 40,000 miles. Oil leaks from the top of the engine are common on 1.6-litre cars, but rarely cause any serious engine damage, as long as they are spotted early. The power-assisted steering system is not reliable on 216GSi versions made from October 1989 to January 1990. The problem is sticking valves which cause the system to suddenly stop working. Most of the defective versions should have been replaced by now. Check the gearbox for noisy rattles when trying to change gear, a result of worn bearings. This is more common on 1.4-litre cars than 1.6-litre versions and usually only shows itself after 80,000–90,000 miles. Bodywork and paintwork is first class, though on the first of the

new cars (from October 1989) rust can take hold along the tops and down the seams of the front wings. Electrics are generally good, but on all cars with central locking check this works properly. After around 15,000 miles some of the systems fail to work properly, only locking the driver's door. Check that the door mirrors work properly, especially on the Twin Cam cars.

**Verdict**
The Rover 200 and 400 are cars which hold their value well, thanks to good build quality. The earliest 200s are very inexpensive now, but they don't have very resilient bodywork. Today's 200 is a fine car, but make sure you check the service history, because most of these cars are used as company cars, and they quickly accumulate miles. Best choice is one of the 1.6-litre cars, but not the Twin Cam – it's rather overpriced, and not as quick as it sounds.

**ROVER 400**
Front-wheel-drive saloon version of the Rover 200 hatchback.

**History**
*March 1990* Range is 414Si, 414SLi, 416GSi, 416GTi.
*November 1990* 416SLi, 416SLi.
*April 1991* 418SLD turbo diesel, 418GSD turbo diesel.

**Fault Finder**
The 400 should be examined for the same faults and potential problems as its hatchback brother, the 200. The diesel and turbo diesel 400s use Peugeot diesel engines which are very reliable, as long as they are serviced regularly.

**Verdict**
A high-class saloon which oozes more quality than the Ford Orion or Vauxhall Astra, second-hand prices for the 400 can vary, depending on whether the car has been used as a salesman's car (average to low second-hand value) or as a private motorist's car, in which case the recorded miles will dictate the value.

**ROVER SDI**
Rear-wheel-drive hatchbacks.

**History**
*January 1982* Range is completely revised. New range is 2000, 2300, 2300S, 2600S, 3500SE, 3500 Vanden Plas (VDP).
*June 1982* 2400SD turbo diesel with Italian VM engine.
*September 1982* 2600SE launched, plus trim and equipment update for 2000, 2300, 2300S, SD, and 2600S.
*October 1982* V8 engined Vitesse launched.
*July 1984* Revised versions of 2600 and VDP launched to replace SE models. VDP EFi launched with same V8 engine as Vitesse, but with a standard automatic gearbox and without the Vitesse's sports suspension. All other models get major trim and equipment update.
*October 1984* More major revisions for all models, including new electronic fuel injection system, and heated electric door mirrors and electric sun-roof on 2000 and 2300 models.
*September 1987* Range discontinued.

## Fault Finder

Before October 1984 there were problems with some fuel injection systems. Often they would deliver the wrong amount of fuel to the engine, causing either misfiring at high speeds and when accelerating hard, or flooding the engine when starting. If any of these original SDIs do still exist then it's likely that they have since been fitted with the Mk II injection system. Many police authorities complained that when chasing villains at high speed the brakes on the police Rovers would often fade completely. This is down to the design rather than any inherent fault with the parts, but do make sure that you check the brakes over carefully. There should be good progression when the pedal is depressed, and once the car has been stopped, the brake pedal should stop going down. There are two common brake problems: the first is leaks in the braking system. These can be spotted by looking for air bubbles in the brake fluid reservoir, low brake fluid level, and brakes pulling to one side, usually to the nearside. The second problem is worn brake pads, causing scoring to the front discs. This is common on the Vitesse and VDP and EFi, cars which have heavier engines and higher performance than the other models. Engines are generally fairly strong, especially the V8 unit, but on the 2000 you need to check for smooth running. For the first year of the revised range – January 1982 onwards – when the 2000 engine was reintroduced there was a problem with a small wire inside the distributor cap which would burn out with monotonous regularity. As a stop-gap measure it was possible to put a piece of thick electrical wire in its place. That allowed the 2000 to run fairly well for quite some time. The only long-term cure is the fitting of a later-design distributor. If the engine on the 2000 you are looking at does not run smoothly it is likely that you have the original distributor. On all versions look for excessive black smoke from the exhaust – a sign that the valves are worn. This is a most common problem on the 2000 and 2300, simply because these are big cars and these engines are quite small and relatively inefficient. This means that they are often pushed very hard, with consequent damage to the engine. Automatic gearboxes can be reluctant to change up a gear when accelerating hard. If this happens on your test drive it's best to leave that Rover alone, it does herald serious problems in the near future. Power steering pumps fail regularly, making this large and heavy car virtually impossible to steer, especially around town. If there's a lot of groaning from the steering when turning it can mean that the system is low on fluid. However, there's seldom warning when the system is going to fail completely – there's usually a bang and then the pump falls to pieces. Water leaks are very common and they can affect all parts of the car. Look in the boot, particularly under the carpet, for any signs of corrosion or any standing water. Similarly, check the windscreen rubbers for any leaks, and evidence of staining caused by leaks. Always check inside the glove box on the passenger side, water almost always leaks into here from the screen above; a common fault on all Rover SDIs. Worn shock absorbers, especially at the rear, are very common. This can easily be spotted because the rear of the car will sag down on one side. Replacement is not expensive. Check the exhaust system carefully because these wear quite quickly in the middle, and they are expensive to replace. Electrics should also be examined carefully, especially electric windows and sun-roofs because they tend to stop working with monotonous regularity. If you are opting for a Vitesse never try and close all of the four electric windows at the same time (it is easy to do this with one hand because the buttons are all grouped together) because it invariably blows the fuse which powers the windows and the sun-roof. Check also for a good dashboard fit, in particular where the instrument panel joins the dash, because there are often gaps here, caused either by bad installation or by warping of the rather thin plastic at the base of the instrument panel.

## Verdict

A full service history is desirable on these cars, but you may not get one, because by now most will have covered very high mileages and be on third or fourth owners. But, if you can find one with reasonably low mileage, adorned with a Vitesse badge and alloy wheels, then you will have a good performance car with plenty of interior room and sure-footed handling. Try and avoid 2000, 2300 and 2600 cars, their engines are not reliable and they are not good performers.

## ROVER 800

Front-wheel-drive saloons and hatchbacks.

### History

*July 1986* Saloon range is launched first. Range is 820i, 820Si, 825i, V6 2.5-litre Sterling.

*October 1986* 820E, 820SE.

*February 1988* 827Si, 827SLi, Sterling 2.7-litre.

*May 1988* Fastback hatchback range launched. Range is 820, 820E, 820i, 820Si, 827Si, 827 Vitesse.

*November 1989* Major trim and equipment revisions to all models.

*September 1990* 820 models get new 16-valve engine. 825 turbo diesel Fastback launched.

*April 1991* 820 Turbo 16-valve saloon and hatchback.

*January 1991* Range discontinued and replaced by new range.

### Fault Finder

The first advice is to buy an 800 made after 1988, when the quality improved somewhat. On all Rovers check for dodgy electrics. This means everything. Check door mirrors, windows, sun-roofs, dashboard dials, cruise controls, warning lights, headlights, sidelights and indicators. Rover 800s built since January 1990 have improved, but still make these checks. Engines are quite strong but 820 16-valve units can have rattling timing chains, and gearboxes which have a very short life. Check for a smooth gearchange and smooth engine performance. Any hiccuping or hesitation when accelerating can point to faulty engine management boxes, a problem which has only been sorted out in the last two years. Power steering pumps fail with monotonous regularity, especially on cars built from the start of production until the end of 1988. Brake calipers can seize on all models up to January 1989, and less regularly on later models. Interior trim fit and finish varies tremendously from car to car. Check that there are no rattles or squeaks because if there are, they will be hard to banish.

## Verdict

The quality of Rover 800s prior to 1988 was abysmal. Since then the cars have improved beyond measure and today's 800 is a very good car. Second-hand values are very attractive for buyers but beware, you must have an 800 with a full service history, and if there are any electrical faults, expect more to occur later. Best choice is an 820i with full specification.

## SAAB 99/90

Front-wheel-drive saloon.

## History

*September 1982* Revisions to the 99, with new five-speed gearbox. Model range is GL two-door and GL four-door.

*October 1984* Saab 90 launched to replace the 99. Available only as a two-door. Front of the 90 is from the 99 while the rear is from the then newer 900.

*March 1985* Range deleted.

## Fault Finder

Check for excessive black exhaust smoke, a sign that the engine valves, or the valve seals, are worn. This can be a problem on very high mileage models, though generally speaking these engines are quite robust and many people keep these cars far in excess of 100,000 miles. Gearchanges are quite heavy and quite notchy, but given a hefty push they should slot into gear cleanly. If there's any crunching or resistance then there could be major gearbox problems on the way. As with the 900, the engine's core plugs can blow out when the weather gets very cold. These are designed to blow-out to prevent freezing water cracking the block, but they tend to drop out far too frequently, even when overnight temperatures are not that low, so allowing water to flow out of the cooling system. It is therefore wise to check for any warping of the cylinder head which might have occured due to consequent engine overheating caused because there wasn't enough water in the system. In both the 90 and 99 this is best done by checking for globules of water on the dipstick. If there is any there it means the head gasket is not making proper contact with the block and is letting water into the oil. Eventually this will cause the engine to stop, and could cause more permanent damage to the engine block itself. Brake pads last a long time on these cars, so there is rarely a problem with worn pads, but it's still wise to check the state of the discs and rear shoes for any scoring of their surfaces. Rust has not often been a problem but there were some paint application problems on cars made between 1981 and 1982 which caused the paint to blister and flake, particularly on the roof and front bonnet. It is highly unlikely that these cars have not been resprayed by now, but nevertheless it's important to check that the bodywork is in good condition, and if it has been resprayed, that it's been carried out properly. Check for wear and tear inside, especially on the seats, because these cars are very robust and very well built. Any worn seating or trim will point to an uncaring former owner, and these are often the type of people who will also neglect servicing. Lastly, try and get a 99/90 with a full service history; although these cars are strong and can go on for at least ten years, they do suffer if servicing is neglected.

## Verdict

These cars are not pretty, but if you can forget about that you can make the most of their robust character, good interior roominess – the 90 is the best in this respect – and relatively low running costs. The best choice is as late a 90 as you can find, hopefully with a full service history. It must also be said, that if you can find a good Saab 900 it is a better buy than this car, simply because it's better looking, slightly more modern and retains a better resale value. And early 900s will not cost much more than a pristine 90 or 99.

## SAAB 900

Front-wheel-drive saloons and hatchbacks.

## History

*January 1982* GLi saloon.
*September 1982* GLi five-door, SE Turbo three-door, CD Turbo Auto saloon.

*March 1984* 900i two-door.
*October 1984* Range is revised. All carburettor models badged 900, fuel-injected models badged 900i, Turbo models called Turbo 16.
*October 1985* 900 two-door, 900 Turbo two-door.
*January 1987* Turbo 16 convertible.
*May 1988* Turbo 16S two-door.
*November 1988* 900S 16-valve three- and five-door hatchbacks, 900S convertible.
*April 1990* 900i convertible with power hood.
*September 1990* New version of the 900S with new 16-valve turbo engines.

## Fault Finder

Paintwork on all models made before 1984 should be checked over carefully, because there were cars produced whose paintwork did not stand up to day to day wear. Look for paint peeling, rust in the roof rain channels and blistering paint on the bonnets. These problems beset some colour of cars more than others, the worst affected being the dark brown finish. On all 900s check for engine overheating. This can be caused by the engine's core plugs blowing out when cold weather strikes. The plugs are designed to come out if water begins to freeze in the engine so that the engine block is not damaged, but on cars produced before 1985 they were far too sensitive, blowing out when the temperature dipped near to freezing. Check the temperature gauge when driving because if the car has been driven for long with the core plugs out, the engine could have overheated and more serious damage occured. Engines are very strong, and easily capable of 200,000 miles, provided the servicing has been regular. Check though for noisy crankshafts, usually signalled by a knocking noise when the engine is gently revved. Listen also for rattling from worn timing chains. These problems are most common on the carburettor models built upto 1985. On turbocharged models check for camshaft belt noise. If you hear this chattering, rattling noise then the belt needs replacing very quickly, before major engine damage is caused by its total failure. Turbo versions have a lot of turbo lag – the delay before the turbo boosts – but the turbochargers themselves are also prone to failure if they are not treated properly, and they rarely are. When the car is stopped after a long run, the engine should be allowed to idle to allow the turbo to whine down. If there is any clattering when the turbo comes off-boost, then there is a problem, usually with the turbo's blades, and it will need replacing. Water leaks from top engine hoses are quite common on cars made before 1986, so check all hoses for signs of chafing. Brakes are efficient and last well, but on Turbo models they do need to be regularly checked, simply because they're subjected to heavier braking. Exhausts do not last very long, they often need replacing after 30,000 miles, so check the system isn't blowing. This is very important on turbo models because a defective exhaust can affect performance. On APC engined cars built after 1987, check for smooth engine running. These cars are designed to run on any grade of petrol but if they have been run on low grade fuel there can be engine hesitation when accelerating. If this fault exists the engine may need decoking to restore full performance. All versions need to be placed in reverse gear before the key can be taken out of the ignition. Reverse is always a little awkward to get into, but make sure it's not very hard, because this points to a worn gear-lever collar. The collar needs to be lifted before the lever can be slotted into reverse.

## Verdict

The 900 is not a pretty car but it has a loyal following thanks to first class build quality and strong engines and gearboxes. Best buy is the 900i because it performs well enough and lacks the complexities and higher running costs of the turbo. 16-valve versions are slightly smoother than their 12-valve brothers, but the difference in smoothness and engine refinement is not dramatic.

## SAAB 9000

Front-wheel-drive saloons (CD versions) and hatchbacks.

## History

*October 1985* Turbo 16-valve hatchback.
*April 1986* 9000i 16-valve hatchback.
*January 1987* 9000 Turbo SE.
*May 1988* CD and CDE saloons.
*July 1988* Improved 9000i hatchback (better equipment).
*October 1988* 9000i Turbo 16-valve, 9000 Carlsson hatchbacks, 9000CDiS, 9000iCD Turbo saloons.

*September 1989* 2.3-litre 16-valve engine introduced.
*January 1991* 9000 Carlsson hatchback, CD saloon, both with new 2.3-litre engine.

**Fault Finder**
Engines are mostly reliable, but check for worn bottom water hoses, and as with the 900 check the turbo versions for any clattering when they come off boost. It's also important to check the turbocharger is working properly when it comes on boost. It should propel the car along smoothly, without any hesitation. Check the power steering system, especially on turbocharged models, because it is under a lot of pressure. Listen for any groaning from the steering when turning the wheel hard to left or right, a sign that the system is leaking. Look at the front wheel rims for signs of excessive kerbing because this can literally loosen the steering box and cause damage to the steering rack and cause leaks in the power steering system. It's very important to listen out for any groaning or clonking from the front suspension, and doubly important on all turbo models, regardless of age or mileage, because if the car has been driven quickly the power can cause the spindles in the drive axles to wear and eventually shear off. This means new constant velocity joints will be needed. Check the front brake discs on all models, but again, especially on turbos, because they wear very quickly. Bodywork should not be a problem, these cars are very well protected. However, 9000s made from the end of 1985 to the middle of 1986 did not have the best paint applications, and some needed resprays. Check the paint carefully on these cars for any signs of paint blister or peeling. Interiors should be in perfect condition because they are hard wearing and very well finished. A 9000 with a tatty interior should be avoided, it is the sign of a car which has not been well looked after.

**Verdict**
Underrated but sometimes rather overpriced, the 9000 is a fine car offering long life and relatively inexpensive running costs. A full service record is a must, and it's best to try and avoid the turbo cars. They are exciting to drive but the fuel-injected versions last longer.

**SEAT MARBELLA**
Front-wheel-drive hatchback.

**History**
*May 1988* 850L, 900GL three-door models.
*October 1988* Revised range is 850 Junior, 900GL, 900GLX.

**Fault Finder**
Early versions must be checked for poor paintwork finish, especially on the bonnet and roof. Check near the window rubbers for any rust which might have taken hold due to moisture underneath, and which has then spread out onto the surrounding bodywork. The 850 engine is not very strong, and suffers from oil leaks, particularly from the top of the engine through the head gasket. Check this carefully because oil leaks on this engine can dramatically shorten its life. All 850s, regardless of age,

have this potential problem. The 900 engine is a bored-out version of the small unit, but it appears to be stronger, and less prone to oil leaks. But it does suffer from crankshaft wear, so listen for any loud rattling when the engine is ticking over. Brakes are not very efficient on either verison, but brake pads do not wear down quickly, so there is rarely brake disc damage. The problems here are seized brake calipers on either side at the front, leading to pulling to one side when braking, and brake fluid leaks on to the discs, which can cause longer braking distances. Gearboxes wear their bearings quite quickly on all versions – you will hear a rattle with the engine on when the clutch is put down. Front driveshafts are not strong, and although the rubber gaiters usually remain intact, the CV joints themselves can wear after as little as 40,000 miles. This fault is slightly more common on the 950. Listen out for any clonking from the front of the car when turning the wheel completely over to the left or right. Check for leaks of fluid from the suspension struts, a common fault on the cars built from May 1988 to December 1988. Check for properly working door locks on all models. They are not strong and the insides of the locks sometimes mesh, making it impossible to lock. Interior trim is not strong, so make sure it all fits properly. Electrics seem quite reliable, but there have been a number of erratic fuel gauges, sometimes suddenly dropping down to empty when the petrol tank is still half full.

**Verdict**
Keen pricing has made these Fiat

Panda clones quite inexpensive to buy, but the earliest versions were not well made, and just how long they will last is something of a worry. The best buy is the bigger engined 900, and go for the best trim level.

**SEAT IBIZA**
Front-wheel-drive hatchback.

**History**
*October 1985* Launch of three-door models, 1.2LE, 1.2L, 1.2GL, 1.2GLX, 1.5GLX.
*October 1986* 1.2 Designer three-door. 1.2L, 1.5GL, 1.5GLX five-door models.
*April 1987* Designer 900 three-door.
*October 1988* Heavily revised range, 900 Disco, 900 Comfort, 1.2 Junior, 1.2 Comfort, 1.2 Crono, 1.5 Crono, 1.5GLX.
*May 1989* Heavily revised range, 900, 1.2 Special, 1.2XL, 1.2GLX, 1.5GLX, 1.5SXi.
*August 1990* 1.7D diesel.

**Fault Finder**
Ibizas made from October 1985 to December 1986 were poorly finished, both in terms of their paintwork and interior trim. Avoid these early models. On all petrol Ibizas check for noisy timing chains, and on the 900 watch for excessive exhaust smoke, because the valve seats are quite soft and wear quite quickly. Cars made from October 1988 are best, but they still need checking for engine oil leaks. The 1.2-litre cars often suffer from poor oil flow into the top of the engine, and this can lead to noisy rockers when the engine is ticking over. On all versions, look

for excessive kerbing of the front wheels. This happens regularly because of the wide track. Such damage can offset the steering geometry, causing premature and uneven tyre wear. The 1.7-litre diesel is very noisy, so it's hard to pick up on any untoward engine noises. But on a diesel Ibiza which has covered over 60,000 miles check for diesel leaks in the engine bay. It's hard to clean leaking diesel away, so it's fairly easy to spot. Inside, check the fit and finish of all trim. A common problem on all Ibizas, and especially those built before 1988, is a groaning steering wheel console when turning the steering wheel, because the plastic moves and then becomes warped. Check also for badly fitting interior door trim, and switches which do not cleanly click on or off. Check the heating/ventilation system for clean operation of all controls. Corrosion is not normally a problem, but poor paintwork can lead to blistering paint, and this can lead to quite bad surface rust if not spotted and dealt with early enough. Again, more a problem on pre-1988 cars than on those afterwards.

## Verdict
A brave attempt by the Spanish car company to compete with the European mainstream, but it only began to look promising when Volkswagen took over control of the company. Best versions are those made in the last two years. Avoid pre-1988 cars.

## SEAT MALAGA
Front-wheel-drive saloon and hatchback.

## History
*October 1985* Range is 1.2L, 1.5GL, 1.5GLX.
*October 1988* 1.2 Touring saloon, plus revised 1.5GLX saloon.
*August 1990* 1.7D diesel.

## Fault Finder
Like the Ibiza, Malaga quality improved after 1988. But on all cars check the paintwork for signs of bad application, paint peeling, blistering, and rust creeping out from under side window rubbers. Check the 1.2-litre engine for excessive valve wear by watching the exhaust for bluey-black smoke. Listen also for rattling rockers, often a sign of insufficient oil flow to the engine. On 1.5-litre engines, look for water leaks from bottom hoses, and listen for rattling timing chains. The 1.5-litre gearbox can also show signs of stiffness, usually caused by wear in the nylon bushes. This eventually leads to very difficult, sometimes impossible, gearchanging. As with the Ibiza, check for excessive kerbing of the front wheels, but on this car it's not as common as on the Ibiza. Make sure all door locks work properly, and that central locking switches work on all doors, this type of failure is common on the 1.5-litre GLX. Interior trim can be appallingly badly put together – it's worst on cars made from October 1985 to January 1987 – so make sure it all fits properly. As with the Ibiza, a common problem is a creaking, groaning steering wheel column, caused by the plastic surround moving, and eventually warping. Check all switches, too, these often fail to engage properly. Finally, check the boot for water leaks. This is not too

common, but a quick check is sensible.

### Verdict
Not the prettiest of cars, but pretty practical. On the face of it the Malaga is quite a good package. Unfortunately, early build quality leaves a lot to be desired. Malagas are not expensive, but bodywork is rarely in good condition. Best model is a 1.5-litre.

## SKODA ESTELLE/RAPID
Rear-wheel-drive saloon (Estelle) and coupé (Rapid).

### History
*October 1982* 120 Rapid.
*January 1984* Series 2 Estelle, 105S, 105Lux, 120L, 120LS, 120LSE.
*March 1985* 130L, 130LSE, 130 Rapid.
*April 1987* 120LX, 120LXE.
*June 1987* 130 Cabriolet Lux.
*August 1987* 130GL, 120L Five.
*August 1988* 136 Rapid.
*December 1989* 135 RiC Rapid.
*September 1990* Range discontinued.

### Fault Finder
Check for engine overheating. This is usually due to broken piping, and it can be cured, as long as it's spotted early enough. Look for oil leaks in the engine compartment. This is doubly important, firstly because leaks from the bottom of the engine are quite common on cars which are not serviced regularly, and also because engine fires often occur in Estelles with oil leaks. Check the condition of all petrol bearing pipes, again because ruptures have occured

here, and they can lead to engine fires. Check for uneven performance when accelerating hard, a trait sometimes found in Estelles built before the middle of 1985. Hard-to-adjust carburettors were the culprits, but they can be replaced with a different design. Erratic starter motors – sometimes they worked, sometimes not – could be found in some Rapid coupé models made between March and December 1985, but most of these should have been replaced by now. Brakes can suffer seized calipers on the front, but this is rare, and where it does occur it can easily be cured. Gearboxes are quite strong, but on Estelles built up to mid 1985 the remote control inside the gearbox could wear and make it very hard to select a gear. Check the clutch because clutch plates wear quite quickly on pre-85 cars. Bodywork can vary, sometimes it's first class, while on other cars the paint can peel and blister. Corrosion is not a big problem, but stone chips on the rather bluff front lead to quite bad surface rust in a short time. Check inside for good fit and finish of all trim. On convertible models look for any holes in the material caused by regular careless folding of the hood. Look for water leaks, especially around the top of the front windscreen and through the seal where the cabrio top meets the rear bootlid.

### Verdict
The Estelle and Rapid are not as bad as they are often made out to be. Performance is delivered smoothly and quietly, and handling is better than early Porsche 911s. Running costs are not high,

and there are plenty of dealers. Prices second-hand vary tremendously. Try and pick a late model Estelle 130GL, a good package of performance and equipment.

## SKODA FAVORIT
Front-wheel-drive hatchback and estate.

### History
*July 1989* 136L, 136LX.
*December 1989* 136LS.
*May 1990* Favorit Forum.
*May 1991* Forum Plus.
*June 1991* 136LS estate.

### Fault Finder
Not many problems with this car, though it hasn't been on the market for very long. Check for noisy timing chains, which you will hear rattling when the engine is ticking-over. If there's more than background rattling then the chain will need replacing. Gearboxes vary, some are very light and precise, others are quite sloppy in operation. So far, there's no news on any gearbox failures. Check all paintwork. Most Favorits have a good paint finish, but some of the earliest L and LX cars suffered from poorly applied paint, especially around the door seals, and inside the door jambs. This can blister and crack, leading to small amounts of rust which if left can spread. Body fit must be checked carefully. Examine the seals around the doors, because there have been a number of Favorits with out of line doors. As speed increases the front edge of the door, where it meets the window pillar, moves out and causes excessive wind noise, as

well as causing a draft inside the car. Likewise, check the tail-gate for a good seal, and listen for wind noise from the tail-gate area at high speed. Interior trim is tougher than normal from East European cars, and there have been few electrical problems.

### Verdict
The Favorit is easy to drive, performs quite well, and comes along at a sensible price. Second-hand values are holding up quite well, so because the car is not too expensive to begin with it means you can buy with a fair degree of confidence.

## SUBARU JUSTY
Four-wheel-drive, three- and five-door hatchbacks.

### History
*December 1986* Range is SL, SL2.
*January 1989* Revised SL2, new GL2.
*October 1989* 1.2 4WD ECVT Auto five-door.

### Fault Finder
Check the four-wheel-drive system for leaks. These are not common, but poor or irregular servicing can lead to problems here. When cornering, listen for creaks from any of the wheels – it's best to try and listen when the car is freewheeling – a sign that one or other of the driveshafts could be binding, due to lack of lubricant. Check also for uneven tyre wear, a way of checking for any misalignment of the four-wheel-drive system. This is not common on this car, but excessive kerbing of the rear wheels can cause the four-wheel-

drive to move out of alignment. Even a small movement is enough to cause problems. Look under the car at each axle, making sure there are no lubricant leaks. Gearboxes are not the toughest, so check for any crunching when trying to get into gear, a sign that the nylon bushes are wearing. On the automatic model, check for slipping gears, though this is a rare problem.

## Verdict
Due to import restrictions, a mere handful of these cars have been sold in the UK, so prices will always remain fairly competitive. Best choice is the GL2.

## SUBARU 1.6/1.8
Front-wheel-drive and four-wheel-drive saloons, coupé and estates.

## History
*November 1984* 1.8GL, 1.8GTi front-wheel-drive saloons.
*December 1984* 1.8DL 4WD, 1.8GL 4WD estates.
*April 1985* 1.6DL front-wheel-drive saloon and estate, 1.8GLSE 4WD Auto saloon, 1.8GLSE FWD estate, RX Turbo 4WD saloon, RX Turbo 4WD estate.
*June 1986* Turbo coupé 4WD.
*December 1990* Range rationalized to 1.6DL FWD saloon, 1.6DL FWD estate, 1.6DL 4WD estate, 1.8 4WD estate.

## Fault Finder
The front-wheel-drive models made from 1984 to April 1985 suffer from excessive wheel tramp when accelerating briskly, and this puts lots of strain on the driveshafts. Listen for any

groaning from the front when pulling slowly away from rest. If there is any delay between moving off and the wheels turning, accompanied by a clonk sound, then the drive shafts are wearing and should be replaced. On four-wheel-drive models the same problem can occur, but more importantly, take a look at the rear axle to check for any oil spills, and listen for a whining sound at high speed when the four-wheel-drive system is switched in. Check the centres of all wheels for any lubricant leaks, caused by worn bearings. Make sure that the four-wheel-drive lever is working smoothly, and that the wheels lock into four-wheel drive with no more than two seconds hesitation. When driving, check for any wander at low speeds. This can be caused by steering track rod ends being damaged by hard off-road use. Engines are very tough, but they are all rather noisy and when they become older – after around 80,000 miles – they can burn a lot of oil, due to valve seal wear. Subarus with less than 80,000 recorded miles should not have this problem. On versions with power-assisted steering there can be problems with leaking power steering pumps. If the steering whines when it's being turned, and it becomes progressively harder to turn the wheel, this could be the problem. On models with the hill-stop handbrake – from November 1986 – check this is working properly. Corrosion is not generally a problem, but on a 4x4 Subaru which has been used off-road – many are bought by farmers – check for broken paint along the sills, and any rust. Check that the sump guard which is fitted to all 4x4 Subarus has not been severely dented, because in serious cases this can affect the bottom of the sump. On estate versions which have been fitted with a tow bar, check the exhaust for black smoke, a sign that hard work has caused valve wear. This problem is most common on 1.6-litre versions and requires expensive engine repairs.

### Verdict
These Subarus are amongst the most reliable cars on the roads today. And even though the latest Subaru dual range four-wheel-drive system is not the most modern, it's an effective system which loyal owners swear by. If possible, go for a version made after 1986 because the 4x4 system, and engine refinement, are considerably better.

## SUBARU LEGACY
Four-wheel-drive saloon and estate.

### History
*October 1989* 1.8GL saloon, 1.8GL estate, 2.2iGX saloon, 2.2iGX estate.
*March 1991* 1.8GL Eco saloon, 1.8GL Eco estate.
*December 1991* 2.0 Turbo saloon, 2.0 Turbo estate.

### Fault Finder
A full service history is very important here because the four-wheel-drive system demands regular expert attention to keep it in tip-top condition. Check the tyres for uneven wear which can be caused by the four-wheel-drive

system being even slightly out of alignment. This is not a common problem on this car. Body work is good, corrosion virtually unheard of. Check the turbocharger for smooth running, but, again, no major problems so far.

### Verdict
The Legacy is another of those cars which impresses with its reliability. As the range gets older, and owners may neglect servicing, it's possible that more problems will occur, either with engines or the 4x4 system, but for the moment this looks like an excellent second-hand buy. Prices are quite high for 2-year-old Legacys, but first-year depreciation is substantial.

## SUBARU XT TURBO
Four-wheel-drive coupé.

### History
*July 1985* XT Turbo launched.
*June 1987* Revised and slightly restyled XT Turbo.
*October 1990* Discontinued.

### Fault Finder
Prior to June 1987 the 4x4 system was switchable, not permanent, and this system is not as reliable as the permanent 4x4 launched in June 1987. So, check for leaks of lubricant from the four-wheel-drive couplings on each wheel. Make sure that the 4x4 selector lever operates smoothly. It's vital to check the front drive shafts for any groaning or clicking due to worn CV joints because this car is very powerful, and hectic driving can damage the driveshafts. On automatic gearbox versions check for difficulty selecting reverse

gear. This is not a common fault, but some XTs produced towards the end of 1985 had poor gear selectors which could wear after relatively low mileage – around 35,000 miles. On versions produced after June 1987, check for gears failing to change up smoothly on the four-speed automatic gearbox. Again, not that common, but some of the earliest cars had problems with the bushes inside the gearbox, sometimes causing the gears to stick.

**Verdict**
Reliability is always a strong XT point, but the styling of the car made it less attractive to buyers. The earliest models should be avoided – before June 1987 – because the ride and handling were not that impressive and the four-wheel-drive system was not one of the best.

**SUZUKI SWIFT**
Front-wheel-drive hatchback and saloon.

**History**
*March 1985* Swift launched in 1.3GS form.
*November 1986* Totally new Swift launched. Five-door 1.3GLX, 1.3GLX Executive, 1.3GTi.
*March 1988* 1.3GL.
*December 1988* Heavily revised 1.3GTi.
*April 1989* Heavily revised 1.3GLX.
*April 1990* 1.6GLX 4WD saloon.

**Fault Finder**
No major engine problems here, but the twin-cam GTi engine must be checked for noisy camshaft

belts. Ideally, they should be replaced every 36,000 miles, so if this hasn't been done, make sure the work is carried out as soon as possible. GTi models made after December 1988 seem to have longer lasting camshaft belts, and in many cases they can easily go on to 70,000 miles without mishap. On all models, but especially on pre-1988 GTis, check the front driveshafts for wear, and make sure that the rubber gaiters on the shafts are not split, and leaking fluid. Gearboxes are not the strongest, with second gear losing its synchromesh rather quickly. Nylon bushes in the gearboxes can also wear after as little as 30,000 miles, especially if the Swift has been used in heavy town traffic, so listen for any crunching or difficult gear selection. Interior trim is quite flimsy, so check everything fits properly. The cars made after April 1989 are the best, before that, the older they are, the worse they can be.

**Verdict**
Not a bad car, with fine mechanicals and decent paintwork finish. The Swift can be disappointing inside, with early models shedding trim. Best buy is the very swift GTi made after 1988, as long as it comes with a full service history.

**SUZUKI SJ**
Four-wheel-drive multi-purpose vehicle.

**History**
*June 1982* SJ 410 Q soft top.
*October 1982* SJ 410 WV 3-door.
*October 1985* SJ 413 VX.

*March 1987* Spanish-built Santana hard top. Santana Sport soft top.

*August 1989* Santana SJ 410 Sport hard top.

*July 1990* Samurai SJ 413 long wheelbase hard top. SJ 413 becomes Samurai SJ 413.

### Fault Finder

SJs built between 1982 and 1985 suffer from poor engine noise suppression. The engines should be examined carefully for oil leaks from the top of the engine. Check the dipstick for bubbles of water mixed in the oil, a sign that the head gasket has failed, this is a particularly important check on any SJ which has covered more than 50,000 miles. Check the front wheels for correct tracking and balance, as regular kerbing affects the steering and tracking geometry. Look at the front drive differential for large oil leaks. This is very important on the SJs made during 1982 because underside protection was not great. On all models check the freewheeling front hubs for smooth operation, because if they are not working, usually due to corrosion, the four-wheel-drive cannot be brought into action. Check for smooth operation of the four-wheel-drive lever, because lack of servicing can cause the lever's mechanism to seize. This is a particularly important check if the SJ has been used regularly off-road where mud and water can get inside the differential box, causing corrosion which stops the system working. The Santana versions are Spanish-made and their quality is not as good as the Japanese-built SJs. Check for poor paint application and shoddy trim inside. The gearboxes in the Santana do not seem to last as long as the units in the SJ. In particular, check for severe rattling when the clutch is depressed, a sign that gearbox bearings need replacing. On all soft-top models check the condition of the fabric. The material is not too tough, and is susceptible to rips. Check also for corroded hood attachments, especially where the hood latches onto the side of the body. In the cargo decks, check for corrosion to the steel floors, a vitally important check if a farmer has been a previous owner, because anti-corrosion measures have only been stepped up in the last two years.

### Verdict

The SJ/Santana is a classic case of attractive, chunky looks allied to a noisy engine and poor on-road suspension. None of these vehicles are that pleasant to drive, performance is limited and space inside is cramped. But, off-road this little machine is a match for any other mud-plugger. Best buy is the reasonably comfortable Samurai.

### SUZUKI VITARA

Four-wheel-drive multi-purpose vehicle.

### History

*October 1988* JLX, JLX SE hard tops.

*August 1989* JLX soft top.

*December 1989* JLX SE Auto.

*July 1991* Revisions to SE models, giving them more power, improved sound insulation.

*December 1991* Five-door JLX long wheelbase estate.

## Fault Finder

Very reliable, but check for smooth operation of the four-wheel-drive lever, a light and smooth gearchange, and if the Vitara has been used off-road, have a good look underneath for any damage. The JLX and SE models made in October–December 1988 sometimes have problems with seized brake calipers on the nearside wheel. If this problem exists the Vitara will pull to the left when braking. Repair is inexpensive. Pre-1991 versions sometimes suffered from poor oil feed and this could make the engine rockers noisy. Listen for a clattering sound when the engine is gently revved. Check the back of the rear seat for rips caused by dogs. Many Vitara owners have dogs, and they can easily cause damage to the flimsy plastic seat backs.

## Verdict

So far, reliability has been very good, with very few faults occurring. The best buys are the five-door model which has better suspension than the three door version, and more room, or the three-door SE, which offers a high equipment level. Best versions are those made after July 1991, because they are more powerful, and more refined.

## TOYOTA STARLET
Front-wheel-drive hatchback.

## History
*January 1985* 1.0GL.
*April 1990* New Starlet 1.0GL.

## Fault Finder
Some of the earliest metallic

painted models, those produced in early 1985, suffer from chipping paint around the headlamps. The clutch is a hydraulic system, so there is no clutch cable. This seems to work well, and there have been few cases of failure. If the clutch lacks feel, there could be a leak, but this is rare. Mechanically this car is a marvel. As long as it is serviced according to the schedule there should not be any problem. Even at 100,000 miles the engines are still going strong, sometimes consuming a little more oil than when new, but there is no history of serious valve or crankshaft wear. Carry out the usual checks for oil leaks, and check for smooth operation of the gearbox. Interior trim is strong, electrics last well, and as long as the bodywork is well looked after there should not be any problems.

## Verdict

Stunningly reliable, it's usually hard to find anything wrong with the Starlet. Even after 100,000 miles it's rare for anything to go wrong, and that includes the smallest fault. The only potential problem area over really long-term ownership will be the condition of the bodywork. Do watch for metallic colours which have faded, usually on the bonnet and fronts of the wings.

## TOYOTA TERCEL
Front-wheel-drive and four-wheel-drive hatchback and estate.

## History
*October 1982* 1.3GL three- and five-door.
*March 1982* Four-wheel-drive estate.

*February 1985* Revised 4WD estate, with body changes and revised gearbox.

*September 1984* 1.3GL discontinued.

*October 1988* 4WD discontinued.

**Fault Finder**

On the front-wheel-drive 1.3GL, listen to the engine carefully for rattles when it's ticking-over. Tercels built in 1982 and early 1983 sometimes suffered from poor oil flow to the engine rockers, and eventually this can cause damage to the top of the engine. Check all water hoses, especially the bottom ones, for chafing and wear. This is a check which has to be carried out on all Tercels. Gearboxes on 4x4 Tercels built between 1983 and 1985 feature a crawler gear in addition to the usual five forward gears. Perhaps because of the additional complexity of the gearbox, there have been cases of worn bearings, and even gear stripping which has caused metal to float around in the gearbox, sometimes causing so much damage that the gearbox has to be completely replaced. Check for any rattling when the clutch is depressed, and if it's hard to get into any gear, try another Tercel instead. Check both axles very carefully on 4x4 Tercels for any signs of leaking fluid, either from the driveshafts, or the axle differential. Check the front suspension struts on all Tercels built between 1983 and 1985 for leaks, and check the rear suspension system for sagging, especially if a tow bar has been fitted. The rear suspension was not tough enough, and could be damaged if heavy loads were regularly hauled. On all Tercels before 1986 check

the paintwork carefully. It was rather thin, and this could lead to surface rust, most commonly on the front wings and at the bottom edges of the front doors.

**Verdict**

The Tercel never became one of Toyota's top sellers, but the 4x4 is a useful machine with a good level of comfort, equipment and performance. Best choice has to be one of the 1986 to 1988 4x4 versions.

**TOYOTA COROLLA**

Front-wheel and four-wheel-drive saloon, hatchback, estate, rear-wheel-drive coupé.

**History**

*September 1983* 1.3GL saloon and Liftback (hatchback).

*February 1984* 1.6GT coupé (rear-wheel-drive).

*February 1985* 1.3GL, 1.6GT hatchbacks.

*August 1986* 1.3GL Executive Liftback.

*September 1987* Totally new front-wheel-drive Corolla range. 1.3GL hatchback, 1.3GL saloon, 1.3GL estate, 1.6GL Executive hatchback, 1.6GTi hatchback.

*March 1988* 1.6 4WD estate.

*October 1989* Heavily revised equipment and trim, 1.6GTi gets more powerful engine.

**Fault Finder**

Engines are mostly reliable, but it's very important to check the condition of the camshaft belts on the 1.6GT rear-wheel-drive coupé. The cam belts are quite reliable but they do have to be changed regularly, and that's something which is often ignored by the second or third owner. Check the service history to find out when the belts have been changed – it really should be about every 36,000 miles – and if there is no record and the car still sounds sweet, get it done as soon as possible. On the other hand, if the engine sounds rattly on tick-over it's best to look for another car. Another area to look at on the coupé is the condition of the rear axle. This is a very powerful car, and the driveshaft takes a real pummelling. Listen for any grumbling or whining from the rear of the car at average speeds, and at low speeds listen for a soft knocking sound from the rear. If either of these are present the repair costs will be high. The 1.6GTi needs similar care, but it's less likely to have the camshaft belt problem. The front driveshafts need checking over because on hard driven GTis the shafts can wear quite quickly. It's easy to spot; a knocking sound when the steering is turned fully to left or right at slow speeds, and a delayed lurch from the wheels when you pull away. On Corollas built between 1983 and 1987 check the front tyres for uneven wear. The steering and suspension is relatively sensitive, so that even hitting potholes at speed can cause the steering geometry to go off-centre. Bodywork on all models is usually good, a rusty Corolla will be one which has not been well looked after.

**Verdict**
A good, honest car, the Corolla is not going to set anyone's pulse fluttering – with the notable exception of the hair-raising GT Coupé – but it is reliable, both versions still

look modern, and it is capable of very high mileage without any mechanical problems. Best all round choice is a 1.3GL hatchback.

## TOYOTA CARINA
Front-wheel-drive saloon, estate and hatchback (Liftback).

**History**
*April 1984* 1.6GL, 2.0GLD diesel saloons, 1.6GL Liftback.
*March 1988* New Carina range, 1.6GL saloon, 1.6GL Liftback, 1.6GL estate, 2.0GL Executive Liftback.
*March 1990* 1.6XL saloon and Liftback.
*February 1991* 2.0XL diesel saloon and Liftback, 2.0 Executive saloon, 1.6GL estate, 1.6XL estate.

**Fault Finder**
1.6-litre engines can burn rather a lot of oil once they've covered high mileages – 70,000 miles plus – so look at the condition of the exhaust to see if it is black inside, a sign of excessive oil-burn. From March 1988 all Carina engines are very good, with no known history of excessive oil consumption or serious oil leaks. Check manual steering on all pre-1988 Carinas for heaviness. Some cars have suffered lubricant leaks from the steering racks, causing the system to become heavier. Cure is easy, and not expensive.

**Verdict**
Quite uninspiring, but exceptionally reliable, and for many people that is the major plus about owning a Carina. The best are those made after 1988, before then

the Carina was not very pleasant to drive, with ponderous steering and a poor suspension set-up. Best model is a 1.6XL Liftback.

## TOYOTA CAMRY
Front-wheel-drive and four-wheel-drive saloon and estate.

### History
*May 1983* 1.8GL saloon.
*April 1984* 1.8 diesel turbo, 2.0GLi saloons.
*November 1984* 2.0 Executive saloon.
*October 1985* Turbo diesel gets 2.0-litre engine.
*January 1987* New Camry launched, 2.0GLi saloon, 2.0GLi Executive saloon, 2.0GLi estate.
*March 1988* 2.0GLi 4WD saloon, 2.0GLi Executive estate.
*March 1989* V6 GXi Auto saloon.

### Fault Finder
Some 1984 diesel turbo Camrys had problems with the turbocharger. Check that the turbo boosts in cleanly, without hesitation, and that when it comes off-boost it does so without rattling or loudly wheezing, the former a result of the loose turbine blades hitting the sides of the unit, the latter a sign of an air leak in one of the turbo's main pipes. On V6 Automatic GXi saloons, make sure that the gearbox changes up smoothly. Although not a common problem, there have been a few cases of the electric selector switch becoming stuck, so holding the car in a low gear. This is an erratic problem which does not occur all of the time, and seems mostly to have affected some 1989 V6 models. On V6 models, check the brake discs because this car has quite an appetite for brake pads. If the car is regularly serviced this should not be a problem, but scored discs are often the result when servicing is not carried out regularly enough.

### Verdict
Another of Toyota's very reliable cars, the Camry has evolved into a well equipped, very desirable car. Unfortunately, prices have marched ahead, too, and when coupled with this car's inherent reliability it means second-hand prices are high. Best model is a V6 GXi, but if that's rather expensive, the 2.0GLi Executive is well worth looking at.

## TOYOTA MR2
Rear-wheel-drive, mid-engined sports coupé.

### History
*March 1985* MR2 launched.
*October 1986* MR2 T-Bar.
*April 1990* Completely new MR2. MR2GT (more powerful version) GT T-Bar.

### Fault Finder
Regular servicing is a must. Check for a full service record. Engines are reliable, but only if the oil has been changed at the set service intervals. If the oil looks dirty, or the engine rattles noisily on tick-over, the oil could be thickening, and affecting engine performance and longevity. Performance should be smooth, refined, and free of hiccups. If there is any hesitation it may point to lack of servicing. Check for accident repairs as many

of these cars have been driven too quickly by inexperienced drivers, resulting in accidents. Tyres and suspension should be checked. Tyres for any undue wear, and also for their condition. This car demands good quality tyres, and they should all be the same make. Suspension mounts have been known to become sloppy with hard driving. Check the car when cornering; it should be taut, with no body roll. The gearchange should be precise, light and smooth. If it is sloppy it may need no more than the gear-lever tightening-up, but if there is any tightness when changing gear it could signal imminent gearbox failure. This is not common, but on poorly maintained, or hard driven MR2s it's not unknown. Any lurching or hesitation when moving off from rest can signal worn engine mounts – not usually something which occurs until around 80,000 miles – but easily replaced. Make sure they are replaced as soon as they are suspect because running the MR2 on worn mounts can cause the premature death of the exhaust system. Again, because of the performance, items such as brake pads wear quickly – a set may last no more than 10,000 miles. If the MR2 you're interested in has anything less than very quiet, smooth and efficient brakes there could be a problem here. Repair or replacement is not too expensive, even if a new set of discs are needed. Sometimes you will see an MR2 with one headlight up, one down, a symptom of a failed motor, but it must be said that this is a rare occurrence. Electrics are mostly reliable, but electric windows have been known

to fail on the earliest cars. Not because of motor failure but because the window is operated by cable, and this can sometimes jump off its pulleys and become tangled. Wheel bearings suffer as a result of hard driving. They can be heard as a low rumbling from any of the wheels when travelling at low speeds, building to a whine at higher speeds. Check the exhaust, because repair and replacement is quite expensive, but on the plus side, the system should last for around 80,000 miles. Rust is not normally a problem but because the car is close to the ground it does pick up a large number of stone chips on the bonnet and the tops of the pop-up headlights.

### Verdict
Essentially reliable, holds its value well but it has taken a knock because of the new MR2, even though that car is in a different, more expensive class. Best model is the Targa which allows open-topped motoring, plus all the benefits of the hard top.

### TOYOTA CELICA/SUPRA
Front- and rear-wheel-drive, four-wheel-drive sports coupés, convertible and sports hatchbacks.

### History
*February 1982* Rear-wheel-drive 2.0ST coupé and three-door Liftback.
*August 1982* Celica Supra 2.8i.
*February 1984* 2.0XT, 2.0XT Liftback.
*November 1985* New front-wheel-drive Celica 2.0GT Liftback.
*July 1986* Totally new rear-wheel-drive Supra 3.0i.

*March 1987* Celica Cabriolet.
*March 1988* GT-Four coupé with four-wheel drive.
*January 1989* Supra 3.0i Turbo.
*February 1990* Totally new front-wheel-drive Celica. GT, 4WD GT-Four.

## Fault Finder

No major engine problems with these cars, it's rare to get an engine oil leak, even with high mileage. Make sure that on 2.0-litre and 3.0-litre cars the camshaft belts are replaced around 36,000 miles, just to be on the safe side. The GT-4 has a double overhead cam engine so it's doubly important that the camshaft belts are in good condition. Listen for any undue rattling from the engine on tick-over and spend just as long scrutinizing the service history to see if the belts have been changed. If any of these cars have covered more than 60,000 miles without a belt change it should be carried out as soon as possible. On the GT-4 models, check all of the drive couplings for any leaks, or groans when cornering, and listen for any knocks from the front when going over bumpy surfaces. This can point to wear of the bottom suspension points, a problem on high mileage GT-4s. On Supra models, check the rear axle for any rumbling at low to medium speeds. This is a common problem on high mileage (70,000 plus) Turbo versions where wear to the driveshaft has resulted from hard driving. Gearboxes are very reliable, but on all of these cars hard driving may have robbed the gearbox of synchromesh on second gear. While this is not terribly serious in itself, it does point to an unsympathetic driver.

## Verdict

The Celicas and the Supras have a loyal following. Both cars are very reliable, but there are a number of them, especially Supras, which have been involved in accidents, due to that handful of over-enthusiastic but poorly skilled drivers. Choose carefully.

## TOYOTA SPACE CRUISER

Rear-wheel-drive people carrier.

## History

*April 1983* Space Cruiser launched with 1.8-litre petrol engine.
*February 1985* New 2.0-litre engine replaces previous unit.
*September 1990* Discontinued.

## Fault Finder

Check the 1.8-litre engines for overheating – look closely at the temperature gauge during the test drive – and examine for oil leaks. Because the engine is slung under the front seats, cooling is not too efficient, so the engine runs very hot. This can lead to oil leaks forming at the bottom of the engine, so check underneath, as well. The 1.8-litre engined Space Cruiser's engine mounts can wear within 40,000 miles. If this has happened you should feel the movement of the engine as you're driving along. Check also that the exhaust manifold is intact, because if the mounts have gone the engine movement is often enough to snap the exhaust's manifold bolts. The gearchange is not the best, with assorted distances between each gearchange. This meant that many drivers were less than sympathetic with the gearchange, so stripping metal off the cogs, eventually leading to damage inside the gearbox. Check the rubber cover at the bottom of the steering column, between the clutch and brake pedals, because this can wear and split, and if it's left like that the steering linkage can get grit in which eventually causes the system to bind. Brakes can bind on the rear, due to malfunctioning brake compensation valves, so try a few quick stops. The 2.0-litre Space Cruiser had modifications to make it safer during an emergency stop. Early models tipped forwards quite alarmingly when braking hard. Check the electrics because although generally reliable, in 1984 there were a batch of 1.8-litre versions with faulty relay switches, which meant that the electric sun-roofs sometimes worked, and sometimes didn't. Most of these switches should have been replaced by now. Check the bodywork over carefully, because although paintwork was always very good, the length of the Space Cruiser is awkward for many inexperienced drivers, so the rear three quarters panels often become dented. Check the tail-gate catch to make sure it closes and locks properly, most of them wear and the latch eventually refuses to engage.

## Verdict
The Space Cruiser was one of the first people carriers and it proved very successful. But it has quickly been overtaken by newcomers which are much more purpose-built, rather than being based directly on a van, as was the Space Cruiser. If you can find a good one, the model to aim for is the 2.0-litre,

this has the best engine, better suspension and retains a healthier resale value.

## TOYOTA LANDCRUISER
Four-wheel-drive multi-purpose vehicle.

### History
*July 1981* Landcruiser estate with 4.0-litre diesel engine, 2800 saloon.
*March 1988* New Landcruiser, called Landcruiser II. Short wheelbase estate with 2.5-litre turbo diesel engine.
*June 1990* Landcruiser VX long wheelbase with six cylinder 4.2-litre turbo diesel engine.

### Fault Finder
On all versions built before 1988, check the four-wheel-drive system carefully, starting with a look underneath for any lubricant leaks from the drive axles. Look also for damage caused by hard off-road use. The steering has lots of play in it, but there have been problems with worn track rod ends. If the steering makes a clacking sound when travelling on a bumpy surface it needs attention. On models with power assisted steering, turn the wheel over full left, then full right, listening for any creaking or groaning. It will hiss, this is normal, but it should not make any other sounds. If the power steering gets heavier when turning, then there may be a leak in the system. On models made before March 1985, check the front suspension for leaks, and if the Land Cruiser has been regularly used off-road, check the suspension for undue sideways movement, a common

problem with the earlier models. Prior to 1985, the gearboxes were strong but prone to losing synchromesh in second gear. Again, before March 1985, check that the lever to change from low- to high-ratio four-wheel-drive works smoothly. Some do not, simply because they've become corroded. On models after March 1985, Toyota fitted a dashboard mounted electronic switch to go from low to high ratio. Check that this works. There have not been any major problems here, but on some Land Cruisers the electric solenoid has failed on this switch, thus rendering it useless. This problem applies only to a few vehicles produced in mid 1985 and by now all should have been cured. From April 1988 a new four-wheel-drive system was fitted. This is an automatic version and it's very efficient, but it does demand proper and regular servicing to keep it in first-class condition. So check the front and rear axles, and the centre diff, for any oil leaks. On the move, listen for any loud rumbling or whining from the diffs. Bodywork on pre-1985 models need a careful look because rust took hold under the wheelarches and often ate right through the wings, and the tail-gate is also very prone to corrosion. On versions built from 1985 to 1988 the rust problems are less acute, but check anyway. On post-1988 models anti-corrosion protection is first class.

### Verdict
The early Land Cruisers, anything before 1985, should be avoided. Land Cruisers built between 1985 and 1988 were an improvement, yet still not as refined as most rivals. Since 1988 this Toyota has come of age, and the latest version is as good as most competitors. Choose as late a model as possible, but don't dismiss the early ones, at least they are inexpensive, and mechanically they are fairly sound.

## VAUXHALL NOVA
Front-wheel-drive hatchback and saloon.

### History
*April 1983* Range of two-door saloons, three-door hatchbacks launched, 1.0, 1.2L.
*September 1983* 1.0L, 1.2, two-door saloons and three-door hatchbacks.
*January 1984* 1.2GL saloon and hatchback.
*May 1985* Revised range, two- and four-door saloons, three- and five-door hatchbacks. Range is 1.0, 1.0 Merit, 1.2 Merit, 1.2L, 1.3L, 1.3GL, 1.3SR.
*August 1986* 1.0-litre five-door.
*August 1987* 1.3L three-door.
*July 1988* 1.6i GTE three-door.
*October 1989* 1.4-litre engine replaces 1.3-litre.
*November 1989* 1.5TD turbo diesel three-door.
*November 1990* Completely revised range, 1.0 Trip, 1.0 Merit, 1.2 Merit, 1.2 Luxe, 1.2 Flair, 1.4i Merit, 1.4 Luxe, 1.4 Flair, 1.4 SR, 1.5 Merit TD, 1.6 GSi.

### Fault Finder
Most care needs to be taken if choosing a 1.0, 1.3 or 1.6-litre car as all of these engines either suffer from bad oil leaks, or they consume camshafts. Look under the

bonnet for any evidence of major oil leaks – oil which has dripped down on to the chassis members, for example – and listen carefully when the engine is ticking over. This is very important on 1.6-litre cars because they get through camshafts quicker than most other engines. Listen for a knocking sound when the engine is idling, because many Novas made from 1983 to 1986 had faulty fuel pumps. You may also notice this when driving the car because it will give jerky performance when accelerating hard. This is a particular problem with 1.2 and 1.3-litre cars. The gearboxes are fine in the more humble cars, but the 1.3SR gearbox does not last long, especially if the car has been driven hard, which it usually has. Vanished synchromesh is usually the first sign, followed by a reluctance to slot into gear, and then progressively worse crunching as the gearbox gets older. On all Novas made from 1983 to 1986, check the front driveshaft gaiters because they tend to split quite easily, allowing damage to be caused to the CV joints. Interiors on all but the latest Novas – those built during 1990–2 are very flimsy and not well fitted. Check this over carefully because there have even been cases of the dashboard becoming completely detached from the car's bulkhead. Rust is not usually a problem, but stone chips can make a nasty mess of the bonnet. Also check under the rear wheelarches to see if rust is forming, and trying to eat its way through the rear wings. On saloon versions, look under the floor covering in the boot for any signs of rust caused by leaks into the boot. On the outside, look for rust on the edge of the bootlid.

## Verdict
In many ways the Nova is a tough car, but the flimsy dashboards on early models, the camshaft problems and those knocking fuel pumps mean that buying second-hand is not as easy as it might be. But, avoid the troublesome cars and you can end up with a faithful and fairly solid hatchback. Best versions are the 1.6iGTE and the excellent 1.5 turbo diesel.

## VAUXHALL ASTRA AND BELMONT
Front-wheel-drive hatchback, saloon, estate.

## History
*May 1980* 1.3L five-door.

*October 1980* 1200E, 1200L two-and four-door saloons, 1300L, 1300GL three-door hatchbacks, 1300L three-door estate.

*January 1982* 1600L, 1600GL five-door hatchbacks.

*February 1982* 1200E, 1200L three-door hatchbacks, 1200L five-door hatchback, 1300E estate.

*June 1982* 1600L diesel three-door hatchback, 1600L diesel five-door estate.

*September 1982* 1600SR three-door hatchback, 1200 hatchback, 1300GL estate, 1600GL estate.

*April 1983* 1.8GTE three-door hatchback, 1600L diesel five-door hatchbach.

*October 1984* Totally new Astra/Belmont range, 1200, 1300, 1600 three- and five-door hatchbacks and estates in Base, L and GL trim, plus 1800GTE three-door and 1600SR hatchback.

*January 1986* Belmont four-door saloon version launched. Range is 1300L, 1300GL, 1600L, 1600GL, 1600GLS, 1600LD diesel, 1800GLSi.

*August 1986* 1.2 Merit, 1.3 Merit, 1.6D Merit three- and five-door hatchbacks, plus estates, replace Base versions. 1.6LD diesel hatchback and estate, 1.8SRi three- and five-door hatchback replaces GTE. Belmont 1.6GL diesel.

*January 1987* Belmont 1800SRi.

*March 1987* 2.0GTE three-door hatchback.

*April 1987* 1.6 convertible, 2.0GTE convertible.

*August 1987* Belmont 1.3 Merit.

*May 1988* 2.0GTE 16-valve three-door hatchback.

*January 1989* Heavily revised trim and equipment on all models, both Astra and Belmont, 1.8iCD five-door hatchback and Belmont launched. Diesels get more powerful 1.6-litre engine. 1.8iLX estate.

*September 1989* 1.6 Merit Auto three and five-door hatchbacks and Belmont.

*October 1989* 1.4-litre engine replaces 1.3-litre. 1.4LX three- and five-door hatchbacks, 1.6LX five-door hatchback, plus Belmont versions of each.

## Fault Finder

Engine camshaft failure is common on many 1.2, 1.3 and 1.6-litre petrol models. Some only last 30,000 miles, while most fail at 50,000–60,000 miles. If not spotted early enough the resultant

damage usually means a new engine is needed. Listen for excess whine and thrash from the engine when revved, look for major oil leaks on the top of the engine, both are signs of potential camshaft trouble. 1980–2 – Saloon versions should be avoided (two- and four-door) because quality control was poor. From 1980–5 there were car-burettor problems on 1.2 and 1.3-litre cars, making for poor running and heavy fuel consumption. If there is a problem here the car-burettor may need to be changed. During 1984–5 there were problems with paint adherence. Some of these cars may have flaking paint, or bad resprays, there could also be rust. From 1984 onwards, rust should not be a problem. If it is, the car may well have been involved in an accident and not been repaired properly. The exception are high mileage examples (100,000 plus) which can suffer from rusty front wings. Between 1980–3 some Astras have leaking fuel pumps. Check for signs of weeping petrol around the pump, in the engine bay. Replacement is not expensive, and it's a quick job. On cars produced during 1982–4 engine spark plugs often didn't make proper, clean contact, so causing harsh running. In severe cases the car will keep stalling, and often prove impossible to restart. On Astras/Belmonts produced during 1980–4 body resonance and booming mechanical noise means passengers in the back of three-door versions can rarely hear those talking in the front at speeds above 60mph. On models made during 1989–91 there is a petrol evaporation problem with fuel-injected models. When the engine gets hot, sitting in traffic for example, the fuel injection can cut out. Once it's cooled back down, the engine can be restarted, and runs smoothly again. This problem can only be checked by letting the engine idle for at least half an hour. On GTE models there have been occasional problems with the digital dashboards. This can easily be checked by looking over the digital information. If there is a fault there will be a tell-tale sign; the speed reading going backwards, or the temperature gauge climbing to hot as soon as you turn the engine on. If there is a problem it can be expensive because a dealer will put a whole new unit in, it's too high-tech to be repaired at a Vauxhall dealership. On all models, make sure you check the rubber boots over the front driveshafts on each front wheel. They should be intact and not suffering from any leaks. All models can suffer with this problem if the boots are neglected or damaged. Check by driving slowly around a corner and listening for clonking or groaning from the front. Also, when moving away from rest, if there is a hesitant lurch at the front there could well be a problem, and it could be expensive. Front disc brakes easily become damaged because brake pads have a tendency to wear quickly, especially on high performance SRi and GTE versions. Check for any damage by running a finger from the inside to the outside edge of each disc. If less than smooth, they will need replacing. Check for regular servicing, it's a must because oil must be changed regularly, otherwise there can still be problems today with engine camshafts and engine

bearings. You will usually hear the problem, a deathly rattle from the engine when revved hard. Oil should be changed at least every 6,000 miles, even though the service interval is 9,000 miles (4,500 miles for a diesel). The engine temperature sensing unit can become rusty, and so lead to rough and temperamental running. Check by driving at least 10 miles. The nearside rear tyre has a tendency to wear before any of the others. It's a problem which can be cured by proper service attention, when the tyres should all be checked for correct balance. But any such tyre wear could also mean that the car has been involved in a serious accident which has bent the floorpan. Check the underside of the car for any creasing of the floorpan. If there is any, leave that car well alone. On Convertibles, check for rain damage inside the car, although leaking Astra convertibles are very rare. Rear vision with the roof down is abysmal, a car can easily be hidden behind you, so take care when reversing. A badly creaking convertible should be avoided, but expect some minor creaking, especially when cornering, and especially on early versions (1987 models).

### Verdict

A sound family car with a large choice of models. Relatively little goes wrong. Best choices are 1.4-litre models introduced from October 1989, 1.8-litre SRi and 2.0-litre GTE. The 16-valve GTE is hardly worth the extra cost over the basic GTE. Diesels are good performers and economical on fuel, but demand servicing every 4,500 miles, so service costs can be quite high.

## VAUXHALL CAVALIER
Front-wheel-drive and four-wheel-drive saloon, hatchback and estate.

### History
*September 1981* Range launched, consisting of two- and four-door 1300 saloons, 1600 saloons, five-door 1300 and 1600 hatchbacks. Trim levels are, Base, L, GL, SR, GLS.

*June 1982* 1.6L diesel four-door saloon and five-door hatchback.

*September 1982* Equipment improvements across the range.

*October 1982* 1800CD, 1800SRi saloons and hatchbacks.

*September 1983* 1600 Base, L, GL five-door estates, plus 1300, 1600 five-door hatchbacks.

*April 1984* 1600LD diesel five-door estate.

*January 1985* 1800GLi, GLSi saloons and hatchbacks.

*February 1986* 1800i two-door convertible.

*August 1986* 2.0iCD saloon and hatchback, 1.8-litre engine becomes more powerful.

*March 1987* SRi 130 saloon and five-door hatchback.

*August 1987* SRi models get more powerful 2.0-litre injection engine.

*October 1987* 1600LX, 1800LXi saloons and hatchbacks.

*October 1988* Totally new front-wheel-drive Cavalier replaces previous models. Range is 1.4, 1.6, 1.7 diesel, 2.0i. Trim levels are Base, L, GL, CD SRi.

*January 1989* 2.0i 4x4 saloon.

*September 1989* 1.8L and 1.8GL.

*October 1989* GSi 2000 16-valve, GSi 2000 4x4 saloons.

*September 1990* 1.8iL, 1.8iGL in saloon and hatchback.

*April 1991* 1.7GLD diesel saloon and hatchback.

### Fault Finder
On 1.6-litre petrol versions made from 1981 to 1987 it's very important to check on the condition of the camshaft. First, listen for a growling noise from the engine when it's gently revved. Check the service record to see if the camshaft belt has been replaced. It's wise to do this about every 36,000 miles, especially on a car which is covering a high mileage very quickly. Check for oil leaks from the top of the engine. These can be quite serious and on some cars it results in the engine being coated in oil. Most second-hand buyers are likely to see the car once the engine has been steam-cleaned, so check carefully for leaks of oil. Gearboxes are very hard wearing, and it's rare to find a manual gearbox with any problem – they don't even lose their synchromesh very easily – they just get lighter and slicker as the miles go by. It's not unusual to find a Cavalier with 100,000 miles on the clock with a perfect gearbox. It's always worth pushing the clutch down with the engine running, and listening for rattling from the bottom of the gearbox, but there is always some noise, it's only when it's very intrusive that you should worry. On automatic gearbox versions you must check for gear slipping, or gears being held on to for too long. This was a problem with some 1.6-litre cars produced from 1990 to 1991. On manual steering

systems the track rod ends can wear quite badly on cars which have covered over 70,000 miles. If there is more than a few centimetres of play in the steering at the straight ahead position, or the steering makes a clacking sound over bumps, this is likely to be the problem. Repair is not expensive. Check the rubber covers which the steering rods go through, in the engine compartment. These often become virtually shredded on high mileage cars, and it means that water can get into the engine compartment, causing possible damage to the alternator. Check the brake discs because Cavaliers from the 1.6 upwards have a voracious appetite for brake pads. Careless owners will have left them until they begin to score the discs. Check for this by running a finger over the front discs. If they are scored they will need replacing. Check the automatic choke because it doesn't always work, this is a particular problem on all 1.6-litre cars, even the newest, and the problem becomes more regular the older the car becomes. On cars which have covered more than 60,000 miles it's important to check the condition of the shock absorbers. If the car is very floaty, and yet crashes over bumps, the shock absorbers need changing. On cars with electrically operated door mirrors it's common for the switch to malfunction. A faulty one will still push the door mirrors outwards, but it won't bring them back towards you. Interior trim should be in good condition; Vauxhall's quality control on the Cavalier is first class, almost as good as an Audi, so if the trim is shabby, or bits are broken, look for another car because this is a sign of an uncaring owner. Paintwork on all cars can become very flat, losing its shine. This is a particular problem on solid blue Cavaliers which have covered 70,000 miles plus and it usually occurs along the sides of the wings and on the bonnet. Check for corrosion creeping out from under the window rubbers, especially on the back doors, and also check the bottom of the back doors, particularly near the wheelarch because this is a favourite area for rust to begin from. And finally, a word of warning, many Cavaliers are used as company cars, so mileage is normally very high. Check the service records to make sure that the mileage is genuine.

### Verdict
Currently the UK's best selling car, and with good reason too. The Cavalier is well made, good to drive and will last for at least 100,000 miles without major trauma. Some of the best versions are those with the 1.4-litre engine, a gutsy performer which also offers good fuel economy.

## VAUXHALL CALIBRA
Front-wheel-drive and four-wheel-drive sports coupé.

### History
*June 1990* 2.0i single overhead cam and 2.0i 16-valve twin overhead cam engines.
*September 1990* 2.0i 16-valve 4x4.
*May 1992* 2.0 Turbo 4x4.

### Fault Finder
The engines in these cars are tried and tested units, but the 2.0-litre

single overhead cam engine is a unit which demands regular oil changes to keep it in tip-top condition. If regular servicing has not been carried out by a Vauxhall dealer, then look elsewhere for a Calibra. On high mileage single-cam models – 50,000 miles plus – check for any undue rattling on idle, a sign that there is camshaft problem. This is not a very likely problem if the car has been properly looked after, but the Vauxhall 2.0-litre engine is susceptible to these problems, if it's been neglected. Likewise, look for any oil leaks from the side of the engine on the right-hand side as you look into the engine bay. Such a leak will have spread oil down on the chassis members. This type of leak is fairly easily cured but the shortage of oil this has caused may have caused damage to the engine, if it hasn't been caught soon enough. Check for smooth acceleration, without any rau-cousness from the engine. On any high performance car the gear-change should be thoroughly checked over, and the Calibra is no exception. The change on the Calibra is smooth and very precise, so if there is any resistance when trying to slot into gear there is a problem. On a few Calibras there have been worn gear selectors, especially on second gear, and this stops the gear-lever sliding smoothly into gear. These selectors can be replaced fairly easily, but they can also point to hard driving and that may well have had an effect on other parts of the car, notably the engine and brakes. These cars have a large appetite for brake pads, especially so in the case of the Turbo. It is vitally important to make sure that the pads have not been allowed to wear right down and so score the brake discs, because replacement discs are rather expensive. On four-wheel-drive models it's vital that you check the driveshafts on both front and rear axles for any leaks. The problem is a rare one, but again, if regular servicing has been skimped on, problems can occur in this area. Another check to make on the four-wheel-drive models is for uneven tyrewear, often a sign that the four-wheel-drive system is out of alignment. This can happen if the car's wheels have been bumped against kerbs too often. Bodywise, there should not be any problems. Rust is not a problem. Do check for any accident damage, though, because by their very nature these cars tend to be driven more quickly than more mundane machinery.

## Verdict

These cars are still quite rare, so few common faults have shown themselves so far. But, the Calibra is based on Vauxhall Cavalier mechanicals, and .by and large that's a very reliable car. Calibra second-hand prices will continue to hold up well, simply because this is a rare car, so if you are offered one cheaply, walk away, there will be a good reason. The best choice is definitely one of the Turbo models, simply because it provides real value-for-money performance motoring. The base 2.0-litre is just like driving a Vauxhall Cavalier, except that more people look at the Calibra's smooth design than ever looked at a Cavalier.

## VAUXHALL CARLTON

Rear-wheel-drive saloon and estate.

### History

*November 1986* Range is 1.8L, 1.8GL, 1.8iL, 1.8iGL, 1.8iCD, 2.0iGL, 2.0iCD, 2.3LD diesel, all available in saloon and estate form.

*March 1987* GSi 3000 saloon.

*November 1988* 2.0iCDX saloon and estate.

*September 1989* 3.0iCDX estate.

*October 1989* 3000GSi 24-valve saloon.

*September 1990* 2.0iL saloon and estate, 2600iCDX saloon.

*October 1990* Lotus Carlton saloon.

*December 1991* 2.3L turbo diesel, 2.3GL turbo diesel estates.

### Fault Finder

On cars made between 1986–90, 1.8 and 2.0-litre petrol engines had problems with camshaft failure, usually caused when camshaft belts snapped. Listen for any undue rattle from the engine, especially when revved hard. A full service record is essential on all Carltons, mostly because oil changes must be carried out at least every 9,000 miles. Sensible owners will complete an oil change every 6,000 miles. On Carltons made during 1986–8 the manual gearboxes were not the strongest, often suffering from crunching, due to worn synchromesh. Sometimes the problem can be more serious – total gearbox failures are quite common on high mileage cars. Check for any tightness, or reluctance to go into gear. Good Carlton manual gearboxes should have a light and precise gear-change. On all models, cylinder head gaskets can leak quite badly. Any oil leaks in the engine bay should be examined carefully. If they are from a gasket this is not too much of a problem, but it can mean that the car might have been run on low oil for a while, and this may have affected the engine. On tick-over, all Carlton engines should be quiet, virtually inaudible in the cabin. If there is any rattle from the engine – particularly in four-cylinder models – it can be the camshaft, loose timing chain, even engine bearings, all quite serious problems. Many four-cylinder Carltons suffer from hardening of valve stem seals. This can be spotted when revving the engine. Any streams of blue smoke will highlight this fault. It's not a terribly expensive problem to cure. However, if there are intermittent clouds of smoke this could indicate piston ring wear, which is more serious and quite costly to rectify. Look for evidence of tyre kerbing by examining the wheels carefully. Excessive kerbing can cause the steering box to come off its mounts, so if there is more than about half an inch of play in the steering, this could be the problem. Any undue loud whirring noise from a power steering system when turning the steering at low speeds could mean the pump is soon to fail. Because these are heavy cars the disc brake pads wear quite quickly. Check for any scoring on the discs by running a finger over them. Scored discs spell trouble because they will have to be replaced, and this can be quite expensive. Check all electrics. The most common fault is for the electric door mirrors' switch to stop being able to pull the door mirrors back towards you. Electric windows should all be checked, as the replacement unit for each window costs more than £200, and central locking can also fail, frequently only locking the driver's door. This can happen to Carltons with as little as 20,000 miles on the clock.

### Verdict

Not quite as well built as a Mercedes, but far more interesting, and rarer, than a Ford Granada. 2.0-litre Carltons are no fireballs but they drive smoothly, handle well and give a superb ride. Best choice is a 2.0CD.

## VAUXHALL SENATOR
Rear-wheel-drive saloon.

### History
*September 1987* Range is 2.5i, 3.0i, 3.0iCD.
*October 1989* 3.0iCD 24-valve.
*September 1990* 2.6i.

### Fault Finder
All models show some similar faults to the Carlton. These include, oil leaks from the valve cover gasket, and brake pads which wear quickly, as well as problems with the electrics for central locking and electric door mirrors. Check the brake discs for scoring and look carefully in the engine bay for any evidence of oil leaks. If engine tick-over is not smooth and steady there could be a leak of air into the fuel-injection system, this is particularly common in older six-cylinder Senators. On the six-cylinder-engined cars oil can sludge, and there can be wear in the camshaft. On

tick-over listen for any noisy tapping, this could well signal camshaft problems. The colour of the oil should also be checked. If it is dark grey and looks very dirty there could be problems with bad oil circulation. The oil filter must be changed every 9,000 miles. If possible, see the full service records, which will show if this has been done. If these oil changes have not been carried out, the life of the engine could have been seriously shortened. Rusty front shock absorber turrets (under the bonnet) will herald potential problems with the suspension. Check efficiency of all shock absorbers, they tend to wear quite quickly. Original four-speed automatic gearboxes were not too reliable. Check all the gears engage properly and that when the car does engage a higher gear it does so smoothly, without jerking. On early Senators check for play in the steering because there are problems with steering column bolts working loose. This should not apply after 1989. Body rust is not a problem, aside from small amounts on the sills near the back wheels. If there is rust anywhere else it may signal earlier accident damage which has been badly repaired. Check that the tyres are the correct ones. On 24-valve Senators they should be ZR rated, on others, VR. If cheaper tyres have been fitted they may not be able to cope with the Senator's high performance, and could be dangerous.

### Verdict
A lot of car for the money, the Senator is grander than a Ford Granada and top models are

VAUXHALL                          VOLKSWAGEN

packed with just about every extra
you could think of. A well maintained example will last years and
will not cost a lot to run.

## VOLKSWAGEN POLO
Front-wheel-drive        hatchback,
saloon and coupé.

### History
*December 1981* Range launched,
   1050C, 1100C Formel E,
   1100CL, 1100GL – all three-
   door hatchbacks.
*March 1982* Polo Classic saloons
   launched. Range is 1100C,
   1100C Formel E, 1100CL,
   1300GL.
*January 1983* 1100 Coupé.
*October 1984* Major trim and
   equipment revisions. Coupé S
   launched.
*September 1985* Fox coupé, plus
   more powerful engine on Base
   and C hatchbacks and saloons.
*September 1986* 1.3CL saloon.
*October 1986* 1.3 Ranger, 1.3CL
   hatchbacks.
*August 1988* Fox three-door
   hatchback.
*October 1990* All saloon versions
   discontinued.
*November 1990* Completely new
   Polo range, consisting of 1.05
   Fox hatchback and coupé,
   1.05CL hatchback, coupé and
   saloon, 1.3CL hatchback, coupé,
   saloon, 1.3GT hatchback and
   coupé.
*May 1991* G40 coupé with supercharged engine.

### Fault Finder
Suspension joints, particularly the
outer ball joints, and constant
velocity drive shaft joints, need
checking for wear. These problems
will be highlighted by clonking

noises when going over even small
road bumps. If the CV joint is
leaking from its rubber boot it may
already be damaged inside. You
can tell by driving forwards slowly
and feeling for any hesitancy to
pull from the front wheels. The
camshaft cover gaskets often leak,
and they can drip oil onto the
alternator, which will mean a
replacement. The fuel pump can
also leak, and it's a leak which is
not always easy to spot. There can
be serious oil pressure loss with
the corrosion of the pipe between
the crankshaft and the oil pump.
You can hear this because a cold
Polo engine with this fault will
make a rattly noise when idling. If
spotted early enough and rectified
it is not a problem. Failure to act
will mean complete engine failure.
This fault is only likely on Polos
which have covered over 60,000
miles. After 1984, thicker brake
pads were fitted, and they usually
last for 45,000 miles or so. But
even on new Polos pads sometimes
only last 6,000 miles because of
warped discs. If there is vibration
at the front end, get your dealer to
examine the discs carefully.
Bodywork is good, so if there is any
major rust it could mean the car
has been in an accident and has
been badly repaired. Rust spots do
start around the headlamps where
stones often score the paintwork.

### Verdict
A well-built small car which
retains high second-hand values
on account of its basic reliability
and refinement. A cheap used Polo
has something wrong with it, there
are no bargains here. Best models
are the 1.3-litre cars, the 1.0-litre
models have often been pushed

174

hard, and suffer accordingly, and they lack equipment.

## VOLKSWAGEN JETTA
Front-wheel-drive and four-wheel-drive saloon versions of the VW Golf.

### History
*July 1984* Range is 1.3C, 1.3CL Formel E, 1.6CL diesel, 1.6GL, 1.8GLX.
*September 1985* 1.6TX replaces 1.6GL. 1.8GL launched.
*March 1986* 1.8iGT.
*October 1988* 1.8 Syncro 4WD.
*January 1990* 1.6 diesel gets new Umwelt turbo diesel engine.
*February 1992* Range discontinued.

### Fault Finder
Check for clonking noises from the front driveshafts, especially on the 1.8iGT. Normally, the shafts are long lasting, but hard driven GT models put a lot of strain on the front axles, sometimes causing the metal splines to wear, causing loss of traction. Gearboxes are tough, but on 1.8-litre cars second gear seems to be more fragile than other gears, with the result that synchromesh can wear, even after fairly short mileage – around 40,000 miles. On Syncro models, the four-wheel-drive system is part-time, coming into operation when the wheels hit slippery ground. If possible, drive the car on a wet road surface at high speed. If there is a clunk when the 4x4 system starts operating there is a problem with the viscous couplings. But this is a very rare problem, and likely only to be found on cars which have missed

several service stops. Bodywork is good, paintwork excellent, but check on all cars with side-rubbing strips for rust creeping out from underneath, where moisture has become trapped.

### Verdict
So little goes wrong with these cars, but you still need to be careful because there are high mileage ones which have not been very well looked after. Jetta second-hand prices are not as stable, or as predictable, as they are for the Golf, but Jetta GT and GTX versions retain quite healthy residual values. The four-wheel-drive Syncro is not as popular as it deserves to be.

## VOLKSWAGEN GOLF AND CONVERTIBLE
Front-wheel-drive and four-wheel-drive hatchback and convertible.

### History
*October 1981* Range is 1100C three-door, 1100C Formel E five-door, 1300CL five-door, 1500GL five-door, 1600CD five-door, 1600GTi three-door, 1600GLi convertible.
*October 1982* GTi and GLi convertible both get 1.8-litre injection engine.
*March 1984* MK II Golf replaces old models, with exception of the convertible, which continues. New range is 1050 base model, 1.3C, 1.3C Formel E, 1.3CL, 1.6C diesel, 1.6GL, 1.6GL Auto, 1.8GTi.
*February 1985* GTi five-door.
*September 1985* 1.6CL, GL gets more powerful 1.8-litre engine, CL turbo diesel launched.

*September 1986* 1.3C five-door, GTi 16-valve three-door.
*April 1987* 1.8-litre (carb) Clipper Convertible.
*March 1988* Major trim and equipment update for GTi, both hatchback and convertible.
*October 1988* 4WD Syncro.
*January 1990* 1.6GTD turbo diesel gets new Umwelt 'clean' diesel engine.
*February 1992* Range discontinued, replaced by new range.

**Fault Finder**
Golfs suffer from the same faults and problems as do Jettas, but on Golfs you should also make the following checks. The brakes on pre-1988 Golfs are always rather spongy, a result of having to change the brake servo system for a smaller one to accommodate changing the steering wheel to the right for UK drivers. But if there is a lot of travel before the brakes bite, check the system for leaks. Look inside the brake fluid reservoir for any bubbles, a sign that air may be getting into the system. On convertibles, check for rust spreading from the side rubbing strips – this is a particular problem on cabrios made during 1983–5, but it is usually only surface corrosion. Check the gearchanges on all cabrios because it's still the original gearbox which is gated for left-hand drive. This means that many drivers habitually crash the gears, at least until they get used to the slightly slanted gearbox pattern, and this can strip metal off the gear cogs which eventually gets down into the gearbox and can cause premature wear. Check this by making sure that the gear-lever always slots into gear smoothly,

and that there are not any crunching noises. On cabrios made from 1990–2 check the mechanism of the electrically operated hood. These are normally reliable, but they do demand normal regular service attention to keep them in smooth working order. Check the general condition of the hood. They are very well made and hard wearing, but envious vandals often slash them with knives, and repairs are seldom good enough to hide the damage.

**Verdict**
One of the best hatchbacks, or convertibles, you can buy second-hand, as long as the service history is complete and the car has not been abused. There are countless Golfs with badly chipped wheel rims, tatty interiors and worn tyres, but there are also some near pristine models. Just take your time looking. Best choices are the famed GTi in 1.8-litre form, and the Umwelt diesel, a vastly underrated car.

**VOLKSWAGEN PASSAT**
Front-wheel-drive saloons and estates.

**History**
*June 1988* Range is 1.6CL turbo diesel, 1.8CL, 1.8GL, 1.8GT, 1.8GT 16-valve in estate and saloon form.
*September 1989* Major trim, equipment and engine changes across the range. More powerful engines for CL, GL, GT 16-valve.
*February 1990* 1.8L saloon and estate.
*August 1990* All Passats, except for

the L, get the more powerful 2.0-litre engine, plus numerous trim and equipment improvements. Turbo diesel GL is launched.

**Fault Finder**
Four-cylinder engines can burn rather a lot of oil, especially when they are quite new. A year-old model may consume as much as a litre every 3,000 miles. However, after bedding down, these engines are usually no more thirsty than any other comparable unit. On five-cylinder models check for erratic engine timing. There's always a slightly uneven engine beat – a feature of a five cylinder arrangement – but if the engine is hunting up and down on tick-over the injection system needs adjustment. Check front shock absorbers for leaks on 1.6 turbo diesel models made in 1988. On estate models which have been fitted with tow bars check the rear suspension system for any sagging. This is rare, but it can happen if the Passat has been overloaded. It's also worth looking for excessive exhaust smoke, especially from 1.8-litre petrol engined estates fitted with tow bars. The 1.8 is a fair engine, but lots of heavy hauling can cause the engine valve seals to wear.

**Verdict**
Very little goes wrong with the Passat, so second-hand prices are relatively high. A full service history is a must and because the Passat is another car which is regularly used as a company car, make doubly sure that the mileage is correct. Best choices are a petrol 2.0-litre, or a turbo-diesel.

**VOLKSWAGEN SCIROCCO**
Front-wheel-drive, three-door coupé.

**History**
*December 1981* Range is 1.5CL, 1.6GL, 1.6GTi.
*October 1982* 1.8GTi.
*March 1983* CL gets 1.6-litre carburettor engine.
*October 1983* GL gets a 1.8-litre carburettor engine.
*May 1984* 1.8i Storm with high equipment level.
*October 1984* 1.6GT replaces CL, 1.8GTL replaces GL, 1.8GTX replaces 1.8GTi.
*September 1985* 1.8GTX 16-valve left hand drive to special order.
*August 1988* 1.8i Scala.
*October 1991* Range rationalized. Single remaining model is 1.8 carburettor GT II.

**Fault Finder**
The major check on any Scirocco is to make sure that the front driveshafts are working properly. When driving off, listen for any groaning from the front wheels, or a clonking noise. Check under the car for split driveshaft rubbers. Also check the gearchange. It should be slightly rubbery but precise. Sciroccos made between 1981 and 1983 often suffered from worn synchromesh, but this need not be too much of a worry. However, if the gearbox crunches at all when trying to get into gear the gearbox is nearing the end of its life. The steering rack on 1.8-litre cars made between 1983 and 1986 can leak oil, making it progressively harder to turn the steering wheel.

## Verdict
Another Volkswagen which is essentially very reliable, the 1980's Scirocco never had the following of the previous model, but it is a very good second-hand buy. The best choice is any 1.8-litre model, and the carburettor-engined cars perform almost as sweetly as the injected versions.

## VOLKSWAGEN CORRADO
Front-wheel-drive three-door sports coupé.

## History
*May 1989* Corrado 16-valve 1.8-litre.
*April 1991* G60 supercharged Corrado.
*February 1992* 16-valve version gets 2.0-litre engine.

## Fault Finder
The earliest 1.8-litre cars are not terribly smooth performers, due partly to low ratio gearing, so they tend to be pushed hard. So, check for noisy gearbox bearings, and missing synchromesh, usually on third gear. Check suspension struts all round for any sagging. This is not a common fault, but if the Corrado has high mileage it usually means enthusiastic drivers have subjected it to extreme cornering speeds, and this can affect the condition of the shock absorbers. Check that the wheels are the correct alloys because they are often stolen and owners may have replaced them with cheaper wheels. If you buy the car, make sure you fit wheel locks. If looking at a G60 supercharged Corrado, listen for rattles from the engine on tick-over. If it is

there, there could be a problem with the supercharger belts. This is not a known problem, but lack of servicing could well lead to such a problem developing, the point being, check for a full service history.

## Verdict
There was nothing very wrong with the first 1.8-litre Corrados, but they were not as refined as they should have been, hence their replacement with the 2.0-litre cars. The G60 offers train-line performance but servicing is expensive.

## VOLVO 300
Rear-wheel-drive hatchback and saloon.

## History
*September 1982* Range is 1.4-litre 340DL, 1.4-litre 340GL, 2.0-litre 360GLS, 2.0-litre 360GLT hatchbacks.
*October 1983* 360GLE and 360GLEi four-door saloons.
*October 1984* Low friction engine for 360 range.
*October 1985* 1.7GL three- and five-door, 1.7GLE saloon and five-door hatchback, 360GLS hatchback replaced by 360GL.
*October 1986* 340GL 1.7-litre saloon.
*January 1987* 360GLT saloon.
*October 1988* 1.4-litre Base versions of the 340 hatchback.
*October 1991* Range discontinued.

## Fault Finder
Gearboxes suffer from a poor linkage, and with high mileage this can lead to an increasingly sloppy gearchange. In extreme

cases the linkage can disconnect, leaving the car stuck in gear. A good Volvo 300 series gearchange will be a little notchy, but quite precise. If it's hard to find a gear, there's almost certainly a problem with the linkage. On cars with the DAF designed automatic transmission there are often complete transmission failures, caused by the main belt snapping. Any automatic 300 which has covered over 60,000 miles should have its belt checked. The first signs of trouble will be a delay between choosing forward or reverse and the gearbox moving into the gear. This is usually accompanied by a sudden lurch from the gearbox. The rear brakes can sometimes bind, usually as a result of seized calipers, but sometimes because the brake pads have worn down too far. Check the brakes all round for wear. Rust was a problem on some of the cars built during 1982–3, due to poor paint application which led to paint blistering and sometimes cracking, especially along the windscreen/door pillars. Check for this, and look closely to see if a patch-up paintwork job has been carried out because it means there may be other parts of the car where there is the same paintwork problem.

## Verdict
The best engines are the 1.7 and 2.0-litre units, they are robust and fairly economical, though no 300 series engine is particularly refined. There are very good rivals which can be bought for the same price as many later model 300s and many of those rivals are considerably more modern.

## VOLVO 440/460
Front-wheel-drive saloons (440) and hatchbacks (460).

## History
*April 1989* 440 range is fuel injected 1.7-litre, GL, GLE, GLT, Turbo.
*July 1989* Carburettor engines launched in 440, 440GL, 440GLE.
*April 1990* 460 range launched, consisting of, carburettor 1.7-litre GL, GLE, fuel-injection 1.7-litre GL, GLE, Turbo.
*October 1991* New range is 440Li 1.6-litre, 440Li 1.7-litre, 440Si, 440GL, 440GLT, 440 Turbo, 460Li 1.7-litre, 460Si, 460GL, 460GLE, 460CD. 1.7-litre is slightly bigger, more powerful than previous 1.7-litre.

## Fault Finder
One common problem on all 1.7-litre engined models is a loose wire on the rear fuel pump. The 440/460 has two fuel pumps, one in the engine bay, the other under the rear of the car, near the fuel tank. This rear pump's connector wire is the culprit. It's inside a rubberized covering so the connecting end cannot be seen unless the rubber is removed. The pump can only work when the wire is properly connected, but when it becomes warm – once the engine has warmed – it can work itself loose and not provide a proper contact. It's not possible to discover this until the car fails to start, and that's usually after you've warmed the engine by driving several miles. But, this fault can also start off by giving erratic engine running, eventually becoming so bad that the car stalls, and then will not restart until the

engine – and more specifically, that wire on the fuel pump – cools down again. Faulty electrics are common in these cars, mostly giving false warnings. The most common is a constantly lit door-open red dashboard light, which stays lit even when the door is firmly closed. Another is faulty central door locking, sometimes leading to just one door locking or unlocking. It's usually not long before door trim begins to come adrift on cars made from 1989 to 1991, and interior door handle surrounds often fall off. Paintwork on 400s made during 1989–90 was not always good. Blistering paint, fading metallic colours and badly fitting door window rubbers were common. Later cars are much better. Check the boot lock to see if it works properly because many locks stick.

**Verdict**
A solid car, but the early 400s were not up to the traditional Volvo standards of build quality. The cars made during the last eighteen months are much better, and the Turbo in particular is a fine car. Be careful when buying, do not assume just because it's a Volvo it will be in good condition.

**VOLVO 480**
Front-wheel-drive        three-door coupé.

**History**
*June 1987* 1.7-litre 480ES.
*February 1989* 480 Turbo.
*October 1991* 480S.

**Fault Finder**
Check for faulty electrics, mostly

false warning signals, electric windows which aren't working, and central door locking which sometimes works, sometimes doesn't. The cars built from 1987 to mid 1988 also had paintwork problems with fading metallic colours, cracking paintwork around windscreen rubber surrounds and minor paint blistering on bonnets. Check the trim inside, especially on the doors, because the whole panel often comes off on the driver's door. Listen for creaks from the dashboard. They are common on pre-1988 cars and once there, they are hard to banish.

**Verdict**
The 480 is the second Volvo sports car produced in any numbers – the first was back in the 1960s – but it's far from the most successful. Early models suffered from a variety of niggling faults and while the newer cars are much better, this Volvo has still failed to make a major impact on the sports car scene. Second-hand prices are extremely varied, depending very much on condition of trim, rather than just on mileage. The Turbo is the best version.

**VOLVO 240**
Rear-wheel-drive    saloon    and estate.

**History**
*September 1981* 245GLT estate joins 244GLT saloon and estate, DL, GL saloon and estate.
*September 1982* Badging change, all models become 240 in both estate and saloon form. GL gets bigger engine (2.1-litre).
*March 1984* Basic 240 estate launched.

*October 1986* 240DL estate gets 2.3-litre engine.

*January 1987* 240GLT saloon and estate get 2.3-litre engine.

*January 1991* Range cut to just one model, 240SE estate.

## Fault Finder

As with any car with an overhead camshaft engine, it's vitally important to listen for any grumbling noises from under the bonnet, a pointer to possible camshaft wear. Check when the camshaft belt was last replaced, and if it's tens of thousands of miles ago, get it changed. It is a fact that Volvo cambelts are just about the least likely to snap, and wear is usually progressive, rather than sudden, but always check the condition of the cam belt, just to be on the safe side. Oil leaks are not normally a problem, so if there's lots of oil on the engine bulkhead, then there may have been a split oil feed pipe, a problem on some cars produced in 1985. If this has happened there's a possibility that the engine could have been damaged because it's been run on low oil. Check for this by listening for any rattling noises on tick-over, a sign that engine bearings are worn. On some 2.3-litre engines made during 1987 there was a problem with sub-standard water pumps. If the pump is soon to fail you will hear a knocking sound from the engine when it's ticking-over, although, again, it's likely that all of the bad pumps will have been replaced by now. Gearboxes are strong, so if there is a problem here – any crunching noises, difficulty getting into gear – then the gearbox may need replacing, and a 200 with this problem is worth

avoiding. Alternators on a batch of 1982 saloons and estates were faulty, but these will all have been replaced by now. Corrosion is not normally a problem, but the 200 is not completely immune from rust. Check the rear tail-gate in particular because this rusts along its bottom edge.

## Verdict

This is the Volvo which doesn't go wrong. Well, there are some problem areas, but not many. For many buyers the only sure thing in life is their Volvo estate. The best models are not always the most powerful. The 240DL is well loved, and as an estate it provides very practical transport.

## VOLVO 700

Rear-wheel-drive saloons and estates.

## History

*September 1982* 760GLE saloon with V6 2.9-litre engine.

*April 1983* 760GLE turbo diesel saloon.

*May 1983* 760 Turbo saloon with new 2.3-litre engine.

*October 1984* 740GL, 740GLE, 740GLT launched with new low friction 2.3-litre engine.

*October 1985* Estate versions launched, Range is 740GL, 740GLE, 740GLT, 760GLE, 760 Turbo.

*October 1986* 740 turbo saloon and estate, 740 turbo diesel estate.

*October 1987* 2.4-litre 740 turbo diesel estate, 740GL gets 2.0-litre injection engine.

*February 1988* 740 Base estate.

*November 1988* 740SE saloon, 740SE estate.

*August 1989* 740GLT saloon, 740GLT estate with new 16-valve twin overhead cam 2.3-litre engine.

*September 1990* Range cut to 740GL saloon and estate.

*November 1990* Range discontinued, replaced by 900 series.

### Fault Finder

These cars rarely show their age, so a full service record is a must because mileage could have been tampered with. Estates – look carefully for any damage to the cargo carrying area, and the roof inside, often damaged by large loads, or a family's dogs. Rust is not a problem, but the bonnet is large, and therefore attracts stone chips. Check carefully for any respraying as many 700s are finished in metallic paint, and the match might not be perfect. Turbo versions are the most unreliable because the turbo often fails. Proper and careful servicing is essential here. Ironically, the older the Turbo 700, the better because early turbos were very unreliable and will all have been replaced by now with the newer, tougher design. All 700 series engines are rather noisy, but any undue rattling on tick-over, especially on V6 versions, could well be a sign that the camshafts have worn. Repair is expensive, around £700. This will not necessarily happen if the car has been serviced regularly because regular oil changes are the key to stopping camshaft wear in this engine. Check for oil leaks from the engine. Shock absorbers become sloppy around 70,000 miles maximum and must be replaced, otherwise the 700 becomes dangerously unwieldy

when cornering. Disc brakes seem to eat brake pads. The higher the performance, the greater their appetite. Check the discs for scoring – replacement is not cheap. On automatic gearbox versions check that the change is reasonably smooth. 700 autos have always lurched from second to third, but if there is a major clunk when going up through the gears there could be gearbox failure just around the corner. Likewise, if there is hesitation to engage reverse, followed by a clunk. Check for oil leaks from the gearbox. This is very important if the car has been used for towing, when extra mechanical strain will have occured.

### Verdict

Given regular servicing these cars are strong as they come, and they will still look good ten years from now. Best choice is the 740 estate, which is both practical and virtually unbreakable. Avoid the Turbos, especially the early 740 which was harsh and unreliable.

### VOLVO 900

Rear-wheel-drive saloons and estates.

### History

*October 1990* 900 launched. Range is 2.0-litre 940GL and 940SE, 2.3-litre 940GLE, 940GLE 16-valve, 2.3-litre 940 Turbo, 2.3-litre 960 Turbo, 2.4-litre 940 turbo diesel, 3.0-litre 960 24-valve, saloons and estates.

### Fault Finder

Beware of estates with tow-bars fitted, they may have been hard used. Check interior of estates carefully for wear and tear. Full service history is a must, and it's paramount that mileage is checked for accuracy. Too new for any firm news on mechanical reliability, but so far the omens seem good.

**Verdict**
Building on the fine reputation of the 700, the 900 series is set to be quite reliable, as long as it's properly serviced and cared for. Estates are vast and well equipped, and set to retain the best second-hand values of the lot.

**YUGO 45, 55, 65, Tempo**
Front-wheel-drive hatchbacks.

**History**
*May 1983* 1.0-litre Yugo 45, 46GL three-door.
*June 1984* 1.1-litre 55L, 55GLS three-door.
*August 1988* 1.3-litre 65 GLX three-door.
*August 1990* 45 Tempo.
*November 1991* Range changed to 1.0-litre Tempo and Tempo L, 1.1 Tempo L, 1.1 Tempo GLS, 1.3 Tempo GLS.

**Fault Finder**
Early Yugos, those made in 1983 and 1984, did not have good quality control, so look for poor paintwork application, trim falling off inside, and badly finished seat trim. This latter problem was caused by bad stitching which sometimes caused splits to appear in the seat material. The engines should be checked for oil flow. The easiest way to do this is to listen to the engine for any noisy rattling, but also to look inside the oil filter

neck to see if oil is being pumped to the top of the engine. If it is not, there is a problem, usually caused by oil sludging because it's not getting pumped around the whole engine. Up to 1990 model year it's also a good idea to check the front brakes for any warping, or for seized brake calipers, both common faults and both faults which can pull the vehicle to one side when braking. After 1990 a different design was used, and it's far better. Check the tail-gate, the bottoms of the doors, and along the tops of the front wings. Also, look under the rear wheelarches for any rust which might have taken hold there.

**Verdict**
The Yugo was not a really good long term proposition until the 1990 models appeared, and even then the car does not retain a very healthy second-hand value. In many ways, unless you are very short of cash, it's better to look at some of the more modern mainstream European rivals.

**YUGO SANA**
Front-wheel-drive hatchback.

**History**
*January 1990* 1.4 and 1.4GL five-door.
*February 1991* 1.4L, 1.5GL five-door.
*March 1991* Range changed to 1.4, 1.4LS, 1.4GL.

**Fault Finder**
Check the body over carefully, both for paintwork defects – paint runs, peeling paint – and for fit and finish of all panels. There have

been cases of Sanas with doors which don't close properly right around their edges. This leads to a gap between the windscreen pillar and door frame, and this increases as speed increases. On your test drive make sure you can drive quite quickly for a while, and if this problem exists it will then become evident. Engines seem quite strong, but you should check for proper oil flow, and listen for any rattling noises from the engine; in this car's case they are often a sign of worn engine bearings. Listen for a slapping sound, which usually points to piston-slap, though this is rare.

Gearboxes vary in their operation, with some changing smoothly through the gears, while others are much less precise. But it's only if you hear rattling noises when the gear-lever goes into a gear that you should really begin to worry, because then it's a pointer to gearbox bearing wear.

**Verdict**
Much more modern than the Tempo, the Sana is set to keep its value much better. However, beware of poor build quality, even on the latest versions, and look for a full service history.